GNAT BOYS

DEDICATION

This book is dedicated to all those who flew, or continue to fly, the Gnat, a sports car of the skies, and, in particular, we remember, and will never forget, the number of air crew who lost their lives in Gnat accidents. They were all very special people who had earned the right to fly this magnificent aircraft through their abilities as pilots.

GNAT
BOYS

True Tales from the RAF, Indian and Finnish Pilots who
flew the Single-Seat Fighter and Two-Seat Trainer

RICK PEACOCK-EDWARDS
& TOM EELES

GRUB STREET | LONDON

Published by
Grub Street
4 Rainham Close
London SW11 6SS

A CIP record for this title is available from the British library

ISBN-13: 978-1-911667-26-1

Design by Myriam Bell Design, UK
Printed and bound by Finidr, Czech Republic

AUTHORS' NOTE

The publisher has chosen the more modern Oxford Rules style for certain appointments, such as
the Station Commander and Officers' Mess, that we would not normally have chosen. However,
we are happy to concur with the use of the publisher's house style for these and similar items.

CONTENTS

THE CONTRIBUTORS

RAF

Mike Adams, Dave Ainge, Jim Baylis, Al Beaton, Roger Beazley, Bill Blair-Hickman, Graham Bowerman, Geoff Brindle, Derek Bryant, Pete Chapman, Ian Christie-Miller, Dick Cloke, Ray Deacon, John Dickson, Dickie Duckett, Alan East, Bob Eccles, Tom Eeles, Tony Ellender, Mark Fitzgerald, Frank Foster, Ching Fuller, Roy Gamblin, Brian Grant, Stan Hodgkins, Brian Hoskins, Roger Hymans, Sir Richard Johns, Mike Johnson, Peter Johnson, Dim Jones, Danny Lavender, Ian Macfadyen, Ian McBride, Trevor McDonald-Bennett, Doug McGregor, Syd Morris, Dave Moss, Jerry Parr, Rick and Tina Peacock-Edwards, Al Pollock, Rich Rhodes, Black Robertson, Boz Robinson, Dave Roome, Mike Shaw, Roy Sommerville, Mike Sparrow, Dennis Stangroom, Roger Taite, Richie Thomas, Tom Thomas, Jon Tye, Eric Ward, Wyndham Ward, Pete Webb, Jim Wild, Andy Williams and Gordon Young

INDIAN AIR FORCE

Ashok Chibbar, G. M. David, Adi Ghandhi, Manna Murdeshwar, Subramaniam Raghavendran and P. M. Velankar

FINNISH AIR FORCE

Jouko Gullsten, Jyrki Laukkanen, Heikki Nikunen and Reijo Suutala

FOREWORD

AIR CHIEF MARSHAL SIR RICHARD JOHNS
GCB, KCVO, CBE, FRAeS

Air Commodore Rick Peacock-Edwards and Group Captain Tom Eeles are both recognised by their contemporaries as two of the most distinguished pilots of their generation. Their shared addiction to flying, firmly rooted in advanced flying training on the Gnat at RAF Valley was, many years later, to motivate their collection of anecdotal experiences of this unique aircraft in RAF service from 1962 to 1979.

As an advanced jet flying-training aircraft the diminutive Gnat was a most notable advancement on its predecessors in performance, manoeuvrability, technology

Sir Richard Johns with the Red Arrows prior to a display sortie on 17 July 1998.
(Sir Richard Johns)

and sophistication. As such it presented much more demanding challenges than hitherto to student pilots who had completed their basic flying training on the pedestrian Jet Provost. And therein lay the pleasure of instructing on the Gnat as students, all keen and motivated to progress to fighter operational conversion units, got to grips with the aircraft. As a QFI at Valley in the late 1960s I recall with both pride and pleasure my association with students who successfully completed the demanding course before progressing to service at the sharp end of the RAF.

Reading the contributions to this volume recording the story of the Gnat from introduction to service to retirement some 16 years later will remind the reader that the Gnat offered far more to the benefit of the RAF than its primary role as an advanced trainer. And no more so than being the aircraft of choice for the Red Arrows. Contributions from both front and rear-seat occupants make fascinating reading as indeed do the assessments of the Gnat F1 presented by senior officers of the Indian and Finnish air forces. While in service with the Indian Air Force the single-seat variant was established as an outstanding combat aircraft. While the Finnish experience of the aircraft was less satisfactory, a former chief of their air force with 6,000 flying hours on 72 different types concluded that when reflecting on the different aircraft he had enjoyed flying, the first two types that came to mind were the Gnat and the F-18 Hornet. Some accolade.

This volume presents an outstanding collection of memories from various perspectives but I would first refer the reader to the dedication at the front. I could not have written more appropriate words. Nor for that matter can I improve on the assessment of the Gnat's value to the RAF and the reflections of Gnat Boys. Their words admirably present the characteristics of the aircraft and the sheer pleasure of flying such a unique aeroplane.

Some 53 years later I can still remember word perfect the STUPRE(C)(C) drill. Read on.

AUTHORS' NOTE

Readers will note repeated reference to the action following a hydraulic failure using the mnemonics STUPRE, STUPREC and STUPRECC. All are relevant since the actions changed as the Gnat progressed through its service life. The mnemonic started as STUPRE and was later enhanced with one and then two additional Cs.

INTRODUCTION
THE GENESIS OF THE GNAT

TOM EELES

PETTER'S 'POCKET ROCKET'

E. W. 'Teddy' Petter was born in 1908 and was educated at Marlborough and Gonville Caius College, Cambridge, where he studied engineering. He joined the family firm, the aircraft manufacturer Westlands of Yeovil, where he soon proved to be a gifted designer but often a difficult individual to deal with. He was involved in the design of the Lysander army cooperation aircraft, he played a major part in the design of the Whirlwind cannon-armed twin-engine fighter and the Welkin high-altitude interceptor, but none of these aircraft fulfilled the roles they had originally been designated. The Lysander proved far too vulnerable as an army cooperation aircraft but achieved success flying agents into occupied territory, only 114 Whirlwinds were built but it proved to be a very successful ground-attack fighter and the Welkin never entered service as the threat it was designed to combat never materialised. Following disagreements with the board of directors, Petter left Westlands and joined English Electric in 1945. After designing the hugely successful Canberra light bomber he became involved in early design work on the P1 project which ultimately became the Lightning; however, he became disillusioned with the seemingly endless growth in size and cost of combat aircraft. He left English Electric in 1950 to join the Folland Aircraft company as managing director.

At Folland he initiated design work on a small, lightweight fighter aircraft that would be considerably cheaper than a conventional fighter, and therefore attractive to countries with limited defence budgets. At the same time NATO had decided to run a competition to choose a new fighter aircraft to equip the squadrons of the member nations. Petter was very keen to respond to this and he had high hopes that his design would win a large order. His proof-of-concept prototype, named Midge, first flew on 11 August 1954, powered by a Viper turbojet. *Aeroplane* magazine dated 3 September 1954, had a full-page advertisement (see page 11) for Folland Aircraft Limited headed 'The Answer to Europe's Air Defence Problem' and an article headed 'New for Farnborough', which reads as follows:

'The Folland Midge, which first flew on August 11th, will be another exhibit of great interest, by reason of the contrast it makes with the P1 and other fighters on show. Although the present prototype has only 1,640lbs static thrust from the Armstrong Siddeley Viper engine, compared with more than 4,000lbs static thrust from the Bristol Orpheus in future Gnats, some very high subsonic speeds have already been achieved, and there is little doubt that the Gnat itself will be supersonic, in a dive if not in level flight. The private venture Midge and Gnat are light, but in no sense utility, fighters; in production form they will have complete flying and navigational equipment, heavy fire power, and good endurance. In fighter-bomber role, the Gnat can carry bombs, napalm or rockets beneath the wings. Folland claim that five Gnats can be built in the man-hours required for one standard fighter, and that fully equipped the cost is between one-third and one-quarter that of current fighters. A static model display will show how two Gnats, with only their wings detached, can be carried in a Blackburn Beverley.'

The definitive version, the Gnat, powered by the more powerful Orpheus turbojet, flew for the first time on 18 July 1955. It was armed with two 30mm Aden cannon. There was considerable interest in this diminutive fighter from

The Midge first flew at Farnborough in 1954. (*Aeroplane*)

The advert for the Folland Gnat which appeared in *Aeroplane* magazine in September 1954.

both the RAF and some foreign air forces. Six were ordered by the Ministry of Supply for trials. The Gnat was assessed as a potential replacement as a ground-attack fighter to replace the Venom in RAF service but lost out to a ground-attack version of the Hawker Hunter. Twelve Gnats were ordered by the Finnish Air Force and served with it for a number of years and two went to Yugoslavia where a proposal to build the Gnat under licence was made, but no production order occurred. One of these aircraft can still be seen in a museum in Serbia. The greatest success was an export order to India and an agreement to build the Gnat under licence by HAL in that country, where it was further developed as the Ajeet and sometimes referred to as the 'Sabre Slayer' after its performance in one of the India/Pakistan conflicts.

At the same time the RAF realised that there was a need for a new advanced jet trainer to replace the Meteor T7 and Vampire T11, the performance of which was considered to be inadequate for the next generation of combat aircraft, such as the Lightning, TSR-2 and P1154, the latter two never achieving service status. One of the requirements for the new trainer was that it had to be equipped with the integrated flight instrument system (IFIS) that was to be used by all the new front-line fast jets. Folland, doubtless encouraged by a senior retired RAF officer on its board of directors, offered a two-seat version of the Gnat to meet this requirement. The seating would be in tandem, not the RAF's preferred side-by-side arrangement, the Gnat trainer aircraft would be slightly larger than the fighter, with modified flying controls and a bigger fin: it would also have a limited IFIS layout. Apparently Folland claimed that the Hunter T7, the Gnat's only possible rival, could not be fitted with IFIS, but this was false as the Hunter T7A was already flying with a full IFIS display. With hindsight, it seems surprising that the RAF chose the Gnat T1, a much more technically complex aircraft, rather than the proven Hunter T7 with its side-by-side seating, its renowned simplicity and robustness and its proven ability to be equipped with the IFIS. Overall, the performance envelope of both aircraft was very similar, the Gnat having a slight advantage in maximum achievable Mach number, but the Gnat, being much lighter, was considerably more agile. An order for the Gnat T1 was placed in 1957, perhaps as a consolation prize for the fighter not winning the ground-attack replacement competition. The first trainer prototype flew on 31 August 1959, however, Petter retired from Folland at the end of 1959 at the relatively young age of 51 and emigrated to Switzerland.

After initial testing and trials by the manufacturer and Boscombe Down, the Gnat finally entered service with the RAF at CFS and No. 4 Flying Training School (FTS), RAF Valley, in 1962. At Valley two squadrons were formed, unimaginatively named 1 and 2, along with a Standards squadron. The Gnat soon became popular with its pilots who enjoyed its sparkling performance, although it proved to be challenging for students of lesser ability. Being technically complex and so small, rectification of faults often presented difficulties. Taller pilots could not safely fit in it and it proved to be too much of a handful for some of the foreign students who were being trained by the RAF. Availability on the flight line was often less than required to meet the training task so it was not long before a third squadron was established at 4 FTS, ironically equipped with the Gnat's rival, the Hunter, which trained taller pilots, foreign students and any overflow students who could not be absorbed by Gnat courses.

Quite a few of the earliest Gnat instructors had been members of various Fighter Command squadron aerobatic teams, including the legendary Black Arrows. It was not long before they realised that the Gnat offered great possibilities as formation display aircraft and formation aerobatics soon started to be practised, if somewhat unofficially. A team was formally established in 1964, named the Yellowjacks, as their aircraft were painted bright yellow. The higher echelons of the RAF were not overly enthusiastic about this colour scheme or name, but as the Lightning display team was proving hideously expensive to operate it was not long before the Red Arrows were officially formed as the RAF's display team, using initially the Yellowjacks' pilots and an all-over red paint scheme for the Gnat which was felt to be more acceptable. The Red Arrows were an element of CFS, the only other service establishment to use the Gnat in any numbers apart from 4 FTS. Over time they gained a worldwide reputation for excellence with their Gnats and even managed to take them across the Atlantic to display in North America.

NEMESIS

By the late 1960s it was evident that a replacement was needed for the Gnat. Availability was poor due to unserviceability; the loss rate was high and the Gnat's limited endurance was inhibiting the ability to teach more advanced lessons. An initial proposal to use the two-seat version of the Jaguar came to nothing, but Hawker Siddeley's HS.1182, soon to be named Hawk, was selected as the Gnat's replacement in 1971. Flying for the first time in August 1974, it began to replace the Gnat at CFS and 4 FTS in late 1976. The Red Arrows were the last RAF unit to fly the Gnat, finally relinquishing their mount for the Hawk in 1980. Two Gnats carried on flying at research establishments for another couple of years. The Finnish Air Force retired its remaining Gnat fighters in 1972 but the Indian

Air Force continued to operate the aircraft and its successor the Ajeet well into the 1990s.

But this is not quite the end of the Gnat story. Several Gnat T1s were used at RAF Cosford for training engineers in turn round and fault rectification procedures, where the aircraft were kept in a fully serviceable condition but did not fly. When they were replaced by redundant Jaguar aircraft most were sold to civilian owners and returned to flying status on the civilian register. Some found their way to the USA, but none are believed to be flying there anymore. However, in the UK, the Heritage Aircraft Trust, based at North Weald, operates several Gnats and these can still be seen flying at air displays today. Thus, it is still possible to see the diminutive Gnat, Petter's 'Pocket Rocket', flying today, some 66 years after its first flight, an impressive record for an iconic and much-loved aircraft.

CHAPTER 1

THE GNAT TRAINER BOYS

THE FIRST GNAT ARRIVES IN RAF SERVICE

On 2 February 1962 the first Folland Gnat T1, XM709, was flown to RAF Little Rissington, home of CFS, from Dunsfold. It was greeted on arrival by the AOC-in-C Flying Training Command, AM Sir Augustus Walker. By virtue of his appointment as project leader, Flt Lt Derek Bryant became the first Gnat QFI/CIRE. This is his story.

DEREK BRYANT – GNAT PROJECT OFFICER AT CFS

Derek Bryant

My first task was to convert Dennis Yeardley (whose DFC had been awarded for shooting down an Me 262, I believe the first jet kill of WWII) and John Young. On 9 February Dennis and I took off on his first conversion sortie and landed at Kemble where early conversion flying took place. Thanks to our ground crew, backed by a first-class Folland rep, the project made a great start. I flew 25 sorties in the first ten flying days concentrating on team conversion but with two familiarisation sorties for our commandant, Air Cdre Pat Connolly. The 26th sortie on the afternoon of 28 February was to practise close formation on a Jet Provost whilst it took public relations photographs of our aircraft.

This sortie attracts particular attention because it ended in a two-wheel landing, the starboard undercarriage being unlocked. The cause was no mystery...pilot error. I had retracted the undercarriage too soon after take-off. A coincident wing wobble caused the retracting starboard undercarriage to strike the ground; the impact sheared the datum shift link. A starboard red confirmed that we had a problem as did some pitch-control problems caused by unpredictable datum shift inputs (the mechanism was an ingenious solution to a stability problem

Derek Bryant in the front seat and Dennis Yeardley in the back, acknowledge the camera as they taxi XM709, the first Gnat T1 to enter service with the RAF, past the Aircraft Finishing Section hangar at Kemble on 9 February 1962. (Ray Deacon).

introduced by stretching the Gnat fighter to create the trainer). Dennis, in the rear cockpit, and I discussed the control problem and decided to revert to manual, thus regaining positive control of the tailplane. Consequently, we sought advice from Folland test pilots via ATC but, in the limited time available and given

With the damaged starboard undercarriage dangling in the airflow, Derek Bryant burns off fuel in the stricken Gnat. XM709 suffered Category 2 damage and was repaired on site by a Hawker Siddeley civilian working party from Dunsfold. It was two months before the second Gnat, XM706, was delivered and three months before the damaged aircraft took to the skies once again. (CFS, via David Watkins)

the uncertain nature of the damage, there was little they could do to help. We therefore burnt off fuel and prepared for an emergency landing. I would carry out the approach and touchdown; Dennis would then help me to keep the aircraft straight and the wing up for as long as possible. We had a nasty moment on finals when selection of full flap gave us momentarily uncontrollable pitch problems which I instinctively countered by turning and Dennis intuitively re-selected power controls. The eventual touchdown was uneventful, and luck was with me when, on two wheels and a wing tip, we slid between two prominent runway lights and came to rest on the grass.

Having made a textbook two-wheeled landing, Derek Bryant (in greatcoat) walks over to see the damage for himself as civilian staff from 5 MU return the damaged aircraft to the CFS Type Flight hangar. (Ray Deacon)

There was no excuse for my error, but it is an ill wind that blows no good. Subsequently, a 140-knot minimum speed retraction switch was introduced. The control problems experienced on finals heightened my enthusiasm for a modification which transferred tailplane control to the stick-mounted trim switches when in manual. Folland were already promoting the modification at a cost. In my opinion it should have been part of the into-service acceptance standard. In October I flew with Sqn Ldr (later AM Sir) Donald Hall of A Squadron Boscombe Down, who was the RAF test pilot for the Gnat on an informal evaluation of the need for the modification. Later still, my final sortie on the project was to return to Dunsfold to fly a solo evaluation on a pre-production aircraft, XM694, with the modification incorporated. Thus, my project flying neatly came full circle, but more importantly, the modification was accepted by the RAF.

The pre-modification standby-trim system required considerable manual dexterity which has prompted another recollection. Our C-in-C was the then Air Marshal, later Air Chief Marshal, Sir Augustus Walker. As many will know he lost his right arm in WWII in circumstances which reflect his bravery; and his determination thereafter to lead a normal life included re-learning to fly with an artificial limb strapped to the control column. In May 1962 he undertook a brief conversion course on the Gnat and went solo without difficulty. To watch his good

Under the watchful eye of Derek Bryant (left), AM 'Gus' Walker, his artificial limb strapped to the control column, taxies a repaired XM709 for a solo flight from Kemble in 1962. (Tom Thomas)

hand dart about the cockpit was an object lesson in manual dexterity. He did not need the modification.

Although arguably not part of the history of the Gnat project, the aftermath of my accident provides an interesting insight into the attitudes then prevalent in the HQFTC/CFS hierarchy. The commandant had arrived swiftly at Kemble to witness our landing with which he was impressed. He was less impressed to learn from me that it was my fault. Quite properly a Board of Inquiry was assembled with a view to taking court martial action. Having considered the evidence I believe the commandant took the view that my admission of gross negligence clearly established culpability, but that the overriding service interest was the swift introduction of the Gnat. The C-in-C must have agreed because the outcome was a formal interview before him. Thereafter, during later appointments with increasing command responsibility, I never forgot that loyalty is a two-way street.

But I get ahead of myself. Another interesting incident occurred on 28 June. John Young and I were working up an 'unusual attitude' sequence for inclusion in the syllabus. As a matter of principle, I believed that we should explore recoveries from more extreme attitudes than we would include in the syllabus. It was during an 'unload' from a slightly overcooked low-speed vertical recovery that the aircraft fell over backwards, picked up dramatic yaw without significant roll, and we sensed a hint of negative 'g'. We sat still and allowed the airspeed to increase before recovering. Don Hall was informed and the following day he and I attempted to reproduce the symptoms but without success. The upshot was that we curbed our enthusiasm for the esoteric and concentrated more on recovery from those unusual attitudes more likely to occur in real life. That said, John Young devised an absolutely brain-scrambling entry into an unusual attitude taking full advantage of the Gnat's extraordinary lateral agility. In fact, he used to hand over for us to complete a recovery on instruments alone with the aircraft more or less in straight-and-level flight but still rolling. Much to his amusement I, and others, then developed our own unusual attitude whilst trying to unscramble our physiological confusion. I hasten to add that this was a staff only 'treat'.

My logbook reminds me that quite early in our internal work-up we converted a Trapper, Freddie Latham, and Bill Croydon who, halfway through his conversion was promoted and posted elsewhere. What a waste of precious Gnat hours at that stage – an example of Air Staff/P Staff disconnect which was not unusual in those days. On 7 July I performed a modest low-level display in front of HM The Queen Mother as part of CFS Golden Jubilee celebrations. It was a typical English summer's day. Sunshine and showers with some well-developed cumulus clouds around. My display finished with a high-speed run followed by an 'upward

Charlie' (vertical continuous roll). On about the second twizzle I entered a dark cumulus cloud. Soon thereafter, rapidly running out of airspeed and still in cloud, I was grateful for the practice I had had with John Young.

July also saw the arrival of the first batch of advanced instructors who had been selected to start the student training programme at Valley. Thus, they were all competent and well-regarded instructors. I suspect that at times our 'instruction' (perhaps 'guidance' would be a better word) was based on the principle that 'In the land of the blind the one-eyed man is king'. That said, I do not recall any serious disharmony between us either with the content of their own conversion syllabus or that proposed for their students; nor any disagreement with the advice on one's approach to advanced instruction which was to be included in the Instructors Handbook. Indeed, some of the course 'helped' us in our evaluation of training profiles. A low-level profile flown with Al Pollock largely in Northern Ireland was one such sortie which I will not readily forget.

By this time the project had returned to Little Rissington. I had been asked by the commandant if I would be happy with the arrangement and I assured him that I would. The main runway at Rissington was entirely adequate for Gnat operations if the aircraft was flown accurately. As accurate flying is the foundation stone of credible instruction, I could see no good reason for not moving back. I had but one reservation. One of the Gnat's less endearing characteristics is 'earholing' down the runway in a crosswind. This lateral tilt, a feature of the undercarriage geometry, felt most uncomfortable and detracted from efficient braking. But it only became a serious concern if the runway was wet. There was little margin for error at Rissington in those conditions.

My reports to HQFTC forecast possible student problems with fine-pitch control in close formation as we on the team had experienced some early difficulties. In fact, the instructors on the first course did not seem to have much of a problem; successive improvements to the seals and valves in the Hobson unit tailplane motor much improved the breakout response. The Yellowjacks, led by Flt Lt Lee Jones, put to rest any lingering concerns we may have had, although his penchant for misreading his altimeter during low-level formation aerobatic displays did cause me concern in my post-project appointment on the Air Staff at HQFTC!

The Gnat was particularly well equipped (to partial OR946 integrated flight instrument system standard as I recall) with up-to-date instruments and navigation systems. Offset tactical air communication and navigation (TACAN) system and ILS provided useful freedom and a sense of confidence when flying and recovering in marginal weather conditions. It also made the Gnat particularly well suited as a lead-in to Lightning conversion. One of the privileges I greatly enjoyed in April

1963 was a brief command-sponsored detachment to Middleton St George to fly the Lightning T4 and to discuss with the instructors what they felt should be emphasised during advanced training. Received wisdom is that ex-Gnat students usually performed well in the Lightning world.

As Martin-Baker ejectee No. 124 I am second to none in my appreciation of Sir James's achievements. But it would be remiss not to mention the revolutionary lightweight seat fitted to the Gnat trainer. Although, fortunately, its operational performance was not tested during the project, we were involved with IAM Farnborough's efforts to further improve user friendliness and comfort. Amongst other things a Wg Cdr Tony Barwood was trying to create a plastic seat mould compatible with the average male bum (known colloquially as 'the Barwood bum') upon which would be fitted a slim cushion with appropriate compression characteristics. Anyone who has had a communal shower after a rugby or football match will know that an average male bum does not exist. Undeterred, and assisted by our sensitive comments, the wing commander eventually perfected a compromise profile. Thus, to the brilliant simplicity of the Gnat seat was added a user-friendly harness and comfortable seat. Wonderful, especially on the third instructional sortie of the day!

There was no clearly defined end to the project. I suppose it could be said to have ended when we submitted the final version of the various publications and syllabi we had been tasked to produce. I then took over the Gnat Air Staff desk at HQFTC and was thus 'hoist with my own petard'. Actually, the transition from project to routine at CFS was seamless. We had already converted additional CFS and Valley instructors during the validation process and that process continued, albeit with excitements and disruptions ably described elsewhere by others. Conversely, student training at Valley got off to a less-than-ideal start as maintenance and logistic difficulties severely reduced aircraft availability. One of my early staff tasks was to re-write our carefully structured ab-initio student syllabus which had been based to some extent on short-endurance high-intensity sorties. Instead, we had to resort to fewer, longer sorties to take full advantage of any serviceable aircraft. But that, as they say, is another story.

On reflection, many years on one tends to remember high and low points of the project and forget the solid and continuous effort by all involved. But looking back on our success, if that is what it was, considerable credit must go to the HQFTC/CFS hierarchy. They gave a 27-year-old flight lieutenant command of a small, hand-picked team and, within the broad guidelines of probable training resources, also gave the team a remarkably free hand and very full support. We were trusted to liaise directly with all involved in the development and acceptance into service of the Gnat trainer and encouraged to consult widely with, amongst others, users of the end product. Moreover, we had the well-tested Vampire training system as a sound foundation for our work. But above all we were fortunate to be introducing into the service an aircraft which, whilst commanding respect, had the performance and capability to stimulate the sheer joy of flying.

THE GNAT PROJECT:
A TECHNICIAN'S PERSPECTIVE

Chief Technician Tom Thomas sums up his early experience when, as a corporal, he was one of those selected for the Gnat project team.

Tom Thomas

When XM709 arrived at Rissington I thought it looked really beautiful as it flew over but more like a knock-kneed Rhode Island Red once on the ground. The Gnat project commenced straight away. Our boss was Flt Lt Derek Bryant with Flt Lts Dennis Yeardley and John Young completing the aircrew team. Flt Sgt Jimmy Gallagher was posted onto the project but, unfortunately, he had not even seen a Gnat until the day it flew in. Sgt Pip Piper was assigned as the senior airframe NCO but promptly terminated his service to take over as licensee of 'The Inn for all Seasons' on the A40. It soon became our favourite watering hole. So I was the sole airframe fitter for a while until two junior technicians, Pete Durdin and Jack Foley, arrived. Pete was a very quiet, likeable lad straight from his fitter's course, while Jack was a 're-tread' who had served in the RAF then left but as he could not settle in civvy street he re-joined and had to start all over again as a J/T. He was a star, liked by everyone and always had stories to tell.

Referring to the landing accident to XM709 on 28 February, very little damage was sustained by the aircraft in what was a skilfully handled landing – turning the aircraft onto the grass just as the wing gently lowered prevented a more serious outcome. On inspection the starboard main undercarriage radius rod was found to have fractured which allowed the undercarriage leg to swing freely until pushed back into the bay on touchdown. Don Parker was the Folland representative on the project team at the time and although we had only been together for three

Tom Thomas assists Derek Bryant with strapping into XM709 during the first few days of the Gnat project at Kemble, February 1962. (Tom Thomas)

weeks, he imparted so much information about the aeroplane and the Folland Aircraft company that he fired our interest and enthusiasm for the task ahead.

The RAF has a great variety of specialist equipment to call on when receiving aircraft after crash landings but the Gnat, being so tiny, required a simple sling and a crane to lift it. To keep the aircraft straight and level whilst hanging on the sling required myself and Sgt Pip Western to sit one on each tailplane as the crane began a long and slow crawl back to the D site hangar to await inspection. Folland, or Hawker Siddeley as it had become, soon assembled a repair team and they duly arrived at Kemble. My job was to liaise with them and supply any equipment they needed such as hydraulic test rigs, pitot static equipment and inclinometers. Together, we soon removed the complete starboard undercarriage unit. Now, part of the pivot assembly on which the undercarriage rotates houses a small cam plate which, when the airbrakes are selected, operates a hydraulic valve that locks the undercarriage at 35 degrees. This plate was given to me for safe keeping while new doors, seals, hydraulic lines, etc, were fitted to the undercarriage leg. Re-fitting the leg to the aircraft was a time-consuming operation requiring the trimming and shimming of the doors with many undercarriage retractions to ensure a good flush fit once the gear is up. When we eventually completed the job, the new doors were resprayed, before final testing with the cam plate fitted in place. Alas no cam plate. I had lost it – how embarrassing! So, Don obtained another from Dunsfold but my colour still reddens when I recall the loss.

The loss of 709 brought the project to an abrupt halt but it was able to re-start in earnest with the arrival of XM708 on 9 May and XM706 a day later.

Note. The two previous extracts are from RAF Little Rissington, The Central Flying School Years 1946–1976, published by Pen and Sword Books, and are reproduced with its kind permission.

THE SUMMER OF '63

MIKE SHAW

Mike Shaw

Ah! That golden summer of 1963, when a young Cranwell graduate's fancy turned to thoughts of liberty, life, love – and the GNAT!

We lucky few, we of the fast-jet cohort of No. 82 Entry (motto: 'Semper in Excreta') had the good fortune to be the very first course of students to be sent to Royal Air Force Valley, home of No. 4 Flying Training School, to undergo our advanced flying training on that new slippery little pocket rocket, the transonic Folland Gnat.

In fact, our saga had started well before the summer, as we mustered at Valley in mid-February just as the 'Big Freeze' of the worst winter since 1947 was starting to loosen its icy fingers. I had somehow struggled up the M1 and A5 in my diminutive Lotus 6, wearing all my underwear, two flying suits and my bone dome, dwarfed by huge lorries chucking chunks of frozen slush at me most of the way. But the weather broke as I crossed Snowdonia in the dark, giving me a once-in-a-lifetime sighting of a gorgeous silver moon low over the mountains. An omen!

As the 26 of us gathered in the ground school next day, our new pilot officer braid worn self-consciously in public for the first time, we started to meet our instructors and get to grips with the Pilots Notes of this new little beast. My memories of ground school and the Gnat flight simulator are hazy, except for our introduction to TACAN which then seemed like the cutting edge of military science. By then only about a dozen Gnats had been delivered to Valley, but with more coming every week. Sidling up to one in the hangar, my abiding memory is of being able to lean into the cockpit without the help of steps, and I was the runt of the litter, the shortest kid on the course. As many of us said – you didn't climb up into the aeroplane, you just put it on like an overcoat.

Flying it was like a dream, it handled so lightly and the extra speed after flying the Jet Provost at Cranwell appeared perfectly natural. We all seemed to make good progress to first solo and beyond, that is whenever there were serviceable aircraft available to fly – the little blighter seemed to be having more than its fair share of teething troubles. As one wag put it: "Poker player's description of our hangar – Full House, Gnats on Jacks." Those early problems were to persist throughout the course, which was now extended from the planned four months to an eventual eight, right through that lovely summer in Anglesey.

We developed a great rapport with our instructors, some of whom treated us almost as human beings – quite a change from the ivory towers of Cranwell. Notable members of the staff included Lee Jones, who would become the leader of the Yellowjacks and of course the first leader of the Red Arrows, along with the wonderful Henry Prince, Roger Hymans who had flown with the Black Arrows of Treble One Squadron, and the unforgettable Alan 'Nerveless' Pollock, more of whom later. As the course progressed (very slowly) and the spring gave way to summer, life became very enjoyable.

The Gnat's service ceiling was 48,000 feet, and we had reached the high-level handling part of our course. After another dual demo with our instructor, the solo exercise required us to explore the reduced turning ability at these extreme altitudes. This quickly turned into a secret competition among us to see who could get the highest. Ian Dick quietly admitted to getting very gingerly to 52,000 feet whereupon he fell out of the sky, so I was determined to beat this. I just failed

Gnat pilots of 4FTS at Valley in the 1960s. (Ray Deacon collection)

Lee Jones and Henry Prince with a hairy student at Valley in 1964. (Ray Deacon collection)

to do so and can remember vividly the blackness of the sky, the curvature of the earth – and the feeling of vertigo as the little jet rolled itself onto its back and gently plunged back into the atmosphere – and feeling that only my harness and the Perspex hood lay between me and the Skerries and the waves almost ten miles below. Scary.

The serviceability problems of the Gnat did not improve and in July it was decided to send half the course on leave in turn for a couple of weeks. Some of us took advantage of this by doing a lot of sailing locally, being loaned a prototype racing yacht by Saunders-Roe at Beaumaris for the Menai Straits fortnight, and even winning the North Wales team racing series. While we were playing on the water, Ian Christie-Miller suffered a total engine failure at altitude over Llandudno. Air traffic steered him the wrong way, to RAF Sealand, although he was already pointing towards Valley. Gliding down he mistook the disused runway at Hawarden for Sealand, but make a pretty good fist of sticking it down at 150 knots, passing across a road and under some power lines before hitting a submerged water tank, writing off the Gnat and badly injuring himself, sadly ending his fitness for fast jets. On eventually being again cleared to fly he completed training as a helicopter pilot.

In September I was chosen to accompany Alan Pollock to RAF Aldergrove in Northern Ireland for the annual RAF Battle of Britain Air Day. Alan was really grumpy about being put on static display, but we spent the day proudly showing off our little aeroplane to an eager public, who had free run of clustering around. At one point I had to shoo off an enormous Irish woman and her children who had set up their picnic sitting on our starboard tailplane. When we later departed for home, Alan treated me to a thrilling low pass of the tower and then out over a very calm sea at low level at 420 knots.

"OK Mike, you have control, show me 100 feet." Blimey, this was fun, as we had so far only practised down to 250 feet with an instructor, and 500 feet when solo.

"No, you're still too high; that's not 100, I have control, this is 100."

"Gosh, Sir, that feels more like 50."

"Nah, this is 50."

"Struth, this feels more like 10."

"Nah, this is 10 feet."

At this point we passed a small fishing boat at about deck level. Al then pulled hard into a half-loop so that over our shoulder we could spot our pencil-like wake, filling in for miles across the glassy surface of the Irish Sea.

As we now approached the end of our course our thoughts turned towards the subject of our postings. By now we had acquired the beginnings of a swagger as being the aspiring first Gnat graduates. Naturally we were expecting a sheaf of plum postings to the Hunter and hopefully as the initial first tourists on to the supersonic Lightning. The prospects enthralled us all. What we did not know was that Their Airships had other ideas. They were worried about the ageing gerontocracy of the V-Force and had decided that most of our course were destined to be co-pilots on Valiants, Victors and Vulcans! Fortunately for the sake of good morale this was not revealed to us until the very end.

With our final handling tests completed, we had one last presentation for RAF Valley. The Royal Artillery on the neighbouring headland of Ty Croes had a test unit for guided weapons. Their 'gate guardian' was a Thunderbird SAM, which we felt would look better embedded in the lawn outside our officers' mess at Valley. A recce party first went in under cover to partially saw through the support frame. The next night we divided into an assault party, a transport unit, and a digging group to prepare the site in the mess lawn. The transport unit (Pete Crook's Land Rover) drove up past the guardroom to the army mess while the assault team led by Bruce Latton sawed through the rest of the supports under the noses of the guards. The Rover then freewheeled down to the 22-foot missile which was loaded very quietly aboard. The team then set off to Valley, passing a police car which was on a routine visit to the army base.

"On manoeuvres, are you?" asked the police, "we've just passed this big white missile on its little transporter, going down the road." "Nonsense," said the guard commander, "all our missiles are khaki, except for this one on a stand outside the guard…room…oh dear."

By which time, the Thunderbird's base had been embedded in by the lake outside the officers' mess at Valley. Unfortunately the concrete had not set by the time the army arrived to reclaim it. Attempts to delay them by offering trips in the Gnat simulator and tours of the station were ignored so they retrieved their missile, but not before photos were taken, one hung in the bar at Valley for many years. A few weeks later the army returned and stole the old four-blade wooden propeller that hung on the wall in the mess ante room, but no one noticed that it had gone. Eventually the army had to ring up and offer to return it. They inserted a brass plaque recording the details of the abduction in the propeller's centre which can still be seen to this day.

Our moment of triumph at breakfast in the morning before the army arrived, watching more senior officers' eyes pop out over their cornflakes at the splendid sight of our missile stuck proudly in the lawn, was rather dashed as our postings were announced. Ian Dick, Johnnie Pym, and Roger Giles got Hunters, Bruce Latton, Sandy Weaver and Mike Seyd were creamed off to CFS to become instructors, Rod

Members of No. 82 Entry posing with their stolen missile with a plaque that reads: 'With the compliments of No. 82 Entry'. (Mike Shaw)

Brown went to the Canberra, and the rest of us went to the V-Force as co-pilots. For so many of us, what a waste of the Gnat.

PS. By subterfuge and good fortune, and thanks to my short legs, I eventually escaped from the V-Force to fly Hunters and Harriers for the next 14 years. Oh joy. But that's another story.

MEMORIES OF A GNAT STUDENT

TOM EELES

Tom Eeles

My Cranwell Entry, 83, graduated in July 1963, having completed some 180 hours basic flying training on the JP3 and JP4, nice enough aircraft but a bit pedestrian, especially the JP3. Twenty of us were selected to go for our advanced flying training to 4FTS, RAF Valley, Anglesey, where the Gnat T1 was just entering productive service, replacing the Vampire T11 and Meteor T7. We were only the second course to be trained on the aircraft.

When compared to the Jet Provost, Vampire and Meteor, the Gnat was a very different and much more advanced aircraft. It owed its origins to the diminutive Gnat fighter, designed by Teddy Petter, who tried to break the trend of fighter designs becoming ever bigger, more complex and expensive. Not only was it tiny, with its tandem seats, sharply swept wings, hydraulically powered flying controls, advanced flight instrumentation, a blistering transonic performance and an astonishing rate of roll but it also represented a great leap forwards in sophistication and technology when compared to its predecessors. We felt privileged to be able to fly it.

On arrival at Valley we found the first course still there, despite having graduated from Cranwell some nine months ahead of us. The Gnat, still rolling off the production line, was already proving difficult to keep serviceable despite being so new. Valley was a vast building site as the runways, airfield, technical and domestic facilities were all being upgraded. The winter weather in 1963 had been terrible so delays were inevitable. We started in the ground school, which was located in a veritable rabbit warren of WWII-vintage buildings scattered randomly behind the control tower, where we learnt about the Gnat's complex systems, including the ingenious longitudinal control system. It is worth describing this in a little bit more detail, as it will then become apparent why some found the Gnat such a challenging aircraft.

Pitch control was achieved by a slab tailplane, hydraulically powered by a device called the Hobson unit. There was a feel-trim system that enabled the control column to be in the centre of the cockpit when the aircraft was in trim in pitch, whatever the speed. When the fuselage-mounted landing gear was raised or lowered, it travelled some distance fore and aft so generated a considerable trim change, nose up when gear raised, nose down when lowered. This was compensated for automatically by a datum shift mechanism in the pitch-control circuit. All this worked well until the hydraulic system failed. In this event, an accumulator enabled the slab tail to be positioned at the required angle. Once the accumulator was exhausted, the slab was 'frozen'. Pitch control was now provided by small elevators that could be unlocked by the pilot, but they were too small to provide a full range of control, so a standby trim system was provided which moved the slab from its frozen position in the nose-up control sense, but only back to the frozen position in the nose-down sense, thereby assisting manual control in pitch.

Following hydraulic failure the datum shift stopped working so the trim change on gear selection had to be countered by a combination of standby trim and elevators. We soon learnt the vital need to ensure that, following hydraulic failure, the tailplane had to be frozen in the right place so that full pitch control was retained after landing gear selection. Every Gnat pilot will remember the drill, STUPREC, S – speed below 400kts/.85M, T – trim to the ideal sector, U – unlock elevators, P – power cock off, R – raise guard on standby trim, E – exhaust tailplane and aileron accumulators, C – check operation of elevators, ailerons and standby trim. Combine this drill with coping with a simulated engine failure (which produced the hydraulic failure) and you were a very busy pilot.

Another state-of-the-art innovation was the flight simulator, a device that was extremely primitive when compared to today's simulators. It lived in a large caravan, had no visual facility or motion, but it did allow us to practise the normal and emergency operating drills before we got into a real aircraft for the first time. The Gnat's ejection seat was also quite different from the Martin-Baker seat, it was much lighter, had no safety pins but had the same 90kts in level flight at ground-level capability. Instead of safety pins there was a lever with a big red knob on the end at neck level under the head box. When selected to face forwards the seat was safe. To make the seat live, the lever was moved through 90 degrees to the right. If you forgot to do this before take-off, your neck was pressed firmly into the red knob by way of a reminder of your omission as you accelerated on take-off.

At last ground school ended and it was time to fly the Gnat. The flight line was located in a collection of old buildings on the far side of the airfield as the new facilities were still under construction. One advantage was that it was only a short stroll across the dunes to the beach. Another new piece of flying kit that we had to wear was the two-piece grey waterproof immersion suit, commonly referred to as a goon suit. As Anglesey was surrounded by the cold Irish Sea this uncomfortable garment was a sensible precaution and gave much more protection than a flying suit if you landed in the water. In the air the Gnat did not disappoint. Sitting in the front seat, with the long pitot tube sticking out in front was like riding on a witch's broomstick. Everything seemed to happen at phenomenal speed when compared to previous experience in the JP. It was a new experience not to have a QFI sitting right beside you, but just a disembodied voice from behind. It was also a new experience to know where you were at any time, thanks to the wonderful TACAN with its offset facility, a vast improvement to the DME fitted in the JP.

The Gnat handled superbly, that is until the voice behind you turned off the hydraulic cock in the middle of your aerobatic sequence and you were faced with doing the STUPREC drill, probably followed by simulated engine failure and a practice forced landing in manual control, quite a challenging handling exercise. We did seem to practise emergency procedures quite a lot. Transonic flight was easily achievable, Pilot's Notes stated that: 'Well contoured airframes in steep dives approach Mach 1.3.' Remember that each Gnat was essentially hand built so some airframes were better contoured than others.

Gnat line-up on press day at RAF Valley in October 1963. (MoD)

The course was 70 hours of flying and consisted of all the usual activities, general handling, instrument flying, night flying, formation and navigation, plus all the usual test sorties. The instructors were mainly ex-Hunter and Javelin men, the Lightning not having been in service long enough to produce many QFIs. My logbook shows that I flew with Mike Kelson, Tony Doyle, Gerry Ranscombe, Dick Sheridan (RN exchange), Denis Hazell, and flew test sorties with Wg Cdr Edwards and Sqn Ldr Woods. Some of the instructors went on to be founder members of the Red Arrows, via the interim Yellowjacks team that was just forming under the leadership of Lee Jones and Henry Prince when our course graduated in March 1964. Many of our dual-formation sorties ended up doing formation aerobatics, not part of the formal syllabus. I also recall a publicity day at Valley, when all the Gnats were lined up on the hardstanding to be inspected by the gentlemen of the press who were flown up to Valley by Argosy. At the end of the course our postings were a mixture, with the aces being selected as the first ab-initio Lightning pilots. Sadly some of our course fell by the wayside and left to more sedate multi-engine flying training on the Varsity at Oakington.

Off-duty life in Anglesey in 1963 was very different from our relatively cosmopolitan existence at Cranwell, where the fleshpots of Lincoln, Nottingham and even London were easily reached. It took a very long time to get in or out of Anglesey in those days, dual carriageway roads did not exist, the M1 finished somewhere near Birmingham and the A5 followed a tortuous path through the Welsh mountains. The locals spoke Welsh, a language none of us could understand and there were no pubs open on Sundays. The officers' mess was lively and somewhat more relaxed than life had been at Cranwell so inevitably was the centre of our social life. Happy days indeed.

RECOLLECTIONS OF ROYAL AIR FORCE VALLEY

TREVOR MCDONALD-BENNETT

I completed my basic flying training on the Jet Provost at RAF Acklington in January 1965, a month before my 20th birthday. I was desperately keen to fly fighters – the Lightning in particular. It was therefore a huge relief to be selected to continue my advanced training on the Folland Gnat at RAF Valley. We started the course with 18 students. Nine of my contemporaries from Acklington, and the remainder from the other basic training stations.

My first flight in the Gnat took place on 8 March 1965, so I must have arrived on the station three or four weeks before that to complete the technical ground school,

Trevor McDonald-Bennett

some basic simulator training to familiarise with the very different, but excellent new instrumentation, plus heavy emphasis on proficiency with the fairly complex emergency drills and procedures. On our first day at No. 1 Squadron, the boss, a very punchy Sqn Ldr Moors, welcomed us with: "You are here to train as fighter pilots. If you f**k up you will go on bombers!" With some trepidation that became my mission. I was very fortunate to have Flt Lt Perry Edwards as my nominated instructor, although inevitably I flew with several others as the course progressed, including the boss.

So continuing to my first flight. The Gnat was experiencing serious issues with the canopy resulting in a number of spectacular failures during my time at Valley. It was not uncommon to see aircraft landing with it missing completely. Apparently, the issue was the different coefficient of expansion between the Perspex and canopy frame causing large stress levels in the structure. Having strapped in, you can guess what happened next – we couldn't close and lock the canopy in spite of ground crew leaning on it, etc! So out we got and moved to a spare aircraft. Whilst walking to said aircraft Perry said, "bloody hell, look at that" (I think the language was probably a little more colourful!). He pointed skywards to an aircraft apparently performing a simulated flame-out approach, and despite attempting to stretch the glide it looked likely to hit the undershoot. It certainly did, and completely disappeared from view before bouncing onto rocks well short of the runway where it broke it's back but didn't catch fire.

Neither of us saw an ejection or 'chute, so naturally thought the worst. I thought this would be an appropriate time to go to the bar, but Perry insisted that we get airborne as briefed. Dave Ainge the solo student had indeed been practising a practice forced landing (PFL) but had experienced a genuine flame out during the procedure. I recall that a small amount of flap was selected during the practice procedure to produce approximately enough drag to counter the idle thrust. Of course, with no idle thrust his descent rate was too high. Had he raised the flap it could be argued that he might have made it, but for an inexperienced student a very tall order particularly whilst handling the flame-out emergency. He had in fact ejected very late and his only injury I seem to remember was a broken tooth as he was catapulted forward on the first swing of the parachute as he struck the ground. A very lucky chap. The ejection had taken place as we lost sight of the aircraft, so we were unaware that he had thankfully survived.

Back to the spare aircraft, strapped in and canopy successfully closed. Start up and taxi all as briefed, and first real awareness of how close to the ground one feels in this diminutive aircraft. It was standard practice to have a good laugh watching first take-offs for new students with the inevitable wing wobbling from overcontrolling on the super sensitive ailerons. Of course, I wasn't going to be guilty of this was I? Unfortunately I was just like everyone else. Once properly airborne it became obvious what a fantastic, delightfully handling, high performance machine this was. The visibility from the bubble canopy was outstanding, and the flight instrumentation excellent. A quantum leap after the Jet Provost, and an immediate awareness that the course certainly wasn't going to be a walk in the park. The level of concentration and sheer pleasure of some general handling allowed me to forget temporarily the accident which we had witnessed, but once back in the circuit overflying the wreckage on short finals was a different thing altogether. After landing and back on the ramp the ground crew told us straight away that Dave Ainge was OK which seemed hard to believe, but wonderful news. So that was a very memorable first day flying the Gnat.

The course continued normally with no significant dramas. Swept-wing characteristics, high-altitude performance, and transonic flight were all new concepts which I was hungry to understand and master. Perhaps I was becoming a little overconfident, but that all changed dramatically when I came a bit too close for comfort to killing myself. Not something I am proud of and I don't recall the date. It happened on a solo sortie which included practising all varieties of circuit after recovering to the airfield. The incident occurred during a low-level circuit with a fairly strong crosswind blowing towards the runway. I hadn't made any correction for drift or allowed for the different visual perspective of the runway at the lower altitude. This all combined to put me far too close in for a safe circuit. However, I stupidly continued with an ever-tightening finals turn attempting to line up.

I was wearing an uncomfortable immersion suit and was tensing my legs as the approach got hairier. One slippery rubber boot slipped off a rudder pedal and the other tensed foot inadvertently applied full rudder, resulting in a rapid roll to the inverted at low altitude providing a view of terra firma which I never wish to see again. I quickly sorted out my feet and applied full aileron and lots of power, and the good old Gnat rolled right way up whilst I nonchalantly transmitted going around on to the dead side. I was expecting to be ordered to land immediately by the duty pilot in the tower, but astonishingly nobody saw me, so I continued the detail as briefed with much more attention to the effects of the wind. I am still after all these years ashamed of my performance that day, but I certainly learnt a lot from it. Interestingly I still tense my legs like that under pressure. How I can play golf is a complete mystery!

Another incident which I recall involved a solo student from a different course conducting a formation take-off. As described earlier, the Gnat has a very complicated longitudinal control system, part of which is called datum shift and involves automatically changing the tailplane incidence as the gear retracts or extends. The gear moves forward or backwards during the sequence, and due to the small size of the aircraft has a significant effect on the centre of gravity (C of G) and trim. During a formation take-off unless the leader and his number two are perfectly synchronised with gear selection the datum change is likely momentarily to make formation in the vertical plane a little tricky. On this particular take-off the lead instructor retracted the gear in a very sporty way immediately after lift-off, the student got out of synch, and hit the ground as the gear was retracting. He very spectacularly wrote off the recently reinstated ILS aerial which sliced into the aircraft next to an air intake. The aircraft caught fire, the student jumped out and ran like hell with his oxygen tube still attached! It stretched a very long way before detaching itself. My memory is hazy, but I think I am correct in saying that the station commander appeared whilst the fire crews were doing their job. They asked him to leave and not interfere with proceedings, at which point an ejection seat fired and almost hit his Land Rover. He moved quickly after that, and before the second seat followed the first.

Another exciting datum shift incident involved a solo student from the course ahead of us experiencing failure of the system as he selected gear up after take-off. The aircraft pitched up to a frighteningly high attitude, but he had the presence of mind to roll the aircraft beyond 90 degrees of bank to lower the nose, and then selected gear back down which sorted the miss-trim situation out. A very white-faced student entered the crewroom after landing.

My next recollection is that of a terrible day on 22 April about six weeks after my first flight in the Gnat. It involved a fatal collision between two aircraft on a formation practice exercise. The instructor in the lead aircraft was Tim Mermagen with I think (but am not certain) an air traffic controller in the rear seat on a familiarisation flight. The other aircraft involved was being flown by solo student Gavin Priest. Whilst rejoining formation after a practice break away the student lost sight of the lead aircraft in the sun and pulled up colliding with the forward fuselage trapping the instructor's legs in the deformed nose. The passenger ejected suffering leg injuries, but the instructor crashed trapped in the aircraft and was killed instantly. The student attempted to return to Valley with restricted thrust and gear stuck in the mid-extension airbrake position. He was attempting to make a semi-flame-out approach on to the into-wind active runway, but realising that he had insufficient altitude opted to switch to the reciprocal downwind runway where he touched down at very high speed, bounced, and cartwheeled in view of staff instructors and students watching from the squadron roofs. A horrific sight, and he was of course killed instantly.

I understand that the wing commander flying was heavily criticised for not ordering the student to eject from the stricken aircraft. As a result of the number of accidents and incidents there was much media speculation concerning its safety and suitability as a trainer. Word got around that it had been discussed in Parliament, and it would be reported on the BBC evening news. Gavin Priest was on a different course ahead of mine so I didn't know him, but others described his appearance, and I thought I would have recognised him by sight. By the time I got to the TV room the lights were dimmed, and we all anxiously waited for the bulletin. Sure enough there was heavy criticism of the aircraft further impacting on our already sombre mood. The lights were switched back on, and I almost jumped out of my skin when I realised that I had been sitting next to the student I had thought to be Gavin Priest. He understood the shock that I had experienced, and we decided to have a good session in the bar. A really terrible day impossible to forget.

We moved on to the formation phase, low-level navigation and other advanced areas. I must say that it was extremely twitchy to fly in close formation, but as experience was gained the ultra-responsive controls became a delight rather than a burden. I was not looking forward to my final navigation test at all. This was a phase where I was definitely lacking in confidence. The test involved a high-low-high profile with a descent I think over Scarborough for the low-level part. I was incredibly lucky hitting the major turning points and features virtually spot on. A complete fluke, and somebody must have been looking out for me that day.

Compressor-blade corrosion from the humid salt air was an issue, and we were all scheduled for very early morning 'compressor wash' sessions. This was conducted by a ground engineer spraying an oil mix via a probe into an air intake with the engine running at various rpms. The required rpm was signalled by large ping-pong-style bats. It was very boring and was also used for those who had been on the 'naughty step' as a form of punishment. A member of our course was scheduled several times consecutively. He started taking a paperback with him to alleviate the boredom and had a nasty shock one morning. The technician undertaking the wash got too close to the intake and the sleeve of his coat was sucked in to the intake dragging him with it. The pilot engrossed in his book was alerted by heavy knocking on the canopy much like the famous Tony Hancock sketch. Fortunately, it is a long way back to the engine compressor and no injury or damage occurred. The student spent a little longer on the naughty step, and books were banned from the cockpit.

There were a few close calls during practice hydraulic-failure procedures. The all-flying tail was normally hydraulically powered and had very small unlockable elevators. These, plus electric trimming of the stabiliser would be used if hydraulics were lost. It was very important that the elevators were unlocked with the stabiliser at the correct incidence to provide full elevator authority. The complicated (for a student) drill was remembered by the mnemonic STUPRECC. The instructor could select the hydraulics off from the rear cockpit, and when I started the course approaches were flown with load-free pitch. As a result of a number of occasions involving marginal elevator authority to round out, the procedure was changed to fly the approach with an almost fully forward control column. This felt very uncomfortable and unnatural but guaranteed sufficient elevator control for landing. I was relieved that I never had to use it in anger.

Despite everything morale remained high, and mess life was hugely entertaining. The Summer Ball took place while I was there, and there were too many hilarious occasions to mention, including a visit to the bar by a large circus animal which had been 'borrowed' for the occasion!

Another memorable occasion involved a student from a senior course returning to Valley via the twisty A5 in his beloved Jaguar E-Type. It was far from new, but all his spare time and money had been lavished on it. He was overtaken by another E-Type, so the game was on. The inevitable happened as the overtaking car disappeared into the distance, he lost control and wrote off his own. Luckily, he was virtually unhurt – apart from his pride. Not long afterwards there was a call from the officers' mess for him to come and sign for a delivery. It turned out that the other E-Type was being driven by one of the Saudi princes who had just completed the course. When he heard of the demise of the car, he had a brand-new one delivered to him as a replacement.

I completed my final handling test on 16 July, then waited anxiously for our postings. Three of our course members had failed at some point, and of those remaining three went to Lightnings, three to Hunters, one to Javelins, four to Canberras, and four to the V-Force. I was thrilled and relieved that I was one of the three selected for the Lightning, and we celebrated in the customary way. Equally pleasing was that we all got through the subsequent Hunter course and Lightning conversion successfully.

Sadly, just before my departure from Valley on 19 July Roger Cooper a student on the course behind me crashed into the lake just outside Rhosneiger. We never did find out the cause. Roger was a delightful Liverpudlian who used to play guitar at the famous Cavern Club around the same time as the Beatles. It was of course a very sad end to our time at Valley, but a fitting reminder of the somewhat risky profession which we had chosen, but nevertheless one that we wouldn't have swapped for anything.

FLYING THE GNAT AND SOME EXTRA-CURRICULAR ACTIVITIES AT RAF VALLEY

RICK PEACOCK-EDWARDS

Rick Peacock-Edwards

To set the scene for what follows, a few words about my experience on the Gnat. I first flew it in September 1966 when I was a member of No. 27 Gnat Course from September 1966 to February 1967 before being posted to fly the Lightning. I won the flying trophy on my course. There were around 27 on the course, one was posted to the Hunter, six of us were posted to the Lightning, another eight went to fly the Canberra and the remainder to the Vulcan and Victor where they were initially to become co-pilots.

After two flying tours on the Lightning, in June 1973, I attended the RAF Central Flying School Qualified Instructor Course at RAF Little Rissington and RAF Kemble before being posted back to the RAF fast-jet Advanced Flying Training School at RAF Valley as an instructor on the Gnat. I had, initially, been a non-volunteer for CFS and had said from the start that if I had to go and become a QFI then I only wanted to fly the Gnat. I clearly got my way and, ironically, I look back now at a tour that was one of the most satisfying and happy tours in my RAF career. They who made the decision were right, I was wrong. I instructed at RAF Valley from February 1974 through to February 1977 when I was posted back to the air defence world on the Phantom. At RAF Valley, I joined No. 2 Squadron where I quickly became a deputy flight commander and then a flight commander. I achieved my A2 (above average) QFI category during the summer of 1975. On promotion to squadron leader, I became the deputy chief flying instructor in March 1976. I also became the acting squadron commander of No. 1 Gnat Squadron for the months of November and December in 1976 whilst the squadron commander, Sqn Ldr Andy MacNeil, was away on long leave. By the time I left the Gnat I had achieved circa 1,050 flying hours on the aircraft.

I found the Gnat a delightful aircraft to fly, and on which to instruct. It was certainly an aircraft that tested the ability of students. It was a high-performance aircraft and an ideal trainer for such aircraft as the Lightning, but you also had to understand that the aircraft could also cause you significant problems if you mishandled it on emergency procedures. For those who had only flown straight-wing aircraft it was time to learn the different characteristics of a swept-wing aircraft.

BECOMING A PILOT NAVIGATION INSTRUCTOR (PNI)

Undoubtedly, one of the highlights of my time on the Gnat, especially because of my air defence background, was being selected for, and completing, a pilot navigator instructor (PNI) course, and qualifying as a PNI. I loved the large amount of low flying that we did on the Gnat in those Cold War days where this environment was so important to RAF front-line operations, mainly to avoid radar detection and increase the element of surprise.

The Gnat was an excellent aircraft for low-level training because of the high performance and manoeuvrability of the aircraft, elements of the avionics such as an offset TACAN system, and the excellent view from the cockpit. The terrain in Wales offered a quite outstanding training environment, and because of the excellent range and performance of the Gnat it meant that, either via high-low, low-high or high-low-high navigation sorties, the whole of the UK became useable for training. Scotland offered not only some of the most beautiful scenery to be seen but, like Wales, another excellent training environment. I will never forget the beauty of the west coast of Scotland, we were indeed in a privileged position to see the country from the cockpit of the Gnat.

All low-level navigation is demanding, both from a planning and flying perspective, and to successfully complete the PNI course one had to demonstrate a superior flying and navigation skills performance in the most demanding scenarios, an above-average instructional capability both on the ground and in the air, and the ability to cope with the unexpected. In short, to successfully complete the PNI course was a very proud achievement, it was a very demanding and challenging course. Low-level navigation training included what is known as initial point (IP) to target acquisition training, a very important precision-training element of low-level target acquisition.

THE WEATHER CHECK

One of the most enjoyable flights was to perform the daily weather check. The weather check was always the very first flight of the day and regarded as a bonus flight by instructors. The flight involved checking the weather in the local environment, in the low-flying areas, and at all flight levels. It was important because it gave those running the daily flying programmes important information about which training flights could or could not take place. The flying environment around RAF Valley, and throughout Wales, was one of the nicest and most free-flying environments in the country and, whether over the sea or land, at all heights, the weather check offered the opportunity to use your knowledge and skills to great effect, and for your own benefit. The weather flight also provided the opportunity to fly others in the Gnat, those qualified to be flown as passengers. There are plenty of RAF personnel, from other roles and specialisations in the RAF, who can no doubt relate a story or two about their experience on a weather check sortie. Say no more!

A PHOTOGRAPHIC TASK

One extra-curricular task that I am unlikely to forget was when I was one of four aircraft tasked to carry out a photoshoot for a national newspaper using Mount Snowdon as a backdrop. The sortie was successfully completed although for me there were a few moments of excitement in the latter stages. Unfortunately, one of my 'slipper' fuel tanks which, basically, are fuel tanks below the wing, had failed to feed, no great problem if you recover to base and land before the overall fuel weight dropped below a set figure. I cut it very fine on meeting the fuel-landing limit and the result was that, on the final approach to land, I needed an increasing amount of lateral aileron control to keep the aircraft in level horizon flight. Put another way, I was running out of lateral aileron control to keep the wings level. If ever I needed such a situation to inform me why limits are set, then that was the occasion. I landed the aircraft without incident but, obviously, very heavy in one wing. The result was that, as I taxied the aircraft back to dispersal, my Gnat looked very droopy, so much so that the senior air traffic control officer (SATCO) had called my wife. Tina, herself an air traffic controller, rushed up to the visual control tower from her duty that day in radar control so that she could see her lop-sided husband with his aircraft.

AS A STAND-OFF WEAPON

Having just completed two front-line tours in an operational environment related to the Cold War, a tour in Training Command at RAF Valley I thought would be very much away from the operational front line. I was wrong.

In support of certain major exercises, particularly those in which the Royal Navy and the RAF were involved, we would deploy Gnats to RAF Kinloss in the north of Scotland to participate in these exercises, in a specific role. One of the major threats to the UK came from Russian bombers tasked with launching stand-off weapons against targets in the UK, usually from a range of hundreds of miles from the UK mainland. As an air defence Lightning pilot, I had been very aware of the need to intercept these bombers before they could reach a position from which they could launch their weapons. To simulate the Russian bombers in these exercises, Vulcan aircraft were used, accompanied by Gnats. We would link up with the Vulcans and fly towards the UK in a close formation before, at the launch point 'release' by the Vulcans, simulating the launch of a stand-off weapon. We would fly a stand-off missile profile, often targeted at an important Royal Navy ship. We would descend rapidly to very low level and fly towards the target ship at great speed. The Gnat was used for this task because of its comparable size to a stand-off weapon, and the ability to use the performance of the aircraft to best effect. It was good training for those involved in the exercises and, at the same time, it helped keep us aware of current operations in the front-line Cold War environment. After all, most of us would be destined to return to the front line, so we hoped.

DISSIMILAR AIR COMBAT

Another extra-curricular task in which I was involved was as one of the pilots in a detachment of Gnats to RAF Coningsby, to conduct a dissimilar air combat trial with Phantom crews from the staff of the qualified weapon instructors (QWI) course, a part of the Phantom operational conversion unit. Those of us involved on the detachment were, as I recall, all ex-Lightning fighter pilots.

We had an interesting week at Coningsby where, although we encountered weather problems during the detachment, we flew several dissimilar air combat sorties, mainly 1 v 1 and 1 v 2 sortie profiles. The Gnat proved itself, as we already knew, to be highly manoeuvrable. The small size of the Gnat also caused problems for the Phantom crews to remain visual in the close-combat environment. However, what the Phantom had which the Gnat didn't have was a radar and this greatly helped. Two Phantoms against one Gnat made it very difficult for the Gnat in that situation, but the Gnat acquitted itself well in the 1 v 1 visual environment. And, of course, we already knew that the Gnat had proven itself to be a highly effective lightweight fighter in the air combat arena during the Indo-Pakistani War in the 1960s. I didn't expect to be involved in such training on the Gnat but it was a very welcome and interesting experience, especially as the Phantom, overall, had a far greater capability that the Lightning, of which I was very familiar.

A WIFE IN AIR TRAFFIC CONTROL

Finally, in this chapter, I must make mention of the role that my wife, Tina, played in Gnat flying at RAF Valley. I had met Tina whilst flying the Lightning at RAF Coltishall in Norfolk, to where she had been posted following her training as an air traffic control officer. We were married in the weeks before I started my tour at RAF Valley, in fact we married in the station church there and her father, an RAF padre and at the time the resident padre at Valley, conducted our marriage ceremony. The station commander at RAF Coltishall, Gp Capt (later ACM Sir) Joe Gilbert had helped greatly in arranging for Tina to be posted to Valley where she was to become the very first female air traffic control officer at the station, a fact that was not welcomed by the then SATCO at Valley. However, she quickly proved herself to be one of the best air traffic controllers at the station. She would have served a full three-year tour at Valley had she not become pregnant when, as the rule required at the time (1975), she had to leave the WRAF. Her departure was a great loss to air traffic control and, as a mark of the high esteem in which she was

'T' for Tina formation led by Rick to mark Tina's last day at RAF Valley.

held by all pilots at Valley, a surprise formation flypast was arranged to mark her last day at work, and to say farewell. Appropriately, flying a Gnat with the chief flying instructor in the other seat, I led the aircraft formation of four Hunter and five Gnat aircraft, and we flew several flypasts over the air traffic control tower in the shape of a 'T' (for Tina) formation (see the opposite photograph). The other thing that I remember about that day were the dark clouds that were threatening Valley at the time and which, fortunately, and only just, arrived after our sortie had concluded.

A 'GNAT BITE'

DAVE ROOME

Dave Roome

Instrument flying (for real or practice) used to be almost as good as a 100-yard sprint for raising my pulse and I well remember the nerves which accompanied me taking my advanced instrument flying grading (AIFG) on the Jet Provost. This allowed us would-be 'Biggles' to descend to 1,200ft and was – to us, at least – nearly as good as pulling off a blind landing.

However, I digress.

It was late 1966 and I was now on the Gnat course at Valley. With the grand total of 22 hours on type I was sent off into Wales one morning to do some GH, aeros, etc. There I was, throwing my eager craft through footless halls of air when I looked round to see the cumuli build-up over Snowdonia was blocking my view of Anglesey. At about the same time the Valley approach controller reported an increase in the recovery fuel "due to incoming weather". Rather tentatively, I asked Valley if I should 'come home quick' as I was unrated. This caused some consternation and there was a short discussion 'off', presumably to decide whether to divert me to Shawbury. However, the eventual decision was that I should come home now through the TACAN dive procedure, with enough fuel to go to Shawbury if the weather at base worsened.

In those days we used the Menai Bridge as our point alpha or recovery point (110°/13nm from Valley) and, as the Gnat had a superb piece of kit called the offset computer, getting there was like falling off a log. The Gnat was an excellent pre-Lightning trainer – as was the Hawk for the Tornado – and it carried a cut-down version of the OR946 instrument display, also seen on the later Lightnings and on the Buccaneer. The attitude indicator and the nav display were side by side, with the latter giving heading information from a compass rose around the outside. In the centre one could display various things, ranging from nothing (COMP), through ILS, offset TACAN (TAC) and raw TACAN (DL). It is the last two of these that concern us. DL gave the normal TACAN range and bearing to the selected beacon, but if TAC was selected the display changed, depending what one had selected on the offset computer. This excellent bit of kit, the size of 200 cigarettes, had two windows, bearing and range. If you wanted to go to a position 110°/13nm from the Valley TACAN, you set 110 and 13 on the appropriate windows, selected TAC and the display showed a bearing and range to the offset point. So simple it makes you wonder why they didn't fit it to every TACAN-equipped aircraft. In the early Lightnings we used 'TACAN wheels', but that's another story and I digress again.

So, there I was, recovering for a TAC/GCA through point alpha. I ensured that I had 110/13 and set off, confident in the abilities of the kit, if not in my own. With about 10nm to go to the top of the dive, approaching the dive arc from the south, I was already IMC, but I made the appropriate calls and set off down the dive. 75%, airbrakes out, 12 degrees nose down and 300kt, all was sweetness, if not light in the darkness of the cumuli. With about 3nm to go, I went to change to DL to get exactly over the top and...it was already on DL! I had, in fact, dived on Valley and was now about 3nm SE of the overhead at FL55. I still wonder why ATC never said anything; did they not see this odd blip, or did they have a quiet chortle at this student who had piggsed his TAC dive?

Back in the aircraft I was not unduly concerned. I had plenty of fuel (for the Gnat, anyway) and I decided to go back and do it properly. The Ty Croes range was active just to the south-west and, with the airway to the north I knew I had to make a relatively tight turn to the right. No sweat: airbrakes in, power on, change the wings level dive into a climbing right-hand turn...for the next few seconds I'm still not sure what went on but I certainly wasn't in charge of whatever it was. The next thing I saw was Trearddur Bay all over the front screen. I was just short of the vertical, but the wrong side (any pull would take me through the vertical, so it was going to get worse before it got better) with 450kt and the altimeter unwinding at a rate I had never seen before, passing from 4,000 to 3,500ft very quickly indeed. I planted the stick at the back end of its travel and the accelerometer snapped to just over 10g, but I didn't even grey out as I watched the sea get very close very quickly. I was level again somewhere below 1,000ft, breathing heavily and feeling alternately hot and cold, as I realised just how close I had come to reducing myself to my component parts.

That's about it, really, except to say that I made sure all the instruments were erect, went back into cloud on the downwind leg for one of the most accurate GCAs onto RW20 at Valley that I had flown up to that time. I landed, turned off and reported the aircraft "U/S, overstressed", which set the cat amongst the pigeons. When I got into the squadron, my instructor was waiting. I had never liked him: he was a 'creamie' given to showing off in the air and he never made mistakes (at least, he never admitted to any, even though any student could see them). He lost no time telling me that I was 'deep in it' for my mistake and to see the flight commander immediately.

The flight commander had flown Typhoons during the war, part of the time as No. 2 to Pierre Clostermann, and he exuded calm. He took one look at my white face, heard a couple of words, which came out in a shaking and falsetto voice, and sent me off to the crewroom to sit down with a strong coffee, though had he kept a bottle of Scotch in his filing cabinet I think he would have administered some. And me? Did I learn from it? Did I!

I learned that I needed to be a little more painstaking in my navigation and switch selections. Most importantly, though, I learned not to be overconfident of my abilities. Even though advanced trainers are trainers, they can catch out the unwary and ill-prepared very quickly and can bite just as severely as a complicated fighter. I can still see with amazing clarity that picture of the water, framed by the two arms of Trearddur Bay, right now, and it's 55 years later.

1971 TO 1973 – OC 1 SQUADRON, 4FTS, RAF VALLEY

BOZ ROBINSON

Boz Robinson

In 1971 the RAF's advanced trainer was a supersonic, tandem-seat, very small jet. I had been posted as a Gnat squadron commander and must perforce carry out refresher flying, then a Gnat conversion course, flying the latter from RAF Kemble. After 21 hours in the Jet Provost at Rissie I flew my first real Gnat sortie on 3 February with Dave Stuart. Gosh, what a terrific little rocket jet it was. I knew that if I succeeded in conquering that beast, I was in for some great fun over the years, little realising though that I would still be flying it in the next century. My last Gnat trip

Staff and students of 1 Squadron, 4FTS.

was in G-RORI checking out Mark Grimshaw on 8 June 2005. In 1971 I was far from confident of success, it having been nine years since I had said goodbye to the Hunter. Hard work would be necessary to master the Gnat, and to learn to fly it from the back seat. And hard work it was. Happily, the Gnat hangar at Kemble contained not just us but also the RAF Aerobatic team, the Red Arrows who made life exciting. We had some real characters too, on the staff and among the student instructors: Pete Millar, Bill Blair-Hickman, Mike Sparrow, Dave Longden, Bob Eccles, and Roy Gamblin among others. After three months of very intense work and flying, punctuated by idyllic weekends at home, I passed a final handling test with Jock Byrne and was declared competent to instruct and sufficiently proficient to command a Gnat instructional squadron at 4 FTS, RAF Valley.

I took over in May 1971 as Officer Commanding (OC) 1 Squadron from my old 74 Squadron colleague Glyn Roberts. Brian Entwisle was the chief instructor, and an ex-Hunter chap. OC Standards Squadron was Sqn Ldr Holdway whom I had not met before but was soon to be replaced by Glyn Roberts. OC 2 Squadron was an old acquaintance from Horsham St Faith, Hugh Stark, ex-Javelin night fighters. Across the other side of the airfield was the Hunter squadron, 3 Squadron, commanded by Mike Barringer. It felt terrific to be joining such a busy, exciting, and active unit as RAF Valley, commanded then by Gp Capt John Langar whom I had known in Cyprus in 1958 as OC 43 Squadron.

To some extent I was lacking in confidence which may sound odd. My fragile self-confidence was not at all bolstered by the aggressive and semi-hostile manner of some of the Standards Squadron staff members. I have never been very adept at ground school, and when I was being handled by the Standards staff my incompetence at explaining exactly how the flight instruments worked was plain for all to see. However, in my own mind I knew that when instructing in the aircraft, I was as good if not better than most. I decided to take a full-time student to put my ability to the test. Gus Crockatt was the poor victim of my first efforts at passing on the techniques needed to fly a tricky fast jet. Happily, we both made good progress and he passed his tests with the Standards examiners.

One of the joys of that period was the frequent detachments to Kinloss or Leuchars when the Valley weather was bad. Early in the day we would make the decision to take four aircraft away for the day, and operate in Scotland, probably managing three or four sorties there by each aircraft before returning in the early evening to Valley. Sometimes the Valley weather had improved, sometimes it had not. One of my strong memories is of the intense feeling of euphoria on getting into the mess bar with the other pilots after an exciting recovery through cloud. It gave one a huge sense of shared achievement. Once, we got back when the Valley weather had worsened, and we were committed to a descent through 40,000 feet of cloud. We split into two pairs with the lowest on fuel going down first. There was just nowhere else we could go with such low fuel states. There is terrific satisfaction on getting back in those conditions, flying extra smoothly with another Gnat hanging on your wing, and breaking cloud on the ground-controlled approach, well below minima, at 100 feet or lower. Our GCA controllers were definitely some of the best in the world, and we had immense respect for their calmness and capability. In fact, to be a fully certified air traffic controller at 4 FTS was no mean achievement in the ATC world, and it required long hours of training and special qualities of icy cold nerve and immense concentration. Any failure by the ATC staff could result in either loss of an aircraft or death for the crew, the Gnat being so desperately short of fuel, right from take-off.

We clearly did not encounter such situations regularly, always trying, if possible, to avoid them. Had we applied the Air Staff rules to the letter, it would have been impossible to graduate the numbers of students we did. If you like, we were flying on a knife-edge, and the trick was to stay right on that edge without getting cut. So, a squadron commander's post was one which required a big dose of common sense, lots of luck and some sharp judgements. Risk had to be absolutely minimised because the whole operation was filled with a variety of risks anyway. The Gnat has often been described as too much of a handful for a student pilot.

Indeed, it was sometimes too much of a handful for the instructor, as many Gnat accident reports tell. But what was certain was that any student pilot graduating from 4FTS at that time was good at his job and was better prepared for what lay ahead of him than if he had only flown the Jet Provost. In short it was a good training vehicle even though it resulted in us losing many students who simply could not cope with it.

In August 1971 I had around 150 hours flying the Gnat and was settling in well to the squadron commander's job. However, there was always more to learn. It intrigued me that at the morning weather briefings, when two bad weather diversion airfields were nominated, Machrihanish was frequently one of them. I sat in my office and scrutinised our 1 million scale maps, eventually finding Machrihanish on the Kintyre peninsula, near Campbelltown. I studied how to get there and realised that, owing to ATC obstacles like civil airways, it would not be easy. Furthermore, I had not met anyone who had diverted there, or who knew quite how to get there. One of my new staff members was John Blackwell, a punchy young flying officer who had been creamed off from his flying training to be an instructor. Much as they disliked the practice, and only the very best were so selected, they usually proved to be a great asset to any school.

The time came for me to carry out my first flying test of Blackwell. On 17 August I briefed him carefully for a normal sortie profile, climbing into the upper airspace for several instructional sequences for him to give back to me. We taxied out and took off on runway 32. As the wheels tucked up into the fuselage, I said to John: "John, you are to divert to Machrihanish NOW." "Are you serious Sir?" he said. No reply. To give him his due, there was only a momentary hesitation before he turned right toward airway Blue 2, called ATC and started planning the trip while accelerating to 360kts. ATC were also under test, as I had planned. I needed to know just how tricky it was to get a Gnat to Machrihanish, and how much fuel it would need. Any messing about by ATC could seriously jeopardise the practice. To their credit, and to John Blackwell's, mission was accomplished in fine fettle. After 15 minutes we flew across the runway at Machrihanish. I knew how to do it. I knew how much fuel it ought to use, and I knew that we could safely return to Valley with some fuel left to do a few circuits. Furthermore, John's self-confidence was boosted, and all the staff instructors at 4 FTS were suddenly made aware that Machrihanish was a fair bet. Even better, they also realised that to fly with Boz Robinson was to expect the unexpected, there being no better stimulus to get chaps to imagine the worst scenario. The routine of 4 FTS was about to be electrified and serious thought given to preparing for bad times. My next trick had to wait a while, until the winter weather arrived.

Once the sea temperature fell below 10°C, we all had to put aside our thin flying suits and take to the immersion suit to be fully prepared to survive in the cold of the Irish Sea in winter, or worse, in the North Sea. The immersion suit was made of heavy canvas, with a tight-fitting rubber neckband that would keep out the water. It was relatively thin and therefore you needed some more insulation to increase the chance of survival until the helicopter appeared to take you home. The suit itself was uncomfortable and was regarded as a winter curse. During time on the ground you could release the long diagonal zip across the front of the suit, to give some ventilation, but when flying it had to be fully zipped up of course. When I noticed, during my lunches in the aircrew feeder, a dining facility where you could eat in flying kit, that many chaps wore very little under their suit, I knew the time had come to carry out another of my tests.

In conjunction with the senior medical officer, Ben Butler, and the CO of the helicopters, we prepared a surprise for a landing pair of pilots. Late one afternoon, as they taxied on to the hard standing to park their Gnat, a helicopter appeared from nowhere, and I grabbed the crew and told them they were being transported to the Welsh mountains as if they had had to eject; we would tell their families not to worry. They would be given only the standard emergency rations and some signal cartridges carried in their survival pack. No mobile phones in those days. Off they went and were dropped in a pre-planned spot where the SMO could keep an eye on them during the night, and where any escape attempts could be thwarted. We pulled them out after noon the following day, cold and hungry, then brought them into the big briefing room for them to tell their story first-hand to the assembly of QFIs and students. That scheme was most effective in bringing home a lesson to those who neglected their own best interests. Stores reported a sudden rush to collect warm woolly sweaters.

Before my opposite number Hugh Stark was due for posting, my staff helped me in playing a practical joke on him. He was always teasing us that our offices and crewroom downstairs in the operations block smelled less sweet than his offices on the floor above. We bought a box of kippers, waited until all the 2 Squadron chaps had gone home, and then hid our smelly kippers all over the 2 Squadron area. Some were slipped behind filing cabinets, others stuffed into the sofas and chairs in the QFIs' crewroom. Some days later, we noticed a strange smell emanating from upstairs and decided to go to investigate. It really was terrible, but the inhabitants did not seem to notice. Nothing was ever said, but eventually the smell subsided. However, even after Hugh had left, we discovered the remains of a kipper behind his filing cabinet!

In March 1972 it was decided to resurface the runways at Valley so 4 FTS would move to RAF Fairford. In mid-March I carried out a squadron commander's flying check on one of my QFIs, Fg Off Jock Stirrup (later to become chief of the Air Staff and chief of Defence Staff during the period of the Labour government in the nineties). Next, I strapped into a Gnat with Flt Lt Nigel Day my current student only to be interrupted during the pre-start checks by a request from the chief instructor to fly immediately to RAF Brize Norton. I at once delegated Mel Trachta, our USAF officer, to take over my sortie which he did. That was the nearest I think that I came in those years to having to eject. So, I collected an ATC officer, Paul Brain, to fly to RAF Brize Norton. On arrival we were informed that Mel Trachta and Nigel Day had both ejected from the Gnat into which I had earlier strapped myself. Both pilots were safe and well much to my relief. The Gnat's engine had failed and shown a fire-warning alarm, so Mel ordered them both to eject at once. Having landed heavily in a Welsh field, Mel told me that he was disconcerted suddenly to be upbraided as he lay gasping on the ground, by an irate Welsh farmer who shouted at him: "Why don't you buggers give us more warning when you do this sort of thing?" Mel replied that he too would have appreciated some warning. After Mel and Nigel left the Gnat, it circled for a while before doing a perfect wheels-up landing on the airfield at Llanbedr where the fire was quickly extinguished by an astonished fire crew.

Paul Brain and I, now at Brize, had been tasked with coordinating the air traffic arrangements for the forthcoming detachment of the whole of the fleet of Gnats while the Valley runway was resurfaced. Although the 4 FTS aircraft would be operating from Fairford, where testing of the first Concorde was being conducted, the air traffic recovery and approach of our aircraft from the Welsh training area would have to be conducted by the air traffic controllers at Brize Norton. They were quite adept at recovering relatively slow-moving transport aircraft with considerable fuel reserves, but I was somewhat alarmed as to whether they would be able to adjust to recovering much faster planes with critically low fuel remaining. My reservations were in the event entirely justified. It was a tribute to their efforts to adapt and to the energetic and quick thinking of the tower staff at Fairford, which always included a Gnat-qualified duty QFI, that the disasters which so often threatened were successfully averted, often by the skin of the teeth. The situation was compounded by the edict that whenever Concorde was due to take off or to recover, 4 FTS operations were to be suspended. It was not too difficult to work around Concorde's planned take-off times, but her recoveries were rarely punctual, often coming suddenly when a technical fault occurred to the great beast. At that point the duty squadron commander in the tower had to work like a one-armed paperhanger to divert Gnats short on fuel to other airfields, or to get Gnats on to the ground quickly before Concorde appeared from the west.

On one occasion I was tasked with doing an instrument flying trip with one of our students. He was coping fairly well with the sortie though heavy cloud was making things difficult. I preferred to do IF checks in clear air. One item that needed to be covered was 'recovery from unusual positions'. This meant asking the student to close his eyes and then, when commanded, to open them again to assess the aircraft's attitude and recover to straight and level flight as quickly as possible. We were at 7,000 feet somewhere over Gwent and in cloud which seemed to be getting worse. Rather than abandon the exercise, I decided to give him some simple positions from which to recover. He closed his eyes and I put the aircraft into a high nose-up attitude then told him to open his eyes as I gave him back control. He did so and completely misunderstood the situation such that he applied full rudder and elevator.

Needless to say, the aircraft entered a spin at once. I took control. If the Gnat spins below 10,000 feet you are supposed to eject immediately but there was no way I was going to end my career that way! With a yaw doll's eyes showing full white I countered the spin almost automatically, and after some fairly hefty manoeuvres, with me by now holding the controls absolutely central, the aircraft settled into straight and level flight at 4,500 feet, still in cloud. Heavy breathing from both cockpits followed as we made our way gently back to Fairford. Thankfully I had not followed the instructions for a Gnat in a spin to the letter or we would both have been in our parachutes. Not long thereafter, the student went off to fly helicopters.

Early in July we flew to RAF Leeming and the following day, 16 of our aircraft gave a formation flying display at RAF Topcliffe before returning to Valley on the 8th: the Fairford fun detachment was over and our new runway at Valley was nearly ready for action. Well, one runway was ready but the main runway 32/14 was not. The contractors had failed to complete their contract on time. This was very much in my mind in 1979 when I became station commander at Valley and we needed to resurface the runway again. For the next two weeks, flying had to be restricted to the short runway 02/20, with an attendant risk of accident because it had no arrestor barrier. Needless to say the contractors were not popular. Nor were their masters the Air Ministry Works Department, now becoming part of the larger Property Services Agency.

I knew from our conversations that my bobsleigh colleague, Prince Michael of Kent, was keen to fly the Gnat and when he asked to visit us I readily agreed. Then I got cold feet and wondered where my career might go if during his unannounced sortie with me in a Gnat, we had to eject or force land. I was also very uneasy about misleading my splendid boss, Brian Entwisle, so I came out with the proposal to him. He thought it a super idea but then had to tell the pen-pushers at Group HQ. The result was that HRH got his trip in a Gnat but only through an official royal visit to the Central Flying School, RAF Little Rissington, and not with Boz at Valley.

In September, the CFS boys arrived again to do their annual standardisation checks. My friend George Lee, whom I had known many years, said he would do my check and asked if I would prepare to show him how to do a night diversion to RAF Shawbury with a student. All went smoothly – I always love flying at night – and after we had de-briefed the trip, George started asking me lots of questions which I was able to answer mostly without pause. Just a few were tricky enough to reveal my innate inability to explain things technical, but I thought nothing of it. It was not as if I were undergoing an A2 check after all. Then to my utter amazement, George told me that the evening had gone so well, he would award me with an immediate upgrade to A2 from C to I. My long battle with Standards Squadron was over at last. It had taken 18 months, and the fact that George had taken me by surprise – I had no idea that I was under A2 test conditions. In December we said goodbye to dear Brian Entwisle, and hello to another friend, Derek Homer – our new chief instructor and himself new to the Gnat.

In August of 1971 Valley had received a new station commander named Brian Huxley. He was a delightful, quiet and effective leader and was a most popular CO. Brian proved at the time to be a generous host, treating me in a very friendly and trusting manner. With two years' experience in the job, Brian as CO and Derek Homer as chief instructor, I felt very comfortable and confident.

On 5 July 1973 Brian was called to attend a meeting at Group Headquarters and a Bassett aircraft was sent to Valley to collect him. Shortly after the aircraft had taken off with Brian aboard, the crash alarm sounded. The Bassett had crashed just a few miles to the east of Valley. According to the people who arrived at the scene soon afterwards, Brian was not badly injured and was helping to get those more seriously hurt out of the wreckage. The navigator, Flt Lt Peter Lane died. When the station medical officer arrived, he told Brian that despite his apparent lack of injury he should be sent to the Bangor Hospital for examination. Lucky that the SMO did that; on arrival at the Bangor A&E Brian collapsed. He had suffered a ruptured spleen and if he had not been at the hospital, he might have died as a consequence. Needless to say, it took him some time to recover, and we were all very glad to see him return as our CO – alive and well. The subsequent Board of Inquiry discovered that the Bassett had been wrongly refuelled with AVTUR and not AVGAS – jet fuel not piston fuel.

One curious episode occurred in 1973 when advanced flying training was at its peak with around 70 sorties per day being flown from Valley and Mona.

Normally our suspension rate (that is the number of students who failed to reach the required standard) was about 15 to 17% on each course. So, a course of ten students would lose perhaps one or two members, maybe even three. However, 1 Squadron found itself chopping a greater number from one particular group of students, and as the boss I had to call the staff together to try to determine why our chop rate had risen alarmingly, nudging up toward 30% plus. Since it fell to other senior staff from either the Standards Squadron, or other squadrons and frequently the chief flying instructor himself, to conduct 'chop rides', it looked as if my instructors were not doing their job well. Yet I knew that they too were taking pains to examine their own efforts and to cajole problem students into greater effort to succeed. Try as we might, we could uncover no adequate reason for the high chop rate, except to note that the course as a whole seemed not to represent the normal high standard of intake from the basic school, where we learned that the same course had struggled similarly and suffered a higher-than-normal rate of failure. I discussed the situation with the CI and he agreed to seek clarification from the staff at Command HQ. Meanwhile we began to lose even more from that course.

Finally, we finished their training with a chop rate of 37% and all those who succeeded had to be relegated to co-pilot posts on bombers or transport aircraft rather than proceeding to the fast-jet operational conversion units where customarily all our graduates ended up. Then all was revealed. The chief instructor called me and explained that, to prove the system was valid and functioning properly, the Ministry of Defence had decreed that the course of students in question should be made up of potential pilots graded lower than normal at the Officer and Aircrew Selection Centre. Instead of grades A and B with an occasional C, we had been tackling Ds and Es. The news came as a huge relief to me and to my staff.

By the midsummer of 1973 I knew that my time at Valley was drawing sadly to a close and I began to relish a change of scene. Even when you have the best flying job in the whole of the air force, there comes a time when the excitement tends to become routine. You know that nothing could match what you do from day to day but still hanker after a change, knowing that it may well be for the worse. My fellow squadron commander from the floor above, Hugh Stark OC 2 Squadron, had already been posted away to RAF Germany to be replaced by an irrepressible fun-loving Ulsterman, Wally Black, who, when called upon at celebrations, could perform a marvellous cabaret act. Now it was my turn to leave, and to my intense relief I discovered that in September I was to follow Hugh to RAF Rheindahlen to be a member of the Offensive Operations Division at Royal Air Force Germany Headquarters, and thereby a member of the Second Tactical Air Force Tactical

Evaluation team. After a final night test for Flt Lt Shelbourn on the 13th, I handed over my command to an old acquaintance from Canberra days, Dave Coldicutt and drove away to Stonewell for a spot of leave.

DANCING ON THE RUNWAY

FRANK FOSTER

Frank Foster

I will never forget my first flight in a Gnat. The experience was exhilarating. I had never expected such performance from a small aircraft. It had panache, it had style, it had power, it was the sports car of the skies. That was my indelible impression of the Gnat during my advanced flying training in 1969. After the course, I was posted to CFS Gnat QFI training flight as a holding posting before my Harrier conversion. This presented me with a more powerful and interesting aircraft, but I never forgot the Gnat. Imagine my excitement when I was posted back to Gnats as an instructor.

The Gnat was an amazing aircraft. How the designers stuffed so much into such a diminutive airframe always amazed me. While the small size and light weight enabled the Gnat to provide high performance it also gave the engineers some problems. Firstly, the training configuration was adopted from a single-seater design. Inserting a second cockpit without any significant increase in the fuselage size resulted in cosy pilot accommodation. Most pilots found the cockpit space to be at a premium especially during the winter periods when wearing immersion suits was compulsory. Tall pilots found difficulty fitting their legs into the foot wells and applying full aileron was almost impossible especially when using full rudder in a crosswind. A novel solution adopted by some pilots was to shave the heels off their flying boots thus gaining enough space to stop their legs chafing on the lower edge of the instrument panel.

The small size of the cockpit created control problems for the aircraft designers. The cockpit was too short to allow the control column movement and tailplane angle to be fixed, if the tailplane moved the same angle for the same control column movement, pitch control would be too powerful at high speed and not powerful enough at low speed. Folland's engineers cleverly invented CamK, a device shrouded in mystery by ground-school instructors. Basically, it changed the ratio the tailplane moved depending on the position of the control column producing a balance.

Additionally, the designers saved a little weight and space by using the undercarriage doors as airbrakes. When extended, they had to move forward into the airflow. Consequently, the undercarriage extended forward, and this moved the aircraft centre of gravity forward significantly enough to require a large control input from the pilot to maintain a constant attitude. The designer thoughtfully included a control input in the form of the datum shift which automatically moved the tailplane about two degrees to compensate for the change in centre of gravity as the undercarriage extended and retracted.

Another neat design feature included the ability to fly the aircraft without the aid of the powered flying controls. During hydraulic failure or when the pilot selected manual control, a simple procedure could be invoked to allow the aircraft to be flown with a combination of electrically controlled tailplane with the additional help of elevators that could be unlocked from the tailplane. Although the procedure was simple and the aircraft flew perfectly well in 'manual', many students found it difficult to cope and developed a phobia of the hydraulic-warning caption illuminating. When flying in manual, students would forget to manually enter the datum shift changes required as the undercarriage extended until the aircraft suddenly reminded them by pitching nose down. In manual flying mode the Gnat was most probably the first fly-by-wire fighter ever built.

The most amusing characteristic of this little aircraft was its ability to dance on the runway. The Gnat possessed very low crosswind limits compared to modern aircraft and this could be as low as five knots on a very wet runway. The wheel track was just over five feet and it had high swept-wing configuration. In any crosswind the aircraft tried to roll away from the wind while the fin tried to turn it into wind. This meant that the effective weight of the aircraft was always on the leeward wheel. Any braking applied by the pilot would be more effective on that wheel and less on the windward-side wheel. Unless compensated by the pilot this would inevitably swing the aircraft out of wind changing the weight distribution from the leeward wheel to the windward wheel and the whole sequence would begin again in the opposite direction. This runway dance would only happen a couple of times before the nosewheel left the ground and an oscillation began which in severe cases could lead to aircraft damage or loss of control. However, if the pilot kept the wings level on landing this situation would not happen. Unfortunately, the cockpit was so narrow that an average-size person could not physically apply full aileron because their legs were in the way.

The Gnat ejection seat, built by Folland, was completely different to the more common Martin-Baker seat, as described earlier. Unfortunately, there was one surprising feature of which the pilot had to be aware. The aircraft itself could reinforce this whenever the pilot pushed negative 'g'. All seat straps fitted into a quick release box (QRB) that was attached to a fix-length negative 'g' strap. To hold the QRB in a central position a waistband held a thin metal tab that was fixed into the right side of the QRB. Only two other straps fitted into the QRB. The lap straps lay over the legs, threaded through loops on the seat straps and then the shoulder straps threaded through the loops on the end of the lap strap before being secured into the QRB; sounds complicated but it was very easy and quick. The thin tab that first fed into the QRB had to be flat otherwise it would not allow the right-hand shoulder strap to seat correctly. The result was that, if the tab was bent slightly, the right-hand shoulder strap could spring out of the QRB under negative 'g'. A pilot could find himself resting on the canopy. Pilots soon learnt to ensure the thin tab was flat.

There were two things that students could be relied on: not to listen to instructions and their determination to kill their instructor. The Gnat was particularly helpful to the student in this context. Before the low-level navigation phase of the syllabus one instructor decided to give his student an advantage over his peers. He was already in the low-flying area showing the student the correct way to low fly when they approached turning point one of navigation route one. In an instant the instructor decided to fly the first leg in reverse to give his student an advantage over his peers when he flew the route later. Unfortunately, another student on the course was tasked to fly navigation route one and he was airborne at the same time on the same route but in the opposite direction. Not unsurprisingly, what happened when the two jets crossed each other with a closing speed of 720 knots with feet to spare was, to put it mildly, an eye-opening experience.

I was a pilot navigation instructor which meant I flew with lots of students who stumbled around the world with no idea of where they were. Students had taken me to parts of the UK I did not know existed and it was my duty to try and get them back to RAF Valley before they ran out of fuel. One student who had failed his final navigation test twice was in his last chance saloon with me for a third and final navigation test. He planned the sortie well and his map was full of brightly coloured hieroglyphs and folded to perfection. We completed the brief, and I examined his maps, carefully asking what the various areas of artwork represented. Finally satisfied that he may know what he was doing, we walked out to the aircraft. The first thing I noticed at the aircraft was the student had forgotten his map, so I suggested that he unstrap and go back to the squadron and get it; this he did.

However, he needn't have bothered because, once airborne, his flight path never crossed the track on the map. After 40 minutes flying, he had not seen one planned turning point, although he declared he had seen them all, and we had infringed just about every red circle on the map (red circles are areas to be avoided, e.g. small airfields, noise-complaint areas, danger areas etc.). Fortunately, I had checked before take-off that these areas were inactive. On returning to Wales and heading west, the route should have taken us over Lake Bala. This is a long narrow lake orientated NE–SW and is half a mile wide. At 360 knots it should take about five seconds to cross. We came out of Wales over the coast and headed into Cardigan Bay. At this point he shouted Lake Bala and continued for 12 minutes in a westerly direction, some 70 miles over the sea, before I took control and returned to UK national waters and back to RAF Valley. Needless to say, he did not pass the third final navigation test and had he been flying by himself he would have reached land fall in Southern Ireland.

During the course students were taken on a land away to an unfamiliar airfield to see parts of the country they most probably had not seen before. This was a good way to build confidence for the student and give the instructor a chance to see his mates at other airfields. On a trip to RNAS Lossiemouth with an overnight stay my student asked me if I could change our return route to overfly his parent's house. His parents lived on the west coast of Islay, there were no restrictions in the area and very sparse population so no one would be annoyed at the flypast of a single Gnat. I agreed and told him to re-plan his route to make time on target (his mother's house) at 10 a.m. I also told him to phone his mother and let her know that we were coming, not to take any photographs and not to tell anyone else. At 10 a.m. we flew down the coast at Islay and turned up the valley from the sea to the house, climbing parallel to the contours of the valley floor and 'slightly' lower than the 1,000-foot limit at the coast.

When we reached the house, I pulled up sharply to give a plan view of the aircraft to the parents followed by a roll into a downwind position to complete a circuit. As the gear and flaps extended, I looked back to the house to position for a low overshoot when I saw about 100 people in his parent's garden having a party. It was too late to abort the flypast having been spotted by half the population of Islay. I asked the student if he had reminded his mother about not telling anyone about our proposed visit and his reply was, "I told my mother to tell her friends not to say anything". Back at RAF Valley, I had an expectant several days waiting for my invitation to speak with the AOC but to my amazement none was forthcoming. My reward arrived three weeks later when the student returned after a visit home with a flat-sided medicine bottle sealed with a dry cork and full of the most superior uncut Islay whisky I have ever tasted.

RNAS Lossiemouth was also the scene of one of the best aircraft engineering repairs I have ever seen. One of our young instructors did not understand why you trample raised arrestor cables at walking pace in the Gnat. The nosewheel causes the cable to bounce and snag on the mainwheels, damaging the aircraft and often fouling the mainwheel doors. This instructor learnt the hard way. He trampled the cable at 30 knots after a particularly spectacular arrival performed by his student. When he arrived in dispersal the port mainwheel door was dented and bent. However, the flight-line RN officer rang for assistance and within minutes two Wrens appeared with a trolley full of odd-looking tools. They took a quick look at the damage and selected the most appropriate from the many rubber-headed hammers from the trolley. Lying on their backs on the apron, and spurred on by many rude comments from the rest of the ratings, they began to dress out the dents until after a couple of minutes the door shape had been restored. After asking us if we were satisfied with their work they left. It was some time later that we found out these girls were panel beaters from the MT yard who had a few minutes spare and came up to the flight line to assist. Had the RAF known about this there would have been a steward's enquiry, public flogging and the aircraft would have been out of service for months. It cost the pilot a few beers that night to keep the secret to ourselves.

The other great delight we encountered while flying the Gnat was being volunteered for exercises. Some staff officer had discovered the Gnat had a radar signature and maximum speed about the same as the Russian Kh-22 'Kitchen' stand-off missile and would provide realistic training for air defence radars and naval ships. These exercises were welcomed by instructors to relieve the monotony of constant attempts on their lives by incompetent students.

For naval exercises we were volunteered from Leuchars or Kinloss in Scotland to attack naval ships somewhere in the Atlantic supposedly 60 miles from the coast. I say somewhere because we were to be guided by our mother ship, normally a Vulcan, and they were to take us to the target. The idea was that we would fly to a predetermined point in the Western Approaches and formate with a Vulcan. The Vulcan would simulate a Russian Bear and two Gnats would fly below their wings to simulate the Kitchen missile. We always flew two Gnats to each Vulcan and simulated two attack profiles. The idea was to give the Royal Navy training in detecting and avoiding air-to-ship missiles. This all seemed reasonable until it came to the execution of the drill. Two Gnats set off from RAF Valley to rendezvous with a Vulcan 200 miles out to sea, perform an attack against the navy and land at St Mawgan. All this was to be done above cloud, over the sea and using a compass and stopwatch for navigation. We found the Vulcan circling at 30,000ft only because it was drawing smoke rings in the sky. Both Gnats snuggled under the Vulcan's wings, and we headed off in a zigzag pattern towards the fleet.

At the correct launch position, we were given an attack heading and 'launched'. Down we went accelerating to the correct speeds to sea level. Ten minutes later and on time the fleet was spotted. Since the attack profiles were Mach 0.1 different in speed and we penetrated several layers of cloud during the descent we could no longer see each other. Once we had completed our individual attacks it was time to land at St Mawgan. Unfortunately, at sea level we had no idea, within 50 miles, where we were and the erratic approach adopted by the Vulcan had severely confused our mental positional tracking. Up we popped to 10,000ft only to find that we were 120 miles from St Mawgan with very little fuel left. Afterwards we found out that the fleet had decided to sail north-west away from land and neither the Vulcan nor the fleet appreciated that the Gnat was a short-range trainer and could run out of fuel. Fortunately, after a long glide we managed to make it to St Mawgan with only fumes left in the tank. You soon got used to landing a Gnat with absolutely minimum fuel.

Similarly, it was not uncommon to deploy to RAF Kinloss to fly attack profiles for air defence radars in the UK. This entailed flying as far as you could into the Norwegian sea at height and then returning to UK at low level. The first 200 miles could be flown accurately because the TACAN would give positional information but after letting down to low level everything was dead reckoning. The return leg was flown low and fast aiming to land back at RAF Kinloss with minimum fuel. All was going well and four aircraft were inbound at 420 knots skirting around oil rigs approaching the radar heads. All four aircraft flew their own course to give multiple simultaneous targets, and everything was done in radio silence so that the radar defences did not have any clues we were approaching. Once we had overflown the radar heads the plan was to individually make our way back to Kinloss at medium level. One of our formation did not make an allowance for the northerly wind making landfall several miles further south than anticipated. This was further from RAF Kinloss than expected which meant he had less fuel to make the return. This did not faze him one iota because he thought he was at his planned coast in point. On turning north-west for Kinloss he flew close to a red-painted helicopter (a Royal Flight helicopter) on its way to Balmoral; this was definitely a no no. The airways became alive with infringement calls.

However, our trusty pilot did not heed them because he was confident he was 30 miles north of the incident. Popping up to medium level he finally got a TACAN lock on RAF Kinloss and realised his predicament. He calculated he could make Kinloss with about 200lbs of fuel remaining if he did a glide approach and he was not held up for any reason. Gnat callsign 53 contacted Kinloss at 10 miles declaring he was positioning for immediate approach to land. Kinloss 53, a Nimrod with enough fuel on board to fly for days, reported he was 15 miles on the extended centreline, and he declared he was going to land first. A lively discussion ensued with the Gnat declaring he had two minutes fuel to flame out and the Nimrod had enough food and fuel to fly to the Bahamas and return. The Nimrod captain insisted they should divert. The airwaves became blue, and it was evident that Kinloss 53 had lost the argument. What happened was the Gnat landed first and taxied to the end of the runway and shut down to prevent a flame out. The Nimrod landed five minutes later. Back at the flight line the station commander met us and proceeded to tell the pilot not to be inconsiderate and exaggerate his fuel situation, and that he must not upset experienced Nimrod captains. At this point the refuelling crew appeared and asked us to sign for the fuel. I showed the station commander the paperwork. They had put 2,850lbs of fuel into the Gnat which had a total capacity of 2,900lbs. The station commander did not say another word and marched off, we did not hear from him again.

Flying the Gnat as an ab-initio pilot through to QFI flight commander was a fulfilling experience. It had its high points when travelling to work and seeing 20 aircraft on the flight line you knew you were likely to get a sortie that day, and the low points at 10 a.m. the same morning when only five aircraft were left serviceable for the second wave, followed by despair with only one aircraft serviceable for the third wave and that was usually commandeered by Standards Squadron. However, the Gnat looked a graceful, well-mannered aircraft which performed superbly. Well done to Folland for conceiving and building a superb aircraft.

FLYING THE GNAT AS A STUDENT
AL BEATON

First impressions – very excited walking out to the line for the first time. Very small aircraft – looked down into the cockpit. Nose oleo dropped with the weight of two pilots.

Although the Folland seat was quite hard, once strapped in, everything was reasonably to hand and very comfortable. The stick-top tailplane electric trim was a pleasant novelty, the co-location of the throttle and the undercarriage/airbrake was again another Gnat novelty, but it came to hand easily. Flap selection again was neat, simple, and effective. The IFIS dominated the instrument panel, the

Al Beaton

attitude display, which could accommodate the full vertical envelope, was now going to teach us the principles of attitude flying – selected levels of pitch would produce a desired performance which combined with the TACAN range ring circles, was a major step forward in leading us towards front-line fast-jet cockpit management. Zero reader ILS was a complicated internal aids approach – part of the IRT, no wonder it took me more than one attempt to get through that hurdle and onto the best part of the course.

Engine start up – so much more potential Orpheus power than the sound of loose nuts and bolts in a tin can with the Jet Provost Viper. Hands and feet to the flying controls was very natural although the rudder pedals were much closer together than previously used to in a wider two-man cockpit.

First impressions on the first familiarisation flight were exhilarating. Acceleration on take-off was exciting, the rate of climb outstanding and the effects of controls were so light and sensitive for very small inputs. In particular, the rate of roll was superb. In all, this little dart was the epitome of full, total three-dimensional freedom. This was flying taken to another exciting dimension. The first experience and excitement of flying in such a jet was and always will be, totally memorable, unforgettable.

What soon also became unforgettable was appreciating that to operate this complex package of modern avionics and airframe designs that were leading us now towards the complexity of modern RAF front-line jets, was going to be hard work. Being able to do this, essentially in a single-pilot capacity, was going to be tough. So many new things to understand, learn and control, effectively. In particular, the rate at which things happened, it was light years ahead of what we had just been used to at Basic Flying Training School.

Externally, the front-seat visibility, all around, was excellent, very different from side-by-side JP flying – again the sensation of single-seat flying added to the excitement. Sitting well ahead of the wing, slipper tanks just in sight. The realisation that there was very little distance from inside the cockpit to the hostile outside environment, was almost unreal, even unbelievable at 40,000ft, on high-level familiarisation. This small dart of a machine felt so small in the vast natural outside airspace, it was as if I was riding on the tip of an arrow.

Changing from powered flying controls to manual was a novel experience. The unforgettable 'speed, trim and unlock' phrase immediately returns to mind.

The aerodynamic effect of high airspeeds over the flying controls, became an understandable reality. Lack of manoeuvrability emphasised the need for anticipation and configuration setting up became even more important.

On the advanced phase of the course, I do recall my first introduction to low level. As we descended from a medium-level transit towards Lake Bala, I became oblivious to the mouth music coming from the back seat. When he gave me control, his commentary eventually dried up until he finally announced – "you are really enjoying this, aren't you?" With such brilliant all-round visibility and the speed over the ground, it was one of the most memorable sorties of my career in aviation. I often wonder if that first low-level introduction and subsequent low-level navigational exercises, were influential in my being one of the first RAF's first tourists to be posted to the brand-new Buccaneer.

At medium level, I did enjoy the performance of the Gnat. Aeros were a delight revealing that in pure handling, the aircraft was very responsive and covered a great deal of sky, very easily. Yes, the rate of roll was very impressive but sadly overcompensated for by my QFI who one day used a boot-full of rudder to roll even faster – sadly he killed himself when the fin came off during a display at Upper Heyford. The Gnat did build confidence but could also breed overconfidence. I have never since, used rudder to increase roll rate on any other aircraft.

The Gnat was a very good demonstrator of the effects of high level. My recollection was that it was a bit like flying on a razor blade, as soon as you tried to turn, you fell off the blade, with stall buffet and loss of height. A first experience of supersonic flying, Mach 1.1 from a steep 40 degrees nose-down dive, with associated trim changes noticeable over the tailplane. An important practical lesson in high-speed aerodynamics.

In the circuit, usually approached from a run and break, the Gnat was fun to fly but demanded accuracy from the top of the downwind leg – another important lesson applied thereafter throughout the career. The same was true of PFLs, nailing high key at 5,000 feet if not then low key was essential if a landing was going to work. Landing was always a bit of a wobble with such a narrow undercarriage; some into-wind aileron was useful after landing in a crosswind. Braking wasn't a problem even though there was a 'chute although we seldom used it – too much fag in recovering it and repacking it.

The Gnat's excellent handling, manoeuvrability and even stability, made formation flying another rewarding experience. The u/c speed brake was effective although taking your hand off the throttle could be awkward.

Instrument flying – once confidence was built up, the Gnat was a very good internal aids-only capable aircraft. To land off a TACAN dive to ILS, totally based on the procedure, was a rewarding achievement. We certainly learned the value of attitude flying, with known power settings.

Overall, the Gnat was a complex aircraft and a big step up from the Jet Provost, so the learning curve was very steep. Some would say that it was too complex for the AFTS role – I don't agree, I think that this distilled an essential determination in me/us to succeed, which when rewarded with success, turned us out to be well prepared for the next phase of our training towards the front line. I graduated on 8 August 1968. After five months of intense training. I was 20 years old and had a total of 233 hours.

FLYING THE GNAT AS A QFI

I returned to the Gnat on 14 March 1977 – after two Buccaneer tours, as a volunteer for CFS! This was the last Gnat CFS Course – the Hawk was being introduced into the RAF.

All my memories of 40 AFTS Course came flooding back. Flying from the front seat was now a great deal of fun but, of the 53-hour course, only eight were flown from the front seat. Flying from the back was still enjoyable but it was a much poorer cockpit.

The obvious marked difference was the very poor back-seat visibility, not just forward but also from side to side, almost level with the top of the engine intake. Whilst a good trainer for the student, the lack of good visibility for the back seat made the Gnat a more difficult aircraft to operate as a QFI. The front-seat ejection headbox blocked most of the forward visibility, the only gaps looking forward were between the gas pipes either side of the ejection-seat head box.

Demonstration of manual flying from the back seat was extremely difficult, especially as the approach was flapless with a high nose-up attitude. It was helpful to have a crosswind to demonstrate a manual landing as a slightly crabbed approach allowed for some increased forward visibility, until just before kicking straight for touchdown. For a QFI, the most difficult demo was a night landing, in manual, at Mona relief landing ground. I recall my QFI being satisfied when we managed to bounce off the runway, halfway down the strip. He must have been very nervous watching it all from the front seat.

For all exercise demonstrations, the same visibility limitations applied with the exception perhaps of instrument flying. For similar visibility considerations, I recall it was always useful to fly a curved final approach on a visual landing. The less straight ahead flying the better. Otherwise, all the handling characteristics of the Gnat still applied.

I went on to complete my CFS course on the Hunter – an advanced, heavier, higher performing, side-by-side JP style. A better instructional modification of the single-seat Hunter variant, but without the advanced avionics.

It is quite understandable that the Gnat as a trainer, like all modifications of single-seat aircraft, was a poor training vehicle …but just for the QFI. As a trainer for students, perhaps the opposite was true. It was an excellent high-performance AFTS trainer for pilots to understand modern aircraft systems and avionics, swept-wing transonic performance and simplification and anticipation of a task to cope with the rate at which 'things happen' in the front-line fighter/bomber aircraft of its day.

CHAPTER 2

INCIDENTS AND ACCIDENTS

GNAT FORCED LANDING

ROY GAMBLIN

Roy Gamblin

Monday, 19 September 1977, at No. 4 Flying Training School, RAF Valley, on the island of Anglesey, began in much the same way as any other day at the time. The busy training station was in the process of changing over from the Gnat and the Hunter to the Hawk – the RAF's new advanced jet trainer. I was very lucky to have the job of officer commanding the Standards Squadron. My responsibilities called for me to fly all three types concurrently, a fantastic privilege, albeit a very demanding one. The second trip of the day was in a Gnat and was to be a routine instructional standards check for another QFI, Flt Lt Mike Hulyer. Mike was a very competent operator. His check was to be flown as a close-formation exercise in company with another Gnat flown solo by Flt Lt Bill Cope, another fine pilot who went on to become the Buccaneer Force commander during the first Gulf War.

My role was to fly as captain in the front seat of XP540 whilst Mike in the rear seat practised his 'patter' on me as if I was a student pilot learning close formation in the Gnat for the first time. I enjoyed the aircraft greatly. It was an absolute pleasure to fly, especially in close formation. Even though there wasn't a spare inch in the cockpit after I had strapped in my 6ft 3in frame, I felt very comfortable in it – especially in the front seat with its superb view. With two very reliable other QFIs as my companions, the trip promised to be straightforward, easy, and fun. But the fickle finger of fate was to intervene rather rudely. Unbeknown to any of us, XP540 was going to have a bad day.

We were soon airborne from runway 14 and climbing swiftly to the south-east. The sortie proceeded normally over the northern half of Wales for the first 25–30 minutes. Mike's patter was just fine, and I had the pleasure as 'the student' of doing most of the flying after his initial demonstrations. With such a responsive and agile aircraft to fly, I could not fail to get a thrill out of it on every flight but especially during formation aerobatics. We had completed our required manoeuvres in the close 'echelon' positions, including loops, barrel rolls, tight turns, 'emergency' breakaways and rejoins and had just changed to close line astern on the lead aircraft. Mike was now flying the aircraft as we climbed close behind Bill's Gnat to regain some altitude before starting the next phase in the sequence of exercises. We were in clear conditions at about 18,000 feet with blue sky above and 8/8 cloud cover way below us. Our two-aircraft formation was in a turn to the right, passing a northerly heading about eight nm east of RAE Llanbedr, the MoD target facilities airfield on the coast near Harlech that we occasionally used for circuit training. I was very relaxed and was enjoying the view of the lead aircraft only a few feet ahead and above us as I waited for Mike to restart his patter.

Suddenly and unexpectedly, I felt a marked deceleration and decreasing engine noise. We dropped rapidly back out of the formation position. My first thought was that Mike had throttled back to clear formation for some reason. A fraction of a second before that, Mike had noticed an AC/DC warning caption (indicating an alternator failure) but as he had control of the throttle lever he was the first to realise a second later that the engine had actually quit. He called me on the intercom to say that we had flamed out. Simultaneously, Mike closed the throttle and I instinctively hit the engine 'hot relight' button. Mike then called that he was trying a hot relight, so I left him to it, switched on the standby radio and made a brief Mayday call on 243.0 MHz to say that we had flamed out and were heading for Valley. The call was picked up by Bill, who was monitoring the emergency frequency. One of these was my deputy, Pete, who was sitting quietly in the 'local' control room in the Valley ATC tower as the duty instructor. Pete told me later that he listened to a very calm Mayday call (I was glad he thought that, because my mind was racing too fast to even think of trying to sound calm). He immediately began his own procedures on the ground which included informing the OC Flying, the station commander and so on.

Meanwhile, back in XP540, I had taken control as the unsuccessful hot relight attempt ended after the allotted ten seconds. I turned in a gentle zoom gaining altitude on a north-west heading and began decelerating to the gliding speed of 180kts. Simultaneously, Mike and I noticed that the engine rpm gauge was registering zero. Now this was very odd and not in accord with what should have been. Both of us had firmly believed that the engine had flamed out, rather than seized, since there had been absolutely no engine vibration and it had run down in the same way as an engine starved of fuel or flame. We had practised enough with engine failures in the simulator to know the difference. In a flame-out condition, the engine would 'windmill' – i.e., it would turn over at low rpm in response to the airflow through the engine intake. In a mechanical failure leading to a seizure, there would normally be vibration and the rpm would be at zero, or near zero. Our reasoning, and the initial actions, had taken place only in a very short span of about 15–20 seconds from the first symptom, so we now began to take in the conflicting evidence and to try to fathom out what was going on.

The next event, within a few seconds, was a HYD (hydraulics low pressure) warning, which appeared to confirm that we had indeed suffered an engine seizure. If the engine had simply flamed-out and was windmilling, it would be expected also that the idling hydraulic pump would maintain enough pressure to provide power to the tailplane. We now had a more serious condition to confront since, not only did we have a dead engine, we had no flaps available for landing and we would also have to revert to manual control (for ailerons and elevators), using electrical movement of the tailplane, backed up by the small elevators, for pitch control.

So, the HYD warning immediately sparked me off into the STUPRECC memory drill. Halfway through the drill I interrupted it to switch off the fuel booster pump and LP fuel cock, the HP cock having been correctly closed at the end of the relight attempt, an attempt that I was now regretting since that was an incorrect and potentially hazardous response to what by now appeared to be a seizure. Though we hadn't suspected a seizure at the outset.

The memory drills for flame out and seizure are different in many aspects and we had been obliged to start with the one and switch to the other, so I asked Mike to get his flight reference cards out to make sure that we had completed everything necessary under both drills. We had. Somewhere in the middle of all the action, the emergency centre at West Drayton had answered my call with a triangulated position some five miles to the north of Llanbedr, which had just shut for the day (!), though Drayton were trying to contact them to re-open. I could now turn more of my attention to weighing up the two possible options for landing, limited as they were. Not that I had much time for that as I was also aware that, in the absence of the alternator, the battery was advertised as only lasting for 20 minutes – assuming that it was in good shape to begin with.

We had reduced to the gliding speed of 180kts and had drifted back down to the original 18,000ft. Valley was still about 30–32 miles away, with a bit of a headwind at medium altitude and a strong crosswind (18kts – the limit being 20kts) on the only runway, 32, that we might stand any chance of reaching. With its very narrow wheel-track and a high-set and highly swept wing, the Gnat was a bit of a handful in a crosswind, more so in manual. The gliding range even to 32 at Valley, about 1½–2nm/1,000ft in still air, would give us little or no margin for error. On the plus side, there was the fact that the airfield at Mona might provide a last-minute option if we couldn't make Valley 32, but it would prove a late and cumbersome switch onto a much shorter runway and with a significant tailwind! On the other hand, Llanbedr was not only closed but completely obscured under cloud. The only ground feature anywhere in view was a tiny area on the coast near Pwllheli that was of no use to us at all. Llanbedr was also less familiar and had only one runway direction, 18, that was equipped with a jet barrier to stop us if needed. Mike told me unequivocally that he thought we'd never make it to Valley. He was probably right but, before we could enter further debate, Drayton mercifully told us that Llanbedr were re-opening, so it was there that I decided to go.

With plenty of height in hand now, I flew one orbit overhead Llanbedr in the hope of finding even a tiny break in the cloud cover, but there was none. Terrain rises to 2,500ft a few miles east of the airfield, so all initial instrument approaches at Llanbedr were made from over the sea to the west. With that in mind, and to enable full advantage to be made of the excellent radar facilities at the airfield, a special instrument forced-landing procedure had been developed many years earlier. The procedure involved flying from overhead then out over the sea to the west before turning back in under ATC direction to make a 'low-key' position at 3,000ft abeam the downwind end of the runway in use. I hadn't had the opportunity to practise that procedure in a long time but I was well-practiced in visual and other instrument forced-landing procedures as well as in manual flying techniques. So, I was happy enough to set off initially on the westerly heading from about 11,000ft overhead the airfield under ATC direction, still above cloud. Nevertheless, despite the adequate altitude, it seemed a bit unnerving with a dead engine to be heading away from where I planned to land.

As well as being in manual control, which made the aircraft quite heavy and sluggish to handle, I was also having to fly on the smaller and less accurate standby instruments, the main instruments having failed and 'frozen' at their last reading when the alternator came offline. This was normal for our situation and, to cater for it, all Gnat pilots carried a couple of easily detachable sticky patches, usually on the sides of their flying helmets, from where they could be whipped off and stuck over the otherwise misleading and distracting main attitude and direction indicators. However, we had as yet not had an opportunity to set up the standby direction indicator accurately on a steady heading from the wobbly E2B standby compass, so I warned Llanbedr that our headings were not likely to be very accurate. We were given a correction onto heading 240°.

It took a long time to get the actual Llanbedr weather. They had after all only just re-opened so that was understandable. Eventually, as we reached about 8,000ft we were told there was a cloud base of 3,500ft over the airfield, which would not give us much margin over the normal 3,000ft low-key, especially if there were any deviations from the ideal three-dimensional pattern. At that point, at around 8,000ft, still above cloud and about four to five nm out to sea heading away from the airfield, I felt very uneasy about the total picture that was developing and so I decided to bin the procedure, turn back there and then towards the airfield, dive off the height through the cloud and gain speed to give me as much aircraft energy as I could get for visual positioning once we broke cloud. Llanbedr gave me an inbound heading and I turned onto it.

Meanwhile, apart from checking in briefly on the emergency frequency, Bill in the other aircraft had wisely avoided getting involved in the radio chatter as there was little or nothing he could do to help up to that point. I caught a glimpse of him about 200 yards away over my right shoulder just before we entered cloud at around 5,000ft, when he chirped up on the radio with perfect timing and gave us an accurate 15-degree heading correction to the airfield. I could spare him no time, and barely any thought, and not even a quick glance once we were in cloud, but I trusted his judgement implicitly and so left him to it entirely. However, I knew that he had to be flying as close as possible to me to maintain visual contact in the murk and so I tried to keep my aircraft control as smooth as I could, not easy in manual. With no thrust from my dead engine, I must have presented a very difficult reference for him to fly on in close formation. He said later that it was indeed quite a handful because we were "dropping like a stone" at the higher speed. That was the first and last time that I ever had the strange experience of being a formation leader without an engine.

Now we soon had a big problem looming. At 3,000ft, we were still in cloud with no light from below and closing rapidly on the airfield at a mile every 12 seconds. I had to think seriously of zooming for ejection because we were getting rapidly short of height for a successful forced-landing pattern. Moreover, I couldn't know the precise terrain structure beyond the airfield – only that there were spot heights up to 2,500ft at several miles or so to the east. I was also becoming steadily more conscious of a very unwelcome worry as to whether I would make it out of the aircraft in one piece if I had to eject. I had a fear that I might be very close to being too big for a safe ejection. This was a pretty late and stupid time to be thinking about it but I guess it was something to which I had turned a blind eye during the previous years. I should have had myself winched out on the ground, years before, to check the physical clearance but I hadn't wanted to do so in case it brought my

Gnat flying to a premature end – very silly, but true. I fought to keep the thought out of my mind, but it certainly gave me an increased determination to get the aircraft safely onto the runway.

Very suddenly, we broke cloud at 2,800ft, with a speed of 280kts and with about three nm to go to the airfield, clearly in sight to the north-east of us. I wanted to go for runway 18, the only one with a jet barrier at the far end in case I landed too far in and couldn't stop before the runway end. For the second time that day, Mike chipped in to say, "you'll never make it!" Again, I thought he was probably right, but I decided to stick with my plot a bit longer before finally throwing away the barrier option. But it soon became clear that it was not a certainty that I could reach even the minimum recommended low key of 2,500ft for 18, whereas 36 was a certainty, albeit without the barrier. So, I manoeuvred hard right into position for 36 whilst reducing speed to 170kts to get the wheels down using the standby air system, the next very important priority. The good book said that this may take up to 3,000ft of descent and I had to fly below that to maintain my view of the airfield. The book wasn't far wrong – but fortunately the error that day was in my favour. I selected gear down as soon as I could and motored the tailplane by the necessary three-degree nose up to counter the large forward centre of gravity change. Then there was an agonisingly long wait for the gear to lock down during my final manoeuvring to get lined up with the runway at the right height/range ratio. By now I had begun to notice what felt like a metal band tightening around my chest. The stress was reaching a peak. We finally got the third green light descending rapidly through 500ft, about ½nm before the runway threshold. Only then did I feel that we had got to the point where we would not need to eject. Up to then, I had even been half expecting to hear a bang from the back to indicate that Mike had decided independently that a parachute descent was the better option.

From the good position that I had managed to achieve on finals, it was then fairly easy – starting the round out at about 250ft – to achieve a nice smooth, flapless touchdown at 165kts, just in from the painted threshold bars. But our troubles were not quite over. Once the speed had reduced below 160kts, the upper speed limit for streaming the braking parachute in the tail, I called Mike to stream it. He pulled the operating lever, but no deceleration was felt. I gave my lever a tug too, for good measure, but it made no difference. Meanwhile, Bill had continued to fly beside us at a few hundred feet above the runway and was yelling repeatedly at us to "Stream the 'chute! Stream the 'chute". I replied rather dryly that we had done so several times. The brake 'chute had indeed deployed from its container, but it had 'candled' – failed to open – as it often did. I was acutely conscious that we were still hurtling down the runway at a high rate of knots, with no help from the light easterly crosswind, no brake 'chute, no jet barrier and no way even of raising the gear to stop the aircraft.

The ejection option (available down to 90kts minimum) now began to flicker back into my thoughts but was just as quickly dismissed. Not after we had got this far, surely?! I had to be very careful with the brakes which, in the absence of all hydraulic power, were working off the pressure of the ground-charged accumulator. It was essential not to brake too hard or that pressure might be rapidly lost through the action of the Maxaret anti-skid system. As it turned out, the brakes failed totally at about 50kts. I might possibly have been able to keep the aircraft on the runway by an earlier application of full left rudder but, in the circumstances, I was content to allow it to drift gently just off the right side where it stopped nicely on the grass with about 200 yards of runway remaining. With the adrenalin still at maximum flow, and to round it all off nicely, I called for "seats safe!" and a quick exit as there was a possible risk of brake fire. After about 20 yards, I turned around to see Mike some way behind – I guess my adrenalin must have been flowing a bit faster than his. Anyway, there was no fire, so I returned to the aircraft to confirm all the switches safe before handing it over to the care of the fire and rescue services. But, before leaving the scene, I noticed that the engine was gently windmilling in the light breeze. So, it couldn't have been a seizure after all. What had happened, and did we do something wrong?

XP540 after Roy's dramatic landing.

The first person on the scene after the fire crew was the resident RAF medical officer who whisked Mike and me off to the ATC tower for a cup of tea. Meanwhile back at the ranch, Pete and others had been busy. As a precaution, the search and rescue Wessex of C Flight, 22 Squadron, had been scrambled to head down our way in case we needed lifting out of the water or whatever. We had barely started our cup of tea before the yellow Wessex now hove into view past the window, flaring for a landing immediately outside the tower. As we ran out from the tower to clamber aboard for our unscheduled chopper ride home, there was a familiar wave and grin from the captain in the right-hand seat. The crewman handed me a headset to put on and I was greeted on the intercom by the cheery tones of John, a very experienced SAR pilot. He was a good friend and a highly accomplished piano player and raconteur in the bar of the officers' mess at Valley. We were delivered safe and sound less than 20 minutes later outside the line office at Valley where, again for a first and last experience, I was obliged to sign an aircraft back to the engineers having not actually returned it to them.

I made my apologies to the station commander for leaving one of his aircraft in reduced circumstances at another airfield. That done, and having received his congratulations, I turned my attention to Gerry, the senior engineering officer. Gerry guessed immediately that we had experienced an obscure failure that caused loss of the fuel and hydraulic pumps as well as the rpm indicator and alternator. The first item led to the engine actually flaming out but the total loss of hydraulics and rpm indications suggested a seizure. The possibility of that combined set of symptoms had never surfaced in any discussion throughout my years of flying the Gnat, although I subsequently heard that there had been one other such failure. It was certainly not catered for in any of our publications or procedures, so it was not surprising that Mike and I had been a bit baffled by the combination of some symptoms and the absence of others. Anyway, the happy result was a successful forced landing in difficult circumstances and all that was left now for me was the report writing. But first, my wife needed a brief explanation as to what had happened and an amendment to my pick-up time and location. The pick-up was delayed by a few hours and was switched from the squadron offices to the mess bar.

JUST ANOTHER WORKING SATURDAY
DAVE MOSS

It all happened on a working Saturday just a couple of weeks short of my 21st birthday. The conversion phase of No. 41 Gnat Course at No. 4 FTS, RAF Valley had started badly with a run of poor weather and so a full flying programme

Dave Moss

was mounted on 8 June 1968. Did the loss of a day on the beach at Rhosneigr worry us? Certainly not, as young would-be fighter pilots with only provisional RAF wings already on our chests, we had no objections to strapping on the sleek and exciting-looking Folland Gnat T1 and taking the next steps towards productive service on a front-line squadron. So, on down to the flight line for another challenging day getting to terms with this slippery and demanding advanced trainer.

The Gnat's powered flying-control systems were complex and the procedure for reverting to manual control in event of a hydraulic failure required special attention. A lot of time had been given over to this in the ground-school phase of the course and in the simulator. Now we had started flying, 'Effects of Controls 2' was a sortie dedicated to exploring this regime and came as conversion exercise (Convex) 7, to be preceded by a dedicated simulator sortie that I had completed successfully on 6 June. My hugely experienced QFI, who at over 40 years of age appeared so old to my young eyes, was Flt Lt Al Holyoake. He briefed me for this sortie on that Saturday morning that was blessed with good weather and light winds. Moreover, the sea temperature had recently reached the 15°C limit for doing without the bulky old, two-piece immersion suits that we had started the course wearing; this made our flying so much more comfortable.

XR999 at Kemble in October 1966. (Ray Deacon)

As far as I can remember, the start-up, take-off and climb-out in XR999 to around 10,000ft were totally normal. We positioned ourselves in the general handling area over the sea about 25nm south of RAF Valley, with me in control. Al Holyoake used his selector in the rear cockpit to shut off the hydraulic to the powered flying controls which brought on the relevant warnings on the standard warning panel and I then started the procedure known by the mnemonic 'STUPRECC', slowing the aircraft to manageable speed, trimming the tailplane, unlocking the elevator and exhausting the accumulator pressures in the system in order to control the aircraft manually. It was at this time that things started to go awfully wrong. The elevator unlocked normally and the longitudinal trim was set as it should be but, when I exercised the stick rapidly to and fro laterally to exhaust the aileron accumulators, the aircraft started rolling rapidly to port[1]. We were now doing almost continuous twinkle rolls with no response to our control inputs, with the nose dropping every time the aircraft passed through the inverted. I remember Al taking back control and attempting to reapply hydraulic power to the system but with no success. He yelled at me, "This is not normal – put out a Mayday!" I lost no time in doing this as it was becoming very apparent that the aircraft had become uncontrollable in an ever-steepening dive. The roll would sometimes stop momentarily but then start again immediately but seconds later Al gave the order to eject.

We abandoned the aircraft at around 7,000ft and 350KIAS. The 'face-blind' upper ejection handle was the primary means of initiating ejection as the seat pan handle did not automatically jettison the canopy. I did not fancy a trip through the Perspex and so I reached up, straightened my back and pulled the handle[2]. All the automatics worked well and the canopy jettisoned before our seats fired. I was not really aware of going up the rails but was pleased to find myself separating from the seat and quickly under a parachute, in time to see XR999 making like a diving gannet and plunging into the Irish Sea. Looking up again, I spotted my QFI also under a parachute but was surprised to see his life raft also descending, fully inflated, having deployed prematurely from the seat pack and now seemingly suspended by the sea anchor which was acting as a drogue 'chute. Al and I were close enough and with plenty of height in

---

1 Readers who remember seeing the Red Arrows displays in their Gnat days will appreciate that it had very powerful aileron control and rolled very rapidly indeed with full deflection. I seem to remember that the Reds' aircraft actually had the restrictors to the aileron authority removed, but even the standard training aircraft could roll like demons!

2 With the benefit of hindsight, I wished I had had the presence of mind to hang on to the face-blind handle as a memento. Sadly I did not.

hand to have a shouted conversation. Having established that we were both essentially uninjured, Al shouted, "If they pick you up first, tell them I will not be in a dinghy!" I told him I could see his life raft on its way down and then we both concentrated on our drills for entering the water. It was a lovely June day and the water looked almost inviting but first contact made us realise that it was far from 15°C. Once in the water and freed from my harness, I hauled in the seat pack, inflated the life raft and scrambled aboard. Looking in the direction that I thought Al might be, I glimpsed his inflated life raft and had the thought of paddling towards it and getting it over to him. I went as far as pulling in my sea anchor and starting to paddle with my hands but quickly realised that this was a total pipe dream as there was sufficient swell as to make it impossible to keep sight of either Al or his empty life raft. I abandoned that plan and concentrated on getting my little boat as dry as possible and the protective canopy around me.

It was only a matter of minutes before the friendly yellow Whirlwind from C Flight of 22 (SAR) Squadron clattered into view. I was clearly the more visible of the two survivors, being in a dayglo life raft so was soon greeted by the burly winchman on the end of his cable which hoisted us both up into the cabin of the Whirlwind, where I told them of Al's predicament. The SAR crew quickly spotted him and winched him up also. Being so incredibly old and having been in the water with only his Mae West and no immersion suit, Al was really suffering from the cold but the cabin door was quickly shut and a blast of heat helped him. The short transit back to Valley meant that we were delivered to the helicopter spot outside the station medical centre in double-quick time. There I found myself in a rather surreal situation of reclining in a hot bath, with a shot of rum in my hand and the station commander sitting on the nearby toilet seat, being quite solicitous of my health. Once the medics were happy with things, I was ferried back to the mess, and Al to his married quarter.

As is usual following an RAF aircraft accident, a Board of Inquiry, to which we gave our stories, opened on the following Monday. In the weeks that followed, a salvage operation by the Royal Navy recovered a large proportion of the aircraft's wreckage that was spread over the seabed, apparently mixed up with a large collection of empty beer cans, probably dumped over the side from a Holyhead ferry. The cause of the accident was later established as a fracture of one of the aileron servodyne actuators that had the effect of jamming that aileron at full deflection.

I was returned to flying on 41 Course six days later, when I was programmed to fly Convex 8 with the squadron commander, presumably to check that I was fit to continue the course. Four days after that, I was reunited with Al Holyoake who thankfully had also 'DCO'[3] with no further dramas.

It was a memorable experience. Sadly, I did not keep contact with Al, but if he has not already collected his second set of wings, I hope this account accurate enough for my old QFI should he happen to read it. The Folland Aircraft company designed and built their own ejection seats, as the Martin-Baker seats of the day would simply not fit into the diminutive Gnat. Therefore, I was not eligible for membership of the Caterpillar Club, which is restricted to users of Irvin parachutes. The certificate from the GQ Parachute Company whose product I used that day in 1968 hangs on the wall of my study today as a memento, together with a small gold badge that I have never worn. However, some 45 years later, I was invited to attend a dinner in London as a guest of the RAF Survival Equipment Fitters' Association. The story of the accident came to the attention of the chairman of the Goldfish Club[4] who was also attending the same dinner, so now I am pleased also to have a Goldfish badge.

A FAIRLY CLOSE-RUN AFFAIR
DAVE AINGE

Dave Ainge

In early 1965 I was a student on No. 86 Advanced Flying Course at RAF Valley and my instructor was Pete Millard, a Yorkshire man with a great sense of humour who had previously flown the Hunter which I had already set my sights on. After several dual sorties of general handling, circuits and landings and covering possible emergencies, during which I often found it difficult to concentrate on the task in hand due to the almost non-stop jokes issuing from the rear seat, came our solo flights.

I was on my second solo in Gnat No. 15, XR542, on the downwind leg practising a forced-landing circuit back at Valley, when it all went very quiet. The engine had stopped, the hydraulics and electrics had failed and I had lost the main radio. Now the Gnat required some speedy actions because, with hydraulics failure, the powered flying tail immediately froze leaving

---

3   'Duty Carried Out' – the usual annotation in the flying authorisation sheets after a successful sortie.

4   Open to all those who have abandoned an aircraft and landed in water.

no vertical control, that is no 'go up/go down'. Fortunately I had been fairly diligent both in the simulator and listening to Pete and this now stood me in good stead. After releasing the normally locked elevator to allow manual flight, an engine relight was attempted, unsuccessfully, and standby radio selected whilst at the same time concentrating on trying to make the runway. However for practices with an engine running, albeit at idle power, half flap was used as extra drag to simulate a dead engine and the combination of half flap and a truly dead engine resulted in a faster rate of descent than I had previously experienced. With no hydraulics to raise the flaps, my previously perfect profile was thrown into disarray, and it soon became apparent that I was going to have to park it in the undershoot, not ideal as it was a rocky hillside covered in gorse.

After the briefest of Mayday calls, the standby radio having finally warmed up, I resorted to Plan B which was to pull the ejection-seat handle. It was only then I discovered that, being quite tall, I couldn't reach the handle with both hands as my 'bone dome' was nearly touching the canopy. I very briefly considered using the bottom handle but dismissed the idea immediately as it required jettisoning the canopy first and terra firma was fast approaching. I then went for Plan C which was to tilt my head sideways and pull the top handle with one hand which worked just as well. After the briefest of parachute descents (it was estimated at less than a second), I arrived in a heap but still in one piece on the only patch not covered by gorse and only a short distance from a rather sorry looking Gnat. Within only a few minutes the fire rescue team arrived, mugs of tea still in hand and the first question they asked was whether I'd like a cuppa. Silly question.

The fire crew were closely followed by the air-sea rescue Whirlwind with the station doc on board and, having been given a quick once over, saved me having to walk back. As a precaution I was taken straight to sick quarters where a procession of interested parties called by. These included the squadron commander, the OC Flying and station commander followed finally by Pete who had been duty instructor in the tower and had witnessed it all, helpless to do anything and distraught that his student had learned so little about forced landings. The doc finally called a halt and when they had gone produced a bottle of medicinal brandy following which I slept like a log. I am still a firm advocate of Cognac as a cure all.

I had my back X-rayed as spinal compression fractures were common with an ejection but, whether it was the years of playing second row or heaving sacks of spuds about the farm, nothing was found, and I was again cleared to fly. Three days later saw me strapping into the front seat with my flight commander, Roy Clee, in the back to get me back in the saddle and find out if I had lost my nerve. Happily, after a thrilling demonstration of *really* low flying round the Welsh mountains in

Nearly but no cigar; the approach lights and start of the runway on the right, control tower and hangar in the distance.

expert hands, I landed as keen as ever. After all, lightning never strikes twice they say. Fortunately, for me at least, this was to hold true as it was the only serious incident I was to have in over 40 years of flying.

Of course, after any accident comes a Board of Inquiry to determine the causes and to recommend solutions. There is always the possibility of pilot error but

happily for me I was completely exonerated from any blame of my handling of the failure and was actually commended for achieving so much in the mere 50 seconds or so from failure to ejection. The main recommendation to pilots was not to leave the ejection decision so late as it had been a fairly close-run affair; zoom and boom became the catch word on the safety posters.

The cause turned out to be a failure of one small cog in the engine-driven auxiliary gearbox which drove all the main services, fuel pump, hydraulics pump and electrical generator. No

The rear cockpit of No. 15.

wonder it all went quiet, small cogs even in the largest of organisations really can make a difference! This led to a modification and, as far as I know, that was the only such incident of its kind.

I was lucky, my short stay at Valley was marked by several tragic accidents. The Gnat, whilst a superb training aircraft, could be a bit of a handful after the Jet Provost and pilots were sometimes caught out by its responsiveness and the speed at which things happened. On one occasion a solo student collided with the lead aircraft flown by a student and instructor who were both trapped in the aircraft and then crashed in the Welsh mountains and then the solo student crashed attempting to land at Valley, three deaths in one accident. Another lost control turning finals and ejected too late and a fifth died in a further accident. Valley was a sobering introduction to the realities of military flying; when aircraft bite they can bite very hard.

BOB ECCLES

The following citations are included as a tribute to a very fine aviator, no longer with us, and with whom I, Rick Peacock-Edwards, underwent both basic and advanced flying training. We later were also instructors on the Gnat at the same time at RAF Valley. Bob Eccles was not only one of the finest aviators that I had the pleasure of knowing, but he was also a great character and member of the team. He was fun to know and very professional at work. He will not be forgotten.

AWARD OF AIR FORCE CROSS

THAT Your Majesty may be graciously pleased to approve the undermentioned award:
Air Force Cross
Flt Lt Robert ECCLES (2619809), Royal Air Force
On 14 March 1977, Flt Lt Eccles, a Qualified Flying Instructor at No. 4 Flying Training School, was the captain of a Gnat aircraft flying from Kemble to Valley. Fifteen minutes after take-off, at 18,000 feet, there was a brief buzzing sound from the engine which caused Flt Lt Eccles to conclude that it should be treated with caution. He therefore selected a power setting to enable him to descend into a forced-landing pattern over RAF Valley. At 8,000 feet and still above cloud level the engine suddenly vibrated violently and seized. Ft Lt Eccles, while gaining height, transmitted a Mayday call and rapidly completed the complex emergency drills. With an unexpected fleeting glimpse, through cloud, of a local farm, he

swiftly reassessed that he was better placed to land at RAF Mona, Valley's relief landing ground, where there was a more favourable wind down the runway. With exceptional skill and judgement, and only the briefest glimpse of the ground to guide him, he lowered the undercarriage, established the forced-landing pattern and appraised Drayton Centre of his intentions. He broke cloud at 1,500 feet on the extended centreline of the runway but far too high to complete a straight-in approach. At this stage, knowing full well the extreme difficulties and danger involved in executing anything but gentle manoeuvres in manual control close to the ground, Flt Lt Eccles would have been fully justified in deciding to eject his passenger and himself. However, with outstanding coolness, precision and dexterity he side-slipped to lose height and 'S' turned the Gnat to a landing position. These imaginative, daring and unorthodox manoeuvres were completely successful and the aircraft was landed safely with 1,000 feet of runway to spare. Flight Lieutenant Eccles, when confronted with a grave and daunting emergency in the air, chose to reject the option of abandoning his aircraft. His decision to attempt to force land under very adverse conditions was made with the full knowledge of the personal risks involved. Flt Lt Eccles displayed exceptional airmanship and skill as a pilot, together with very considerable courage and devotion to duty during the incident.

Bob Eccles with ACM Sir Rex Roe.

From: Wing Commander A Dawson AMBIM RAF

"THE RED ARROWS"

THE ROYAL AIR FORCE AEROBATIC TEAM
CENTRAL FLYING SCHOOL DETACHMENT
ROYAL AIR FORCE KEMBLE
CIRENCESTER, GLOS.
TELEPHONE KEMBLE 261 EXT 323

Flight Lieutenant R Eccles RAF
No 2 Squadron
Royal Air Force Valley

17 March 1977

Dear Bobby,

Neither of us will forget our flight from Kemble to Mona on 14 March in Gnat T1 XR 998. However I feel I must express formally my deep appreciation of your superb skill, airmanship and captaincy in making a safe forced landing under those extremely difficult conditions after the engine seized.

That initial grumble from the engine gave no more than a hint all was not well but in no way prepared me for the catastrophic failure that followed. Engraved on my mind are your reaction to the engine seizure, your rapid and accurate decision making when you caught a fleeting glimpse of a single ground feature near Mona, your clear thinking under enormous pressure in realising that our best chance was to go straight for low key on Mona 23 runway and not Valley, your judgement of a final turn IMC in a most difficult wind, your handling of the aircraft throughout and particularly after breaking cloud at 1500 ft, in manual with the uncertain drag effect of a shattered engine, and your landing with 1000 ft to spare on a 6000 ft runway. In summary all the elements captaincy, airmanship and aircraft handling of the highest order.

Had I been captain in the front seat I would have had to go for a flame out spiral and would have made for Valley. With a 1500 ft cloud base 30-35 kt wind and without your detailed knowledge of the area, I assess my chances of having to eject with total loss of the aircraft as at least 90% probable.

The facts speak for themselves. Please accept my warmest congratulations on the finest piece of flying I have ever seen in 22 years of flying - and my sincere thanks for saving my arse.

Most sincerely

Ike Dawson

Letter from Wg Cdr Dawson to Bob following the incident that saw him rewarded with the Air Force Cross.

AWARD OF GOOD SHOW 1976

Flt Lt N. S. Champness, Red Arrows and Flt Lt R. Eccles, Red Arrows

Flt Lt Champness and Flt Lt Eccles took off from the Hawker Siddeley Aviation airfield at Bitteswill on an acceptance air test following modification of their aircraft to Red Arrows standard. Flt Lt Champness, the aircraft captain, was flying in the front seat.

During the final stages of the air test, after checking that they were well within gliding range of RAF Wittering, the crew inverted the aircraft at 12,000ft. The fuel caption illuminated at once and the engine started to run down. Flt Lt Champness quickly rolled upright again, attempted a hot relight and although the rpm hesitated slightly at 75% the engine continued to run down. He then handed over control to Flt Lt Eccles in the rear seat for him to set up a forced-

Flt Lts Nigel Champness and Bob Eccles (right), Red Arrows, after their forced landing at RAF Wittering in June 1976.

landing pattern into RAF Wittering while he carried out the drills and checked his actions against the flight reference cards.

They broke cloud at 7,000ft ideally placed and Flt Lt Champness carried out a further two cold relight attempts while Flt Lt Eccles continued to fly the forced-landing pattern from the rear seat. On both relight attempts the rpm increased to only 30% and would not respond to throttle so they continued with the pattern and made a copybook forced landing.

By good cooperation and sensible sharing of the workload both pilots were able to handle a potentially hazardous situation with comparative ease

HE DESERVED BETTER

IAN CHRISTIE-MILLER

On 18 October 1963, Plt Off Ian Christie-Miller, doing his advanced flying training at RAF Valley, set off in his Gnat on a navigation exercise when, in a cruise descent from 39,000 feet, he got a fire warning. He completed the correct fire drill, and now, without his engine, he continued the descent under instructions received in response to his Mayday call. Despite added difficulties, like an unserviceable direction indicator, he calmly followed Northern Centre's directions, until he saw what he thought, and was told, was Hawarden under his wing.

Unfortunately, this was not Hawarden. It happened to be Sealand, a disused airfield, with a short, out-of-wind runway, hazardous obstructions, both fixed (poles, wires, ditches, water tanks, etc.), and mobile (sheep, cows, farmers, etc.). This was an excusable mistake in airfield identification, when you consider that the only airfield in that vicinity, which was shown on his map, was Hawarden. Also, Northern Centre had told him he was in sight of Hawarden (quite rightly), but that darned elusive field happened to be up-sun, and under his aircraft's nose.

He set up a copybook pattern for a forced landing, hitting his 'high key' position on the button at 5,000 feet, and again, his 'low key' at 3,000 feet, with three greens. On finals, at 800 feet and in a good position, his heart must have dropped with a zonk; because he saw the power cables across the approach and realised that Hawarden was never like this. Still undaunted, he reckoned that, even now, he had a good chance of pulling off a landing, so he rejected his immediate thought of ejecting.

He flew under the power cables on a flapless approach and touched down on the runway only 100 yards from the threshold. With normal luck, he

should at this stage have been able to congratulate himself and start to breathe sighs of relief. However, the short runway, and crosswind, and the obstructions, weren't going to allow this to happen. Braking frantically, with the drag-chute deployed, he couldn't stay on the runway, and as he veered off, he struck a hare, a wire mesh fence, a floodlight pole, and a disused static

Below: The damage to Christie-Miller's aircraft after he touched down at Sealand airfield.
Bottom: The furrow leading to Ian Christie-Miller's Gnat after his accident.

From:—Air Vice-Marshal P. T. PHILPOTT, C.B.E., R.A.F.

Telephons:
Boroughbridge 421

Headquarters No. 23 Group
Royal Air Force
Dishforth
Thirsk
Yorkshire

23G/5186/1/Air

20th November, 1963

Dear Christie-Miller,

Personal Commendation

Following your recent accident I received a recommendation from your unit for the award of a Green Endorsement in recognition of your actions. Unfortunately, the order governing the award of Green Endorsements is somewhat circumscribed and restrictive and the fact that the aircraft sustained damage, even though the circumstances were beyond your control, prevents me from making this award.

2. Although I cannot award the endorsement, it is my personal opinion that your handling of the aircraft and your efforts to prevent its loss were in the best traditions of the Service. Please accept my personal congratulations on your excellent performance and my wishes for a speedy recovery from your injuries.

Yours Sincerely,

I. Philpott.

Pilot Officer J.R. Christie-Miller, R.A.F.,
Royal Air Force
VALLEY

Left: Letter of personal commendation from AVM Philpott to Ian after his accident.
Below: The damaged cockpit.

water tank, doing significant damage to the nose area of his Gnat, including the cockpit in which he was sitting.

He was lifted from the wreck by the RAF Fire Service at Sealand; he had his legs broken below the knee, and slight concussion. Taking the bright view, one can imagine that the aircraft could have burst into flames, but didn't; his seat could have gone off, but didn't.

POSTSCRIPT: Ian Christie-Miller spent many months in hospital and recovering from his injuries. He returned to flying duties in April 1965. However, because of his now immobilised right ankle he was unable to operate the Gnat slab brakes and was therefore re-streamed on to helicopters. He went on to have many years of distinguished flying.

CHAPTER 3

SHORT SORTIES AND SNIPPETS

FORBIDDEN FRUIT: THE FIRST GNAT FORMATION AEROS

AL POLLOCK

Flying Training Command was proud of its new Gnat simulator. When a Bristol Siddeley ex-RN photographer, Bob Lomax, came to Valley to photograph the simulator in September 1963, four of us decided Bob should take photographs of real Gnats flying in formation. Boscombe Down had issued a strict instruction forbidding anyone to fly the Gnat in formation, with rumours of soft option courts martial. On 10 September I flew two sorties with Bob Lomax on board. Next day, with Flt Lts Lee Jones as leader (02), Roger Hymans No. 2 (04) and myself No. 3 (08), superbly aided and abetted by Tony Doyle flying

Al Pollock

Bob in his 'camera-ship', we flew a full formation aerobatic sequence.

As No. 3, I saw roving Tony Doyle suddenly snap half-roll inwards as we passed each vertical and Bob took the photo shown on page 88. On the ground Roger and Lee charmingly suggested that I was to chat the chief instructor up – he was not in his office and I left this identical shot with a brief note on his desk. That 'blue touchpaper' photo launched thousands of displays, since ex-CFS Waterfront 'Bill' Edwards was quick to appreciate that increasing Gnats and QFIs meant 4 FTS could work up a formation team – in 1964 this evolved into the Yellowjacks under Lee's leadership. On 29 April after three No. 3 sorties, I was offered the No. 3 slot but by then I was command singleton display pilot and flight commander heavily involved with the new Gnat squadron and syllabus. Later this massively enlarged photograph became the Ops Block's stairway mural.

One of the photographs taken by Bob Lomax of three 4 FTS Gnats breaking the rules by flying in formation before certification was issued by Boscombe Down. The pilots were: Lee Jones in XP502, Roger Hymans in XP504 and Alan Pollock in XR539 (4 FTS).

BILL BLAIR-HICKMAN

Bill Blair-Hickman

Being an advanced flying instructor on my favourite aircraft at Valley was a great job with most of Wales as a low-level flying area. It was certainly gratifying to watch inexperienced students speeding up and becoming genuine fast-jet pilots. After two years instructing at Valley, I was asked if I would like to instruct at CFS Kemble teaching future fast-jet instructors. Normally I would have kept well clear of the training world, but this was something else.

No. 4 Squadron at CFS Kemble was the best kept secret in the RAF. It was a very small detachment at the same base as the Red Arrows in the beautiful Cotswolds. Although accommodated at Little Rissington, each day the pilots would board an RAF bus for the 50-minute journey to Kemble. Although one might assume this was a drag, in fact they got used to it and it was useful for hangover recovery. Very little CFS Rissington supervision was given or necessary. All the Kemble pilots were above average and professional Gnat operators. I jumped at the chance of a posting to Kemble. After being there for a couple of months, I realised what a great choice I had made. The staff worked their way through the advanced-flying syllabus every few months. We would teach lessons to the students in the back seat, they would then fly with another student to practise, then finally teach the lesson back to the instructor.

The students were mainly ex-fighter pilots who found the actual flying quite easy, although we did insist their performance was as good and accurate as possible so that future students at AFS would have plenty to live up to. The tricky part was flying from the back seat while talking and making sure what you were demonstrating was what you were doing. The syllabus was extensive and kept the staff sharp over all types of flying. We covered circuits of all types, the most difficult were flapless manual approaches, particularly at night, and the view from the back was poor. We did extensive aerobatics from 40,000ft down to display aeros at 500ft, supersonic dives and low-level cross countries at 250ft and 420 knots. We did a lot of land-aways including to Karup in Sweden for air shows. A popular destination was RAF Upper Heyford – the homebase for a USAF F-111 squadron. There were many night stops and the odd beer or two. The American pilots persuaded us that we should become a Tiger squadron. I designed a badge of a Tiger jumping through a numeral four. We put the badge on our fins although not strictly approved!

I remember one particular night flight from Kemble...I had managed to get myself some solo SCT on a beautiful night, calm and unlimited visibility. I strapped into or should I say, strapped on the Gnat and connected the anti-g. I then made sure the ejection seat breach lock lever was turned through 90 degrees right, so if I reached 90 knots I could bang out. This system was so much better than Martin-Baker with handfuls of pins for top and bottom handles. The ground crew closed the canopy and started the Palouste air starter. I put the bar forward to boost the fuel and heat the pitot. I opened the throttle to idle position and pressed the relight button. The engine lit up and was soon idling at 38%. I taxied out and lined up on the runway. The throttle was opened to full, and the rpm quickly reached 102%... acceleration excellent... stick back at the 100 knots, lift off at 135 knots, clean up and turn towards Cornwall. In five minutes, I was at 30,000 feet and 36 miles from Kemble. In a rapid descent I could be back at circuit height in two minutes. I descended to 5,000 feet and flew to overhead Cirencester. I rolled over and dived towards the town...landing light on...I recovered by 2,000 feet and light off. This strange behaviour was due to a pretty nurse who lived in Cirencester whom I had promised to visit (airborne). I switched back to professional mode and returned to Kemble to practise various circuits. Downwind was about 200 knots, gear down, flaps ten degrees. I started the final turn at 170 knots and, straight in at 140 knots with full flap. The threshold speed was dependent on fuel weight varying from 125 to 138 knots. The fuel was 700lbs, so the V ref was 127 knots.

While taxiing in, after landing, the tower asked me to give them a ring after I had shut down. I learnt that the Cirencester police had phoned the tower to report a crashing aircraft. They had left a phone number, so I rang and thanked them for their concern and said it was just routine. I invited them to visit the squadron when we could manage it and have a beer in the bar we had built in the corner of one of the hangars. They were delighted.

After leaving Kemble I was posted to Chivenor on the Hunter – another great aircraft – but in my opinion just a little inferior to the Gnat as a pilot's aircraft.

BRIAN GRANT

I was awarded my wings in July 1960 at RAF Swinderby, Lincolnshire, having been trained on Piston Provost T Mk. 1 and Vampire T11. I was one of only two graduates to be selected to fly fighters, albeit night all-weather (Duncan Sands' famous Defence Review), the Javelin and the Sea Vixen (exchange service with the FAA).

After seven years of enjoyable flying throughout Europe, the Near East and, from the deck of HMS *Ark Royal*, the Far East I was posted, in July 1967, to RAF Little Rissington to attend No. 240 QFI Course. The next two or so months were hard as it seemed that I was soon to be instructing on the 'mighty Jet Provost'! My prayers were answered for in October 1967 I transferred to RAF Kemble where Dennis Hazell commanded a detachment of Gnats from RAF Valley. This was the advanced phase of No. 240 CFS QFI Course. Denis ran a 'tight' but fair unit as I and my patter partner subsequently found out. Denis had one aim which was to provide RAF Valley with new QFIs who were capable of instructing students and at the same time had good knowledge and handling ability on the Gnat. To this end we were expected on the last sortie of the day to improve our own skill in the aircraft.

My first trip was with Pete Dodworth on 17 October 1967 in XM706. On approach I was conscious of the compactness of the aircraft, its slightly short fuselage, rather tall tail, marked anhedral and its apparent 'squatting' attitude when on the flight line. Strapping in was like putting on a close-fitting favourite jacket. However, it has to be the first take-off that remains with me. With a high power-to-weight ratio the acceleration was sharp, probably accentuated by one's posterior being no more than three feet above the runway! Once airborne 706 continued to impress with its high manoeuvrability.

Returning to Denis and his relaxed approach. After the last sortie of the day my 'patter partner' and I were debriefing when Denis stuck his head around the door and asked us to call in at his office before securing. Denis started by asking how the sortie had gone and especially the PFLs he had observed. We replied that the PFLs, especially when carried out in manual from the back seat, were quite challenging. There followed a long period of silence before Denis quietly explained that as a result of a recent accident to a Gnat at Kemble whilst it was carrying out manual PFLs an order had been put in place informing pilots that manual PFLs could only be conducted with an A2 instructor in the aircraft. As we left his office, he reminded us to re-read the FOB before our next sortie. Denis had made his point, read, and understand the flying order book (FOB), and we had added to our technical and skill level; a skill level that neither I nor my partner ever had to put to the test.

So it was in January 1968 that, as a shiny B2, I joined No. 2 Squadron (Gnats) at RAF Valley, Anglesey at the start of two and a half years of instructional duties. RAF Valley in the late 1960s was a wonderful station from which to fly and relax. A fighter looking/performing aircraft to fly with immediate access to low-flying areas. Happy hour on Friday evening was always well attended by all. Even the resident swans from the lake outside the bar appeared to enjoy being fed beer-soaked bread rolls.

My major contribution to Gnat operations occurred after an incident I experienced when night flying with a very good student. Because landing the

Gnat after a hydraulic failure required the pilot to remember (a) the STUPRE drill (b) the procedure on lowering the undercarriage and (c) the check on finals, a simulated hydraulic failure was practised at the end of most general handling sorties. On the night in question, with a simulated HYD failure, my student carried out (a) and (b) immaculately. As we were turning finals at about 400 feet and 160 knots my student quietly announced that he could not control the aircraft and asked me to take over. On doing so it was obvious that there was a problem with the tailplane and the elevator. Options seemed limited other than to get away from the ground. Rolling the wings level, applying full power, making an RT call whilst putting the hydraulics back on seemed likely to buy time. As the Gnat screamed upwards, I selected the undercarriage up. In a few seconds we were up at around 3,000 feet and by over banking I traded some height for IAS. Checking in the cockpit confirmed that all the warning captions were out other than the elevator unlock light, but the low-level fuel warning light was now flickering. The Pan call was cancelled and replaced with a request for a fuel priority landing, which was granted. The aircraft landed from a normal circuit and was duly parked back on the flight line. Having completed all the paperwork we retired to the mess for a night-flying supper and a Newcastle Brown ale both of which tasted excellent.

The following day wingco engineering invited me to the Gaydon hangar to see the problem. The engineers had discovered that the pin locking the elevator to the tailplane had not been withdrawn by either of the elevator unlock levers in the cockpit though the warning light had/and remained illuminated as unlocked. The engineers had to check the fleet, and the aircrew got a revised mnemonic... STUPREC where C stands for check the flying controls.

In August 1970 I left RAF Valley, but it was not the last time that I flew the Gnat. I later flew and displayed another aircraft, the Sea Vixen. The owner of that aircraft also owned a Gnat, G-NATY, XR537. This aircraft had been Dickie Duckett's aircraft when he led the Red Arrows and was withdrawn from service in September 1979 and eventually sold in March 1990. On 9 August 2007, after a lengthy restoration I was privileged to take '537' for its first post-restoration air test from Bournemouth International Airport. XR537 made its public debut at the inaugural Bournemouth International Air Festival 2008 when it flew as Red 10 to the Red Arrows. My last flight in a Gnat was in the aircraft in February 2012, at the young age of 73, thus ending 45 years of association with the aircraft.

Would I fly one again? Of course....it never let me down, it is a wonderful aircraft.

It was *too* good for students.

CRIMSON CRABS

JOHN DICKSON (EX-RN FLEET AIR ARM)

John Dickson

My QFI course was with 4 Squadron at RAF Kemble (now Cotswold Airport) on the Folland Gnat. As there was no accommodation at Kemble, morning and evening transport was provided back and forth to RAF Little Rissington, some 30 minutes away. At Kemble, the next-door hangar and flight line was the home of the only other operational flying unit – the Red Arrows.

When not course flying, I took several opportunities to fly in one of the Arrows' back seats and enjoyed the camaraderie. To the extent that I gave them the nickname 'Crimson Crabs', and to uphold the navy end (I was the only navy officer at Kemble), I took every opportunity to 'broadcast' the name when airborne. Of course, the Arrows reciprocated by endlessly asking the tower if the 'fishhead' was airborne.

A few months later, the phone rang in my office at RAF Leuchars. 'JD, the Arrows are planning a dining-in night at Rissington and wonder if you'd like to fly down and join us?' Well, no question about it. But what could I do to enhance the navy tradition? Well, after a bit of thought the answer was obvious and a few phone calls later a cunning plan slowly evolved. I needed the assistance of someone at Rissington and, luckily, I knew the very Baldrick character who had no doubt that he could beg, borrow or steal a small truck from the motor pool for a few hours on the Friday, the day before the dinner.

On Friday, I flew an F-4 from Leuchars to Kemble and jumped on the 4 Squadron evening transport to Rissington. Baldrick was waiting, and we quickly put an 'out of order' sign on a shower stall in the officers' mess and awaited the arrival of the truck carrying a consignment from a couple of fishing boat skippers at Chepstow. Crabs that were normally thrown overboard.

Painting the crabs a crimson red continued long into the night. Just before dinner the following evening, I made sure the two windows I had earmarked were off the latch so the two 'erks' I had paid a fiver to each, could open the windows from the outside and after the loyal toast shovel in the Royal Navy's contribution to the after-dinner speeches.

The guys on the team thought the Crimson Crabs scurrying around the dining room floor a hoot. Unfortunately, this was not shared by the wing commander president of the mess committee who invited me to the anteroom where he made his view quite clear on the conduct he expected from a mess guest. Fair enough. I suppose I half expected it but the wingco's words didn't amount to much as by now we were surrounded by congratulatory team members who reminded him that nothing the navy got up to at mess dinners should surprise him and if he was lucky his car wouldn't end up on the mess roof.

'TIGER SQUADRON'
MIKE SPARROW

Sqn Ldr Michael Sparrow was posted to CFS on 1 February 1971, as OC the 4 Squadron detachment at Kemble. Prior to moving to CFS, Michael had completed a tour with 2 Squadron at RAF Valley.

While at 4 FTS, I had been mindful that our students would soon be in the front line, and that the next best thing to actual experience was to talk to someone who had had that experience; USAF had several bases in the UK, they were at war in Vietnam and they welcomed us with open arms. And so it was that on the last sortie of a Friday afternoon, 2 Squadron Gnats would land at one of the USAF bases, stay overnight and land back at Valley the next morning with student minds full of modern fighter tactics.

RAF Upper Heyford was home to the 20 Fighter Wing USAF and was but a short distance from Little Rissington. Soon it was quite usual for 4 Squadron CFS members to be seen at Upper Heyford whilst USAF members attended all our Kemble parties. It was at one of the parties at Upper Heyford that I was introduced to squadron commanders from many different nations. Enquiries of my host informed me that this was the Tiger Association, it met once

Special photo shoot of 'Tiger' Gnat! Bearing the unofficial 4 Squadron badge on its fin, XS109/A is captured in a vertical climb during the flight on 9 December 1971. (Mike Sparrow)

per year and each squadron had a tiger in its badge. At this time all flew fighter aircraft. This seemed a good way to cement relations with our NATO allies, so I agreed to forward a copy of our tiger badge. Our Gnat aircraft was accepted as a fighter, modified for the training role.

Next morning my two senior students, Dave Roome and Mike Rigg, were 'asked' to oversee the design of a 4 Squadron CFS Tiger badge which, as I recall, was ready by lunchtime. It showed a tiger leaping through a figure four and on its arrival at Upper Heyford assured our associate membership of the Tiger Association.

To record the occasion, we decided to take an airborne photograph of our 'Tiger' Gnat, XS109/A, and this occurred on Thursday, 9 December 1971. It is the only photo to my knowledge of a 4 Squadron Gnat with the unofficial 4 Squadron badge on the tail fin. Flt Lt Bill Blair-Hickman was in the front seat and Flt Lt Des Sheen in the rear. The photo aircraft pilots were me in the front seat with camera and fellow QFI Flt Lt Dave Longden in the rear.

CATCHING CONCORDE

In May 1972, Mike received a priority signal from the MoD stating that approval had been given for a Gnat to fly a photographer to film Concorde as part of a normal training sortie. Arthur Gibson had become a good friend of Mike's over the years, and of course was famous for his films of the Red Arrows and his thousands of photos depicting all sorts of air activity.

The idea of getting photos of Concorde was entirely his and took a great deal of perseverance. The briefing with John Cochrane, who was to fly Concorde during our photo shoot, was short, covering mainly the R/T frequencies and emergencies. 'Flown formation, have you?' he asked. 'Since I was knee high to Pontius,' I replied. 'Ok, don't hit me' – and that was that.

By 18 May I had positioned two Gnats at Little Rissington. Once the initial checks had been carried out on Concorde (ATC Fairford to ATC Little Rissington), Arthur and I lashed ourselves into XS101/H with Arthur in the front seat. When word came that Concorde was taxiing, we started and got airborne. At full throttle we caught Concorde on take-off and stayed with her for an initial climb to around 30,000ft, taking many photos. Overhead Valley we left and Concorde went into the Irish Sea supersonic area. We hurried back to Little Rissington where we leapt at once into the other Gnat, got airborne and caught Concorde coming back to Fairford. Again, many photos were taken, including one from the ground of Concorde in company with a Gnat passing through the overhead of Little Rissington.

Two flashbacks stand out in my memories of that day:

- Arthur: "Ask John to put reheat in so that I can catch the flame in the shot." Me: "Okay." Press R/T. "John, could you engage reheat?" John: "Yes, but I'll have to stabilise JPTs first on these prototype engines." Me: "Roger." What we had not understood was that to stabilise JPTs John had to go to full throttle, sit there for about 10 seconds, then engage reheat. By the time flame appeared, Concorde was about five miles away. Arthur – "Think we'll give that a miss."

- Coming into land at Fairford Concorde increased its angle of attack and condensation was formed as a cloud over its wing, making a fantastic sight from our position. On landing I asked Arthur what settings he'd used on his cameras to catch the wing cloud. His reply was unprintable as he'd been in the middle of changing magazines!"

ROYAL HIGH FLYER

In July 1972, Mike Sparrow was informed that he was to fly HRH Prince Michael of Kent in a Gnat during his visit to CFS. On the 17th a Gnat was flown into Little Rissington from Kemble ready for the prince's visit on the following day.

The ground crew and I were in spanking new overalls, the aircraft positively gleaming. Dawn revealed a dank, drizzly, low cloud day. HRH arrived in his purple Triumph Stag and was whisked off to meet VIPs and carry out the bad weather programme. By 11:00 the portents were good for an afternoon sortie – and so to the official lunch. Now, one thing Little Rissington did extremely well was to look after visiting dignitaries, especially the Royal Family. After all, the Queen Mother was our commandant-in-chief. However, it was with some trepidation that I watched HRH consume his strawberries and good Devonshire clotted cream!

We got airborne shortly after 14:00 and climbed to around FL 150 for HRH to see the general handling he had requested. During the climb he remarked on how quiet it all was, so I set off explaining how our new helmets kept most of the noise at bay. But no, that wasn't it – "The radio is so quiet, nobody seems to be talking except when you want them to," he said. I then explained about the purple area we were in, the strict radio silence in case of emergency and all the radar units watching us. He remarked sadly, "Can't get away from them even up here".

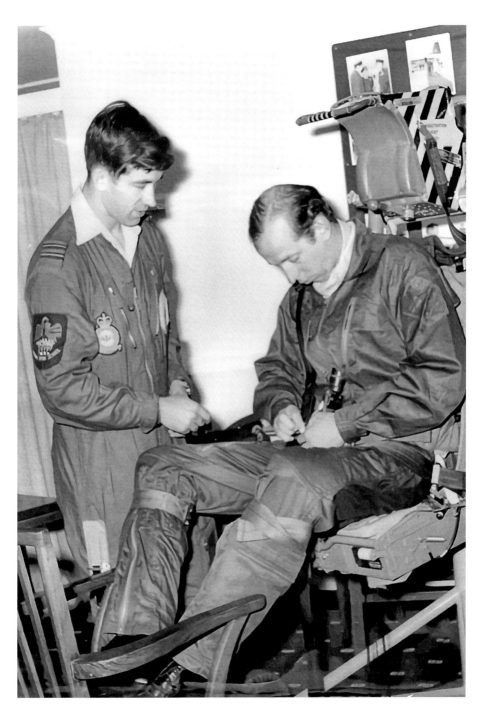

Before being authorised to fly in the Gnat, the Duke of Kent is shown how to strap into the ejection seat by Alan East, followed by instruction on what to do in the event that he was ordered to eject. (CFS Archive)

He appeared to genuinely enjoy the handling of the aircraft and flew it himself on a few occasions. High 'g' manoeuvres and aerobatics caused a momentary silence but an offset TACAN let down to Little Rissington soon got him buzzing with questions. He would have loved a low-level navigation sortie but I was not authorised for that. However, we could do a low-level flypast at Little Rissington at his special request so, after completing two circuits, we flew low over his entourage (not too low) and finally landed. As we completed our shut-down checks, I could see that the low flypast might have caused some consternation among some of the senior officers so, as I helped HRH from the cockpit, I asked him in a loud voice if he had enjoyed the *requested* low flypast. With a twinkle in his eye, he replied in an equally loud voice, "Splendid".

The final twist in this tale came as I said goodbye to Prince Michael in the officers' mess car park. Number 4 Squadron CFS was a member of the Tiger Association, and his beautiful purple Stag was now covered in yellow tiger paw marks! I mumbled something about sending me the bill, but he just laughed and said he thought he had got off rather lightly. I never did find out for sure who had done it."

SYD MORRIS

The summer of 1965 still sticks in my memory: sun, fun and flying the wonderful Gnat. My first trip was on 10 June 1965 with Chas Pringle as my 'creamie' QFI, with whom I flew most of my Gnat trips. My flight commander was the renowned Denis Hazell, who I seem to remember called all students 'closet', or perhaps it was just me? No idea why. My abiding concern on that first trip was how on earth I was going to find the time to complete the downwind checks when travelling at twice the speed of our basic trainer, the Jet Provost. I think it was about 180kts

downwind but I may be mistaken, either way there wasn't much time to get them done before turning finals. The landing was also a bit of a shock which seemed to consist of just pointing the Gnat at where you wanted to land with not much round out or flare. Anyway, we soon got used to it and I found it a totally delightful aeroplane to fly, beautifully balanced light controls, great for aerobatics and low flying. A very comfortable if somewhat snug cockpit. Later it was the late Roger Turnill who told me he had to fly it with his arm going under his leg to hold the stick, it certainly was a problem for tall individuals like him.

Syd Morris

Wouldn't be allowed these days. The instrument display was superb, not bettered in any aircraft I flew until the HUD of the Harrier GR7. We certainly could have done with it on the Hunter and the early Harriers. The only contentious area of the Gnat was the hydraulic system, the tailplane and the emergency follow-up system. I doubt you will find any Gnat pilot of our era who couldn't still tell you the STUPRECC drill for hydraulic failure. Sadly, we had one fatality on our course when Roger Cooper, our Beatles lookalike from Liverpool, crashed into the lake short of the main runway, probably as a result of not fully completing the STUPRECC drill after a hydraulic failure or practice drill [see also page 37]. Not sure which but it certainly served to emphasise the importance of fully completing this drill, although the complexity of this system was perhaps not ideal in a trainer.

Another dramatic incident was on a later formation sortie when, I think it was John Wolff, who was No. 3 in a stream take-off and retracted his undercarriage on the leader's call of "gear up go"; unfortunately it was a tad early for John and his Gnat settled back on to the slipper tanks providing a good imitation of two napalm bombs going off. The newly repaired taxiway where the aircraft came to rest took a fair time to repair. John's exit from the Gnat was rapid to say the least but safe. My last trip at Valley was my final handling test which all went well until arrival back at Valley with a simulated hydraulic failure and in the dreaded 'follow-up' elevator to land on the shortest runway at Valley, which we'd never used before. I managed to slightly over rotate my first roller landing and just touched the tail bumper, which the tower obligingly told us on the next ten circuits I was required to fly by my examiner Mike Vickers, very relaxing (not). Denis Hazell very kindly wrote in my course report that my average FHT result was not a reflection of my true ability, great bloke! My Hunter posting was probably a result of Mike Snelling being more capable than the rest of us and being rewarded with a posting to CFS, lucky chap. He did fly Hunters later when I was one of his instructors at Chivenor and he was still a very good pilot. My final Gnat trip was several years later, 26 June 1977, when I was displaying the Harrier at Greenham Common for the IAT and blagged a trip with the Red Arrows on their 1,000th display. I nearly put Martin Stoner (Red 9) off his stroke when my seat slipped at the bottom of a loop because I hadn't fully engaged the lock, another somewhat belated lesson learnt, but still a great trip in a super aeroplane which I felt very privileged to have flown.

BLACK ROBERTSON

I recall very little about the 78 sorties and just over 74 hours I spent wedged into the Gnat's tiny cockpit. Just two stand out. The first was a formal progress check

Black Robertson

with a flight commander roughly halfway through the course; by then I'd flown some 34 hours in the aircraft. After a few general handling exercises, some low flying, aerobatics and a simulated emergency or two, came the recovery to Valley from high level: a descent flown on instruments that began with positioning for an offset TACAN dive, the geometry and mechanics of which I never fully understood and quite frankly loathed having to fly. To put it mildly, I struggled with this part of the sortie. We then flew a ground-controlled approach, a few practice circuits and 'roller' landings (a 'touch and go' in the US parlance now almost universally adopted) followed by a final circuit and landing. The taciturn rear-seat instructor, Flt Lt Len Morgan, said little throughout the sortie and absolutely nothing as we taxied back. Our return to the dispersal area seemed to take an age – plenty of time to mull over the various options open to me when I was 'chopped', as I felt sure would be the case. I was convinced I'd performed that badly. Deeply frustrated, I felt that I really hadn't done myself justice. If I couldn't fly fighters, nothing else mattered to me. But the RAF would surely want to recoup at least some of the investment made in my training thus far, so I reasoned that I had to think of something.

Rejecting any form of multi-engine aircraft, I thought about helicopters. They seemed the only possible alternative. Yes, I could possibly live with that. Helicopters might not be too bad. Otherwise, I would try to resign my commission, although I had no idea whether this was a genuine possibility. Dejected, I clambered out of the cramped cockpit for what I was convinced was the last time and fell into step with my instructor as we walked back to sign in the aircraft. He still said nothing, nor did he speak as we changed from the cumbersome winter immersion suits designed to provide temporary protection in the event of an ejection over water. I made my way to the crewroom, made him the required standard NATO cup of coffee (white, two sugars) and prepared for the formal debrief and bad news I was convinced would follow. "Well, that wasn't too bad," was my instructor's opening gambit. I could hardly believe my ears and recall absolutely nothing he said thereafter, only an overwhelming sense of relief. So, I might just make it after all!

The second, equally vivid recollection is of an incident two sorties from the end of the course. It occurred during a medium-level general-handling exercise over North Wales with Flt Lt Mike Barringer in the back seat and momentarily shocked me to the core. As I glanced to my right there, filling the entire windscreen and darkening the cockpit, was the underside of another Gnat heading in the same direction. It was belly up to us, turning hard, so close that I could clearly see the oil streaks and rivets on the aircraft's underside. Over in a flash, this brush with death caused my instructor no concern whatsoever; he was looking the other way, entirely unaware of our predicament. There was no time to be scared. Had there been, I would have been absolutely petrified. Just a few feet was all that stood between life and death that day, possibly for four of us. It was far from the first and by no means the last time that Lady Luck was to look kindly on me. With hindsight this experience, pure happenstance, was part of a pattern confirming that, like my father, fate had dealt me a pretty good hand in the game of life. It was also early proof, if proof be needed, of the tenuous hold we have on our existence. The thread on which fortunes hang can so easily be broken, as I was to witness time and again in the years that followed.

MORE STUDENT MEMORIES
PETER JOHNSON

Peter Johnson

I came to the Gnat late. Having passed out of basic training on Jet Provosts at RAF Syerston, I was posted to fly Gnats at RAF Valley. However, a backlog caused by unserviceability resulted in my course being moved to RAF Strubby to complete advanced training on Meteors. Initially hugely disappointed, I won't bore you with how much fun we had flying Meteors especially the single-seat Mk. 8. So, it was following a Hunter tour in Aden, the dismay of a posting to instructor duties and instructor training on Jet Provosts at Little Rissington that I arrived at RAF Kemble to train as an instructor on Gnats. Kemble was where the Red Arrows, then led by Ray Hanna and flying Gnats, were based and I flew with them on a couple of occasions.

When everything worked on the Gnat, it was a delight to fly. Tiny, fast and manoeuvrable, it was something you strapped on rather than in. But when it went wrong it could bite hard.

Just before my arrival at Valley for instructing duties, an instructor had jumped out of a Gnat, together with his student, because of hydraulic failure. His student was OK but the instructor, being ex-Javelins, had pulled his feet back to where the footrests were on the early Martin-Baker Javelin seat. That meant his thighs were slightly off the seat at the moment of ejection in the simple, efficient but gun-only powered Gnat ejection seat. As a result, both femurs were broken and although surviving the parachute landing, he subsequently suffered major embolisms.

A contemporary of mine at Valley was the solo aerobatic display man. I flew with him a couple of times and although he was a very good pilot, his flying could hardly be described as smooth. He used the same aircraft for all his displays and had asked his ground crew to remove the aileron fuses, thereby allowing the maximum rate of roll to increase from around 360 degrees per second to around 450 degrees, significantly enhancing his display. Unfortunately, the combination of enhanced roll rate, very 'energetic' flying and use of the same aircraft led eventually to the fin falling off during a display. He was killed in the subsequent crash.

My first real taste of near disaster in an aircraft was at RAF Kemble on the Gnat QFI course. There we were given model dual lessons by one of the instructors, following which we flew twice with fellow students giving and receiving the same dual lessons. I found myself one night in the front seat of a Gnat with a US exchange pilot in the back 'teaching me' night circuits. After several normal circuits, I told him that I was selecting the tailplane to manual so that he could demonstrate a manual circuit. I did so but then several seconds later the back seater shouted that he had the stick hard back and couldn't stop the aircraft descending. I took control, indeed the stick was hard back, and saw 400ft on the altimeter rapidly reducing, with inky blackness outside. I threw the manual lever back on and the aircraft pitched up violently, popping circuit breakers the while, but fortunately still just under control and not buried in the ground. The back seater had gone through the infamous STUPRE drill but had forgotten the 'U' bit about unlocking the elevators! We very gently completed a circuit to land, and I went to bed that night still shaking.

My other near-accident Gnat incident happened after I'd qualified as an instructor and was in the back seat with a student in the front flying circuits at Llanbedr near Harlech, Valley's relief landing ground. My student in the front of our Gnat was consistently getting too slow on the approach to land. So, I told him to fly the circuit and that I would tell him when to select the flaps to full down, which typically happened halfway or so round the final turn. He flew the circuit; I judged the right moment and said, "full flap now". The next thing I saw was the scenery rushing up at us at high speed. I grabbed the controls, hit full throttle and just about managed to scrape away without hitting the ground. My student had pulled the flaps up instead of down. I shouted at him, probably with some foul obscenity, and he went quiet for the rest of the flight while we flew back to

Valley. Not long after that he voluntarily left the course; I know not what happened to him subsequently but, clearly, he had been frightened off flying Gnats. And I learned a lesson about keeping one hand on the flap lever during the latter stages of an approach.

Two rather more enjoyable times happened whilst instructing on Gnats at Valley. One was whist in the back at medium level pattering one of the early lessons to a new student. I spotted another Gnat, probably flown by another ex-Hunter pilot instructor on a staff continuation training (SCT) trip, clearly aiming for our six o'clock. I wrested control away from the hapless student and turned into the threat, in the process overcooking the pull and flicking into two turns of a spin. However, for some reason the spin stopped, and I found myself nicely in the adversary's six o'clock. That brought huge admiration from the student who I never did tell how much out of control we had been.

The second was during the unusual event of there being two aircraft available at the same time with back seats strapped for SCT. I took one, the other by a hardened ex-Aden Hunter pilot who had survived the years during which six pilots in Aden had been killed on training missions. We were authorised for low-level flying and practice battle and close formation. All went according to plan until we approached the airfield for individual circuits and landings. As we ran in, my gallant leader – several years my senior – said "close formation go" which I promptly did, and we proceeded to perform ten minutes of close formation aerobatics over the field – completely unauthorised. Eventually we split up and landed during which time the enormity of the crime slowly dawned on me. However, nothing happened. We signed back in and had a coffee. Nobody said anything and I guess that everyone thought that we had indeed been authorised for the display. God was on my side that day.

JERRY PARR

November the 26th, 1971 was a Friday and the weekend beckoned.

I was still 'holding' at Valley whilst the RAF sorted out (or tried to) the Spey/Phantom mismatch and my Chivenor course kept moving to the right. Notwithstanding I was getting some flying and was reasonably current on the Gnat however, there were many aspects lacking – procedural IF and all that nause included. This particular weekend the squadron agreed that I could borrow an aircraft to go to Farnborough to spend time with Vicky, my then girlfriend now my wife of over 49 years. My aircrew holdall was packed ready to be strapped into the back seat and I'd put a line on a map, Valley to Farnborough with a few TACAN

Jerry Parr

fixes and some frequencies. The only snag was the weather especially at my destination.

As my departure time approached – my flight commander had submitted a flight plan and all that crap, but the weather got worse – Yellow 2 which was well outside my white card limits. So Martin Johnson stepped up and said he'd drop me off, thus no holdall. In time-honoured fashion I went to do the walk round etc. and strapped in; where's Martin? He appeared from the line hut with my holdall, climbed the steps and put it in the back seat. Farnborough is now Green he said and improving so off you go and have a good w/e. I signed the 700 put it on the floor, shut the hood, got organised if you can call it that and started up; time had moved on however.

Take-off, departure and early transit went well, and I started to relax and enjoy the trip – it was not to last long.

"Charlie 55 – call London Mil on 265.2 – have a good weekend". This I did.

"Good evening C 55 (still no alarm bells) – your estimate for Woburn."

Woburn – where the f*** is that and what is it I thought; no idea was the answer.

"London this is C 55. My TACAN has failed and I'm unsure of my position, radar vectors to Farnborough please." "Roger, C 55 turn right 160 and call London Zone on 131.25." "I do not carry VHF," was my strangled reply as I started to sweat.

I was given a UHF frequency and so unwisely pressed on; the rest of the transit was busy but uneventful then I was given the Farnborough weather. It was not good but there was no turning back now so on I went for a GCA. Plunging into the gloom I felt very uncomfortable. The GCA worked out well once I remembered where the cockpit light switches were and when I broke cloud at about 350 feet it was dark but there was the runway thank God.

Touchdown was a bit hot I seem to remember, and the runway was downhill and it was raining but I slowed (the Maxarets worked well) and turned off the end absolutely drained and shaking from head to foot.

The sequel? Come Monday morning the aircraft had a hydraulic leak, so I had an extra night with Vicky then another aircraft arrived complete with an engineer to fix things.

FROM THE SUDAN TO CFS

DANNY LAVENDER

One fine day in 1964 in Khartoum, Flt Lt Danny Lavender was coming to the end of an exciting two years with the Sudan Air Force having flown over 500 hours in armed Piston and Jet Provosts, Pembrokes, Dornier 27s and Dakotas, when the air adviser summoned him into his office.

He announced my next posting – promotion to squadron leader to command 3 Squadron of the Central Flying School at RAF Little Rissington, with a flight each of Gnats, Varsities and Chipmunks. Whoopee! Not having flown any of them before, conversion onto all three – not only as captain but then to supervise the training of flying instructors – was going to be a bit of a challenge. However, I had an A2 instructor's category and within two months had qualified as an instructor on all three, so I settled down to a busy couple of years.

While I tried to share my time and effort equally among the three flights, the attractions of that tiny, sleek, fast jet, did result in a certain bias! This trainer's pretty economical Bristol Siddeley Orpheus 101 ensured a super performance enabling 40,000ft (12,192m) to be reached in seven minutes, Mach 0.9 in level flight, and Mach 1.15 or more in a shallow dive.

Yellowjacks Gnats lined up in August 1964. (Alex Wickham)

The aircraft handled like a dream but some of the emergencies associated with the longitudinal control system raised one's pulse a bit. Twice it was my sad duty to appear on Boards of Inquiry at RAF Valley when students/instructors were killed while practising forced landings. Instructing from the rear seat at night was also challenging and we used to pray for a crosswind so that the runway could be seen up to the closing stages.

In 1965 I flew to Warton with Sqn Ldr Derek Bryant (known as 'Dr Death' because he used to turn white and then green after a few beers!) to discuss visibility and other factors concerning the back seat: I hope Jaguar instructors appreciate the work that we did for them so long ago. AM Sir Richard 'Batchy' Atcherley is credited with the foresight to recognise that the Gnat would make a good formation aerobatics aircraft. As a result, Flt Lt Lee Jones, to whom we owe so much, formed the Yellowjacks by sheer drive and persistence. After a successful first season in 1964, he was sent to CFS to learn a bit of discipline and to start afresh under the team's new title of the Red Arrows.

These were heady days for me because, with little else to do at the weekends, I would sometimes fly the Red Arrows' spare aircraft, invariably staging through Chateâuroux, to exotic places on the continent for the team's shows. I used to hide my squadron leader tapes, not because I wouldn't have been pleased to be mistaken for the leader of the team but because of the 'blacks' invariably put up at the parties afterwards. It was enormous fun to share some of their experiences with the great

Flt Lt Alex Wickham (back) being strapped into a Gnat by Sgt Huntley. (Alex Wickham)

characters on the teams – I remember entertaining a restaurant full of Italians in Ravenna with a rendition of 'O Sole Mio', which brought rapturous applause.

The runway at Little Rissington was a bit short for the Gnat, if flooded or at night, so Flt Lt Alex Wickham, my outstanding Gnat flight commander, made arrangements to move us to Fairford where the Gnat could almost land across the runway. No sooner had we settled there than our hangar was required for use by the Concorde trials team. Thus began the CFS's long association with Kemble where we were welcomed with open arms. Apart from the routine training of flying instructors, for which the Gnat proved to be an excellent platform, we had other distractions.

One of my most memorable sorties was flying the late King Hussain of Jordan on his state visit to the United Kingdom in 1967. Since it was an official visit to CFS, we had to deploy the Gnat into Little Rissington. All sizes of flying gear were assembled for HRH's arrival, including long johns, which were donned with alacrity. While I was looking discreetly at his head, I recognised that this particular crowned head was unusually large. The bone dome fitting started close to the largest size and soon we ended up having to ram the RAF's biggest size onto his head. Anyway, he did not complain too much and proved to be an excellent fast-jet pilot in our 40-minute flight around the Cotswolds, including a high-speed run low over the Kemble runway. As other RAF aircrew, I had always avoided those purple 'Royal Flights' like the plague but now I found that I was on one. After a slightly fraught final landing, which he insisted on making – the runway was a bit short, particularly for a king – he emerged from the cockpit sounding excited and enthusiastic, also having called me 'Sir' about 40 times.

During my time at Kemble, life was always interesting, with frequent practices and displays from the Red Arrows led by Sqn Ldr Ray Hanna. Occasionally observed would be the odd Gnat 'kangarooing' down the runway when student instructors had become a bit 'ham' with the sensitive control system – even the late Bill Loverseed could not prevent a collapsed nosewheel once. How delightfully nostalgic that the 40th anniversary of the Gnat's arrival at Little Rissington was celebrated by the Delta Jets team at Kemble.

A LUCKY ESCAPE
PETE CHAPMAN

At the time I was a 21-year-old first tour QFI with a total of 200 hours instructing on the Folland Gnat. How did I get to be there, so young and with so little aviation experience? Well, unlike my fellow instructors who had all been on previous operational tours on Lightnings, Hunters, Canberras or Javelins, I had no previous

Pete Chapman

tours, only my flying training. I found myself there because I was the last to leave RAF Valley after my advanced flying training course and whilst packing my car to leave, the squadron commander gave me the news that CFS had asked for a young pilot who had just completed advanced training on the Gnat to join the next course at RAF Little Rissington. This meant giving up my Hunter tour which I was destined for at the time. He promised me a posting of my choice if I took the offer. So, I duly completed the CFS course and six months later I was back at RAF Valley as a newly qualified flying instructor. Nine months later whilst sitting in the crewroom, drinking coffee, I was delegated to fly with a student from the other squadron. Although this was something unexpected, as up until now I had only flown with students from my own squadron, I was keen to help and ready to fly. Anyway, I met with him, only to find that this was his first low-level navigation flight. No problem, I thought. Our aircraft was ready to go and we only had time for me to copy his route map and give a short briefing. The take-off went well as did the first part of the flight at low level as we entered into the low-flying area in the mountains of Snowdonia.

The weather wasn't great, especially for a first low-flying exercise, but the visibility was good under full cloud cover. As we flew along the bottom of the valley, I could see that we might have to execute an emergency abort as the visibility ahead was reducing and the cloud base lowering. I reminded my student of what to do if we had to abort. "Yes," he said and duly repeated everything back to me, word perfect. Flying at 360 knots at 250ft there wasn't a lot of time to make the decision for an emergency climb. So, when the time came, I called to him to abort which he did correctly. He began an emergency climb with full power at the briefed climb angle of 30 degrees. Our safety height in the area was 5,500ft, so it was essential to keep climbing above this height to keep clear of the ground. He continued the climb in thick cloud until, without any warning or discussion, he pushed the control column violently forward. Something I was completely unprepared for. However, I knew how to fly in cloud and so I took over and attempted to regain control of the aircraft.

Unfortunately, that unexpected control input had caused me to lose all sense of orientation with my eyes only able to see the attitude indicator and nothing else. With that amount of unexpected negative 'g' I experienced tunnel vision, meaning that I could only see the one instrument through a 'tunnel'. Which way was up? Was it the black or the white that represented the ground? Were we upside down or the right way up? In my panic I couldn't decide but I knew from the noise that the airspeed was increasing rapidly, so I pulled the control column back at the same time closing the throttle. What happened next I am not sure but I recall climbing, descending and rolling with airspeeds from 200 to 450kts. After what seemed an interminable amount of time trying to regain control I finally reorientated myself. At that point we were descending, the right way up, wings level with increasing airspeed. As soon as I was sure of this I began to pull the aircraft out of the dive. At that moment we broke cloud in a steep descent with the ground approaching rapidly. I applied full power and pulled the control column back as hard as I could to avoid striking the ground. The last recollection I had was a telegraph pole going past the cockpit window. I then flew the aircraft straight back up into the cloud and climbed to 12,000ft at which point we cleared the cloud tops.

Wow! We had both had a lucky escape. My student then thanked me and then told me that I had just given him a great birthday present. What actually happened whilst we were in cloud, I have no idea. All I can say is that the accelerometer ('g' meter) on landing showed readings of -4.5g to +7.5g. Fortunately, there was no serious damage done to the aircraft. I learnt a lot about instructing from that.

'ARE YOU TWO PEOPLE ASTRONAUTS?'

TOM EELES

19 February 1969
Gnat T1 XR544
Self/Lt McManus Valley – Lossiemouth
Self/Lt Gedge – General Handling

After advanced flying training as a member of the second course to be trained on the Gnat, a couple of front-line tours flying Canberras, Buccaneers on loan to the RN and the CFS course I found myself at 4 FTS, RAF Valley, as a QFI on the Gnat. I knew my time there was limited as I was about to return to the Buccaneer, recently chosen to equip RAF squadrons. The RN had offered to conduct the first eight courses of RAF aircrew, so I was to go back to RNAS Lossiemouth for another two years there as a QFI.

On 19 February 1969 OC 2 Squadron at Valley offered me a Gnat for the day, to go to Lossiemouth with Valley's RN QFI, Lt McManus. He needed to sort out some obscure RN admin issue that could only be done at a navy unit and I needed to book a room in the officers' mess, sorry, wardroom. We could keep the Gnat up there all day and I was free to offer any of my RN colleagues a trip if they wanted one. Lt

Tim Gedge, who I knew well from my time on HMS *Victorious*, volunteered and off we went for a brisk general-handling sortie to demonstrate the Gnat's agility. After about 15 minutes, whilst Tim was exploring twinkle rolls, we got a call from Lossie recalling us on the authority of our home base and advising us to use minimum control inputs. I took control and flew back to Lossie very carefully. It took quite some time to find out why we had been recalled in this way, there being no direct-dial military phone facilities in those days, but eventually I got through to Valley.

Apparently that morning the unit test pilot (UTP) was carrying out a minor servicing air test, with a student pilot in the rear seat taking note of all the required readings. There was an item in the air test schedule that required the hydraulic cock to be selected off and a check to be made that at least three reversals of aileron movement were achieved before the ailerons reverted to manual control. As the UTP moved the control column back and forth to exhaust the accumulator there was a sudden 'twang' and a loss of roll control in the front seat. The cable connecting the front-seat control column to the aileron-powered flying-control units had severed. As the back-seat cable was still intact the unfortunate student had to carry out his first-ever landing from the back, not something taught on the course. The Gnat fleet immediately stopped flying pending investigation and remedial action, hence our recall. Rectification was expected to take a long time.

So, there we were, stuck at Lossie, wearing just our old grey two-piece immersion suits, with no money and no personal kit. It was soon obvious that our recovery was at the bottom of Valley's priority list to get us home and that our Gnat would be stuck at Lossie for a long time. We were lent pullovers, enabling us to take off our immersion suit tops and feel a bit more civilised and more importantly allowed into the wardroom bar. Lossie, being a master diversion airfield, provided me with shaving kit and a toothbrush. My bearded colleague only needed a toothbrush. Next day, it was obvious that were going to have to find our own way home to Valley and so rail warrants were provided by the RN and timetables studied. On day three we set off. In 1969 it took a long time with numerous changes en route to get from Elgin to Holyhead by train. Bear in mind we had now returned our borrowed pullovers, were still wearing our full immersion suits which were a bit smelly by now and we were carrying our helmets, oxygen masks and life jackets.

Early 1969 witnessed the increasing pace of the American efforts to reach the moon with the Apollo manned space-flight programme, which was very much in the news. Whilst standing that afternoon on the platform of Crewe railway station, awaiting another connecting train, two small boys came up to us. "Excuse me sir," said one of them, "But are you two people astronauts?"

GUARD FOR STANDBY TRIM SWITCHES

PETE WEBB

Pete Webb

Early in 1976 I was at Little Rissington doing the QFI course on the Gnat. The flying, of course, was done at Kemble. Lloyd Grosse was an instructor but looking back in my logbook I see that I only had a couple of trips with him and neither included any flying in manual. So, it must have been in crewroom chat or maybe in the bar that he imparted a gem of advice regarding the guard for the standby trim switches. The pre-start checklist called for the guard to be 'down'. However, Lloyd's advice was that, certainly when flying in the back seat, the guard should be left up. That just might save a few milli seconds should you need standby trim in a hurry. I took that on board and followed his advice.

Fast forward to 8 October 1976. I had been an instructor on No. 1 Squadron, 4 FTS at RAF Valley for just over five months – a lowly B2. My second trip of the day was with a student I hadn't flown with before and we were to fly Ex17. In those days I could have rattled off what Ex17 involved, sadly, 45 years on, I haven't a clue!

The student did the take-off. Final check in the back seat before we rolled – "trim in the white". As I recall we were on runway 14 so nice and long. We got airborne normally but then accelerated maintaining about 10ft off the ground. Interesting technique I thought. I was about to suggest a little more climb angle would be good when the student shouted, "you have control"! I grabbed the pole and it seemed to be solid. Height still very low, would we clear the barrier? Couldn't move the pole, left hand grabs for standby trim switches – guard was up (thank you Lloyd, and Lord), very soon we were climbing at a pretty steep angle, unlock lever pulled. I must admit the heart rate was high but control in follow-up was good, we left the gear down and following an airborne inspection and low-speed handling check we returned to the circuit for an uneventful landing.

The engineers couldn't find anything wrong with the jet. Maybe the front seater had inadvertently trimmed nose down during the take-off run – I hadn't checked as after engine checks at full power, my eyeballs were outside. I built in another white sector check after this fortunate escape.

MIGRATING TO THE GNAT

ALAN EAST

Having completed a three-year tour on No. 3 (F) Squadron in 2 TAF, Germany, on Sabres and Hunters; and a two-year tour at the Central Air Traffic Control School, RAF Shawbury flying Ansons and Vampires, Flt Lt Alan East was accepted for No. 200 Course at CFS, over the winter of 1959/60.

Alan East

Everybody did the first half of the course on the Piston Provost. Then, according to our ultimate destination – which may not have been what we had chosen – we either stayed on Piston Provost or Chipmunk for the basic phase or moved to the Vampire or Varsity if we were to be advanced instructors. From there, I was posted to Swinderby as a QFI on Vampires before moving on to teach on Jet Provosts with No. 3 FTS at Leeming.

When the opportunity arose, I volunteered for a tour on the Gnat, which was being introduced as the advanced trainer to replace the Vampire at 4 FTS, Valley. There was already the Gnat Evaluation team at CFS: three QFIs, Derek Bryant, John Young and Dennis Yeardley, and three pre-production aircraft, XM706, 708 and 709. In July 1962 I and a few others formed the first conversion course and, including the CFS staff, I became the seventh Gnat QFI in the service. By the time we had finished, the first aircraft had still not arrived at Valley, so we stayed on to help with the conversion of the next batch. Eventually, the first production aircraft were ready for delivery. On 12 November 1962, I flew with Derek Bryant in XP501 to combine an acceptance air test with my instrument rating test (IRT) on type. Later that month, I made my first flight at Valley, in XP502. Our families were pleased to see us home after so long at Little Rissington!

ANDY WILLIAMS

My mind is a little sketchy about a night-flying incident whilst I was on my advanced flying course at RAF Valley in 1966. The incident happened on a night between 3–5 October 1966. I had just landed from a dual sortie and was taxiing back to dispersal. I was aware of blue lights flashing and heading in the direction of the main runway 34/16. When I got back to the crewroom, I learned that a Gnat had burst a tyre on landing and may have slid off the runway. Whatever, the runway was 'black'. The short runway (22/04) was unaffected, so an instructor and his student decided to land on that runway but made a hash of the landing and ran off the end. With both runways now out of action, several dual and solo students were diverted to RAF Shawbury. That's not the end of the story as a solo student who had landed ahead of this 'faff' had been re-routed back to the ASP by the local controller and got himself lost. He ended up being stuck between two blast walls with nowhere to go and had to shut down.

CHING FULLER

Ching Fuller

I was not a great fan of the Gnat's complicated longitudinal control system as it was indirectly responsible for the demise of at least one of my friends at RAF Valley. However, I would like to have flown the Indian version of the Gnat. They christened it the 'Sabre Slayer' because they had so much success with it against the Pakistani F-86s including the downing of Safras Rafiqui an exchange officer on No. 19(F) Squadron and a friend.

DICK CLOKE

Dick Cloke

I was involved with the Gnat early on, having been posted to CFS (to my great disappointment) in July 1964, after four years at Wattisham on Hunters and Lightnings. I flew my first Gnat flight in September 1964 and when I flew my last sortie in August 1967, I had clocked up over 900 Gnat hours. During the early part of my tour the accident rate was bad, we lost around ten aircraft in my first six months along with a number of staff and students. Having said that, I enjoyed flying the aircraft and had very

few incidents apart from once having one wheel stuck up when I came to land. Fortunately, I was able to hold the wings level until I got to a runway junction so when the wing did fall to the ground it merely slid along the tarmac, rather than dig into the grass.

One day I was walking out to fly an SCT sortie with Tim Mermagen, (another sub-5' 6" giant – and unfortunately one of the fatalities) in our normal light-blue flying suits, wearing our white bone domes because it was pouring with rain. Unknown to us, gazing out of the crewroom was one of our fellow QFIs ('Oscar' Wild I think) who exclaimed: "Christ – I thought the mushroom season had started!"

A DENTAL MALFUNCTION

DIM JONES

Dim Jones

Whenever the weather at Valley was deemed to be beyond the capabilities of the student body (a very light shade of green would have done it in my case), we were despatched to the gym, there to have our physiques honed under the tender care of the PE staff. After the obligatory circuit training, some form of team sport malarkey was deemed appropriate. Volleyball was becoming popular at that time, and so it was that our course of ten found itself in two opposing teams of five, separated by a net which was several inches taller than me. After a short while getting the hang of the thing, student over-confidence soon asserted itself, and we started experimenting with advanced techniques such as 'setting' and 'spiking'. One of my colleagues at the back parried a serve from the opposition, and the leftmost of the three of us at the net expertly set up the rebound for the spike. This left a choice of two to do the necessary and, of course, we both went for it at once. My teammate, having a tad more situational awareness than me, anticipated a potentially hazardous outcome, and the need to protect himself from the ensuing collision as I descended on top of him. This he elected to do by raising his elbow, which predictably connected with my face – and, more precisely, with one of my front teeth, which came off very much second best and assumed an unusual angle of attack.

Off I went to the fang-wrangler, who did what he could to repair the damage and save the tooth. After a couple of subsequent appointments, however, he conceded defeat, and said that some root canal work would be required, and that this would require drilling a hole in the back of the tooth. If there are any professional dentists out there, this is from memory, so don't get excited if I have got it slightly wrong. In preparation for the major reconstruction to come, and to prevent any infection, he applied a dressing to the hole he had excavated and sent me on my way.

It chanced that we were at that stage of the course where we were exploring the high-level handling characteristics of the Gnat, and the next ride up was my solo. At the apogee of the profile, I experienced a sharp pain in said tooth, followed by a funny taste in the mouth. The pain and the funny taste went away after a while, and I got on with the rest of the sortie. On landing, it transpired that the funny taste had been blood, and I was despatched to the station medical centre once more, where the dental wizard diagnosed that, under the effect of the rarefied atmosphere in the cockpit, the air pressure in the cavity behind the dressing had increased to the point where it turned the dressing itself into a small-shaped charge, which it then projected unerringly into my tongue.

My erstwhile assailant, he of the sharp elbow and highly developed sense of self-preservation, bore absolutely no responsibility for the original accident, but that did not stop me reminding him of it every time we met. He is sadly no longer with us, and his name shall remain a closely guarded secret; suffice to say that there are not that many who have made a career change from F-4 pilot to Scottish Law Lord.

HOW DULL CAN YOU GET?

When one is not very sharp, 'doing it by numbers' can be a useful substitute for competence – but not always a reliable one. This was never truer than when I found myself as No. 3 on a solo formation ride, the first part of which comprised a stream take-off and join-up to close. For whatever reason, this had not occurred on my dual trip, so I consulted my friendly (and he was, thankfully) QFI for some top tips. When asked how to set up the geometry for the turning rejoin, he advised me to stick the lead aircraft in the bottom corner of the windscreen, just forward of the canopy arch, while keeping a wary eye out for the No. 2 (also solo), whose antics were likely to be as unpredictable as mine. This would ensure that I would not set up any horrific closing angle with which I would undoubtedly be unable to cope. I duly complied but, after a while, it became glaringly apparent even to me that the desired effect was not being had – to wit, the other two aircraft were getting smaller, not larger. I suppose that I must have mastered (or at least been judged to have mastered) the basics of lead and lag during the tailchase phase of Jet Provost training but, of course, when you are doing it by numbers, common sense goes out the window – quite literally in this case. You have no doubt guessed that, when faced with a choice of two corners of windscreen, the dull student will almost certainly choose the wrong one. So it was on this occasion; after a while, a somewhat testy-sounding lead asked when

I might be expected to appear in his vicinity; this coincided almost exactly with the reverberating clang as the penny dropped. I prevaricated with some standard student blather, swapped the numbers technique for a modicum of common sense and TLAR (that looks about right), and managed to join up without further disgracing myself. I can't remember how I explained away the delay during the debrief, but I am pretty sure it was not the truth.

'CREAMIE' THOUGHTS
DOUG MCGREGOR

Doug McGregor

Flying the Gnat from the back seat was slightly awkward because of the difficulty of seeing straight ahead with the obstruction of the front seat. So, one had to get used to rapidly switching one's head from left to right, and still give convincing demonstrations. With the Gnat being a 'lively' aircraft, rapid intervention could be required, especially on take-off and landing, or in the event of an emergency, especially a hydraulic failure, when the correct initial actions were needed, followed by careful electrical handling of the 'slab' tailplane as well as the limited effectiveness of the 'unlocked' elevators. So, it was not easy. It was good for aerobatics, especially from the front seat, where the pitot probe made it easy to select the correct/ desired aim point.

GNAT WHEELS-UP LANDING

Although the total loss of hydraulic control was very unlikely, the absence of an undercarriage lowering function because of a split jack was not something one could practise. So, with the wheels just hanging loosely in the slipstream, I elected to use the long main runway at Valley, despite a significant crosswind. In retrospect, this was not a good choice. After touching down in my high-speed toboggan at some 130 knots, the aircraft did not slow down quickly, and it was not long before the crosswind made the Gnat weathercock and soon slide off the windward side of the runway, at about 100 knots. This was not a comfortable experience, with the high-speed grass a mere six inches beneath one's seat. We opened the canopy at an estimated 30 knots in view of the possible need for a hasty exit. This was not the case, as we then both shortly found ourselves waiting to get off a wing that was doing well over 50 knots! It was no surprise subsequently to see that the canopy had been ripped off. Fortunately, the aircraft eventually was returned to service – including a new undercarriage jack.

GEOFF BRINDLE

Geoff Brindle

A fast-jet posting was what most guys were striving for and so I was pleased to drive down the lane from the A5 into Valley but was a little disconcerted to see two aircraft falling in flames and another trailing smoke heading towards Mona. The sky seemed full of parachutes, and I did wonder whether I had made the right decision. Apparently, a pair of aircraft were climbing out and met a three-ship positioning for a re-join – fortunately all survived including the guys in the aircraft that limped into Mona.

As has been recorded the Gnat was an exciting, manoeuvrable, and complicated jet and as it turned out a great lead-in aircraft for the Lightning. It was a treat to get a solo general-handling sortie – high-level handling, max-rate descent, low flying, aerobatics, and then an instrument approach for an overshoot to then finish with a run-in and break to land. John Leeming and I were briefed up for just such a sortie within a few minutes of each other and agreed to meet up after the low-flying bit and show the flag to Radio Caroline which was moored just off the Isle of Man. We joined up off Point Lynas and set course for the ship – the plan was to cross the ship at right angles with me over the bow and John set up on the stern. As we approached it became apparent that the ship had swung at her moorings and was now in line with our route. We did not want to do a lot of manoeuvring in case we drew too much attention and so we agreed to run down each side as low as we dared. It was not until we were abeam the ship that we saw the aerial cables which ran from the bow up over the mast head and down to the sternpost. We might well have collected them if we had straddled the ship as we originally intended. Our visit did not go un-noticed and the boys in the crewroom heard the voice of the radio DJ complaining about the little silver and orange aircraft that kept 'buzzing' Caroline. Unfortunately, the flight commander also heard the comments, and we were invited in for a one-sided chat post the sortie.

The fire/crash crews were kept very busy at Valley with up to three types of aircraft operating mostly flown by students, and lots of visiting aircraft often using two runways simultaneously hence they had a very demanding training programme to keep them up to speed. It was common practice for one of the last aircraft to land on a Friday being positioned on the runway turn off and the pilot told to feign collapse so the fire crews could gain access, shut down the engine and rescue the pilot. The Gnat had a huge one-piece plexiglass canopy which was a real handful to open single-handed especially with the engine still running. On this occasion the fireman struggled to release the canopy and became very concerned that the pilot seemed in great distress. Not realising this was just a training drill he pulled out his fire axe, reversed it and struck the canopy a mighty blow to release the crew. The plexiglass refused to crack: the axe rebounded and struck the poor fireman on the forehead and tipped him unconscious off the aircraft. The ambulance crew positioned to help the pilot stepped smartly in and quickly attended the injured fireman. The pilot shut down the aircraft and had to wait until all was made safe before he could get a lift back to the squadron. The practice drills were re-organised after that.

GORDON YOUNG

Gordon Young

As the aircraft could go supersonic, one exercise was a supersonic run. We would climb up to around 45,000 feet off Bardsey (the island at the end of the Llyn Peninsula) turn on to south so as to be over the sea, then roll inverted, pitch down about 30 degrees then roll the right way up. The aircraft would then creep over Mach 1 to about Mach 1.2. You would experience the stiffening of the controls before you recovered at around 25,000 feet.

An episode I remember was during a take-off the front-seat IP u/t found difficulty in getting the nosewheel off the ground. When he announced this we were well down the runway and we had to abort and took the barrier at about 40 knots.

Several years later and after two tours I was given the opportunity to return to RAF Valley as a QFI. Initially, we had to go through the QFI Course at RAF Kemble which was also the home of the Red Arrows. I always remember that, as the aircraft pan was split by a taxiway, you had when crossing to look both ways, not for taxiing aircraft, but for high-speed, very low-level runs by the Reds.

As a staff member at Valley we occasionally undertook staff continuation training (SCT). On these we used to carry out land-aways and, with Rick Peacock-Edwards and others, would land away at Leuchars or St Athan then nip off to watch the current international rugby at Edinburgh or Cardiff. On one occasion, we flew to Leuchars, chatted up the local SAR helicopter boss, and hitched a lift to Edinburgh. We had brought Doc McCoubrey up in the back seat and he arranged that we could land the helicopter in the playing fields of Fettes College where he had gone to school. We picked a suitable pitch and landed there. We all got out, jumped over a wall and took a No. 19 bus into town. Throughout the process, a gardener, who had been mowing the grass nearby, never looked up and continued quietly mowing away while we nipped off.

GRAHAM BOWERMAN

Graham Bowerman

One particular memory is of a planned land-away sortie to RAF Kinloss towards the latter part of the course. I was to fly with the Canadian exchange officer, and we planned to transit at 40,000 feet. We took off and climbed, changing frequencies as we went, but as we passed 25,000 feet my instructor seemed to become less communicative. Initially, I took this as a sign that I was doing OK and there was little to be said. However, as we passed 35,000 feet, I realised that I had conducted my last climb check with no response from the rear cockpit. I asked him if all was ok, but heard nothing, something was wrong. I put out a Pan call and carried out an emergency descent. Once below 20,000 feet heading back to RAF Valley I heard my instructor's 'tired' voice and I explained that I suspected he had become hypoxic. He rallied over the next few thousand feet and at 5,000 feet became agitated that we were returning to base because he felt fine. He took control of the aircraft despite my protestations and completed a normal landing from a run and break. The station medics met us and he was taken to the medical centre but released shortly afterwards with no apparent ill effects.

The QFI had suffered hypoxia due to the rear-cockpit oxygen tube becoming detached lower down in the cockpit. I don't recall any thanks for my actions although I did get a telling off for allowing my forceful QFI to take control. We flew the sortie uneventfully the next day.

IAN MACFADYEN

Ian MacFadyen

23 January 1964 was a wonderfully clear night. I was to make my second night solo in a Gnat. The aircraft registration number was XR574 which, by a strange coincidence, is now on display in the museum at RAF Halton. The brief from my instructor, Gerry Honey, was clear: "Climb to over 40,000 feet, do some turns and then set yourself up for a high-speed run (a supersonic dive) before recovering back to Valley for some circuits and landing. Oh, and by the way, you need a target that stands out so your dive aiming point is Menai Bridge."

So off I set. It was a perfect night for night flying with a partial moon. The view from over 40,000ft was stunning and I spent a few moments to take it all in as this was the first time I had been at that altitude by night on my own. One could see as far as Dublin, Newcastle, and London with a few fog patches just visible across England and Wales.

After my practice turns in that relatively thin air it was time to look for my aiming point; it was easy to pick out with traffic crossing the bridge. Diving at 60 degrees at night was quite a challenge and I only just got supersonic before having to make a recovery by 10,000 feet. I have no idea of what took place on the ground and as far as I know no complaints were received. After a few circuits back at RAF Valley I was on the ground ready for a night-flying meal (basically a full English breakfast). So ended 50 minutes of a most memorable night solo sortie.

IAN MCBRIDE

I was on 3 Course behind 82 and 83 Cranwell entries. Availability was a big issue to start with, but it improved by the end of my extended six-month course and formations could be mounted with reasonable confidence whenever Lee Jones and his soon-to-be Yellowjacks did not have prior claim. Before I got there Ian Christie-Miller wrote one off, not his fault but due to circumstance and bad luck, in a forced landing after engine failure but other than that we had no incidents of note other than the occasional datum shift failure. Mine was at night with an 800ft cloud base. Kit Netherton's

Ian McBride

breathing returned to normal remarkably quickly! The ejections all happened after my time. Not much more other than our 'holding' project to dismantle the Vampire in ground school. Just before the final cut, at which point it would cease to be an aircraft, we thought we would do some cockpit drills. To our horror there was still some fuel in it and the bl**dy thing started up and torched inside the wooden building. Most of the station hierarchy were there in seconds but by then we had shut it down and hidden the scorched notices from the walls. Those were the days.

JIM BAYLIS

I have one personal anecdote from my days of flying the Gnat as a member of No. 1 Course. I flew my end of course IRT with Al Pollock (quoted earlier). At the end of the test, he said he had control. Whereupon we left the circuit, and he did a few aeros. Eventually I pointed out that the low fuel light had come on. At this stage, instead of returning immediately to Valley, we descended to very low level over Holyhead harbour. We crossed the harbour at warp speed inverted, with Al muttering something about they can't read our number. I still had the IF visor on, but I can still see the masts of sailing boats flashing past my head! We then broke into the circuit and landed. I didn't dare tell anyone what had happened (it was my IRT after all) but I do recall that the engineers reported to our flight commander about the amount of fuel they had to put into the jet.

Jim Baylis

I loved the Gnat, but after Valley I was sent to fly Vulcans, another aircraft with a great power to weight ratio. I just remember taxiing this little 'racing car' with amazing visibility and such a lightness of touch on the controls. It's a source of regret that I never had a chance to fly the Gnat again.

JIM WILD

I've nothing specific reference the Gnat. Except to say that after talking with other guys we all unhesitatingly said the Gnat transition was the biggest step in training bar none. The moment

Jim Wild

when you took control (sort of!) for the first time was incredible. "How am I going to get to grips with this" was the overriding impression we all thought of then. A wonderful aircraft.

MIKE ADAMS

Mike Adams

I recall a meeting of the vice-chiefs of the RAF and Indian Air Force in MoD at which the VCAS of the IAF gave an entertaining account of an aborted take-off in a Gnat at Valley which resulted in him being taken to a local hospital, where he gave all the usual personal details required by the staff there. Shortly thereafter he was visited by the resident Catholic padre. After introductory conversation, the Indian pilot said, "padre, I'm afraid there's been a terrible mistake, when I arrived here I didn't say I was 'RC', I said 'Parsee'."

MIKE JOHNSON

Mike Johnson

When we were the junior course, we were regularly called upon to report to the flight line just after dawn to taxi the jets to the 'engine wash' pan. There we ran the aircraft engine at different power settings (signalled by an airman with large paddle boards indicating the required setting) while lubricant was sprayed into the intakes to 'wash' the Orpheus engine compressor that suffered corrosion from the salty sea air in the atmosphere at RAF Valley.

One anecdote I have is from the stage on the course when we students were all sent off on solo low-level navigation exercises on a fabulously sunny day. When we returned, we were individually marched into the CFI's office where he demanded to know exactly where we had flown. There had been a low-flying complaint from a lady in Aberystwyth. All professed innocence as the route we followed went nowhere near that part of the Welsh coast. Much muttering and grumbling followed from the authorities, but they had no proof either way or the other. Then, the following evening, the Wales BBC news ran an item about the incident, and we watched it on the TV in the officers' mess TV room adjacent to the bar. The reporter interviewed Mrs Bronwyn Morgan and asked what she had seen and what had upset her. She said, "the jet plane made a dreadful noise and came so low over my house I could clearly see the pilot – but I don't think I would recognise him again!" A few days later we were let off the hook when it transpired that the culprit was discovered to be a Hunter T7 from Chivenor.

GNATS DETACH TO FAIRFORD

RAY DEACON

Ray Deacon

As the number of Gnats using the busy Rissington circuit increased it became apparent that these fast jets were incompatible with the lower speed aircraft such as the Chipmunk, Varsity and Jet Provost and that sooner or later an accident was bound to occur. The solution arrived at was that the Gnat Flight would be moved to another airfield on a permanent detachment basis. As the Americans had vacated the nearby base at RAF Fairford, the opportunity was taken to relocate C Flight to the now-deserted former USAF airfield and the transfer took place in November 1964.

At Fairford, the flight took up residence in a large modern hangar fitted with a domed roof and almost hidden out of sight behind two tin hangars lining the peritrack. It was equipped with spacious office and ground crew accommodation, superb servicing bays and a long gallery that stretched the length of one of the walls, linking the first-floor offices and offering a panoramic view of activities on the hangar floor. An extensive concrete apron between the CFS hangar and the 'tin' hangars provided ample space from which to operate the flight's Gnats.

With the arrival of the Red Arrows Gnats at Little Rissington in early 1965 and the need to practise over the airfield up to four times a day, the decision was taken to move the team to Fairford where it could practise without hinderance from other aircraft apart from C Flight Gnats. They were housed at the other end of the hangar, sharing the facilities with the course Gnats.

RICH RHODES

I was on 4 Course with, inter alia, Mike Bettell, Andy Markell and 'Pritch'. I did win the flying prize, aerobatics prize and ground school prize, but managed it all with

Rich Rhodes

no drama. My instructors were Al Pollock and Roy Booth. I recall Al telling me to go to the AOC's lunch in best bib and tucker and then take the afternoon off. I'd had two pints at the pre-drinks when he rang the mess and told me there had been a change and I was needed for a solo immediately. I told him I couldn't because I'd had two pints. He said: "Bollocks, Rich, get in here ASAP: I'm the authoriser." I did, flew the sortie uneventfully and heard nothing more about it. Another stat, I think, but not one for a book! I give Al Pollock great credit for his adventurous teaching ethos. He was, at the least, unconventional and encouraged initiative. Maybe he should take some credit for my later flying achievements, although flying under Tower Bridge never occurred to me. He certainly encouraged lateral thinking. Roy Booth, who went on to the Arrows, taught me what I'd call 'aggressive' aeros. Never stay still and always use max control deflection.

ROGER HYMANS

Roger Hymans

Sent to Dunsfold to collect a new Gnat I was delayed by a night due to an aircraft unserviceability. The hierarchy at Dunsfold were very hospitable and their sales director – Sir Richard Atcherley – ex-commander-in-chief Training Command, loaned me one of his service blue shirts. Once home the said shirt was laundered and ironed. Unfortunately, however, I passed by the bar at Valley with the shirt which I foolishly identified as being Sir Richard's. It was immediately placed on the bar and signed in biro by all thirty-odd people including our esteemed seniors. Sir Richard was very good about it and said it would be a keepsake.

Later in my tour, someone called me to ask my agreement to a picture of close-formation Gnats (vertical in a loop) in which I was flying No.2 to be printed on the back page of a book about the CFS. He was concerned that, at the time the rather good snap was taken, formation aerobatics were banned, and I might be called to explain myself. I assured him I would be happy to take a chance.

When the Gnat was first made a two-seat trainer it was fitted with UHF radio. This required a solid metal-blade aerial fitted on the belly centreline. Although this worked well somebody decided it needed a second aerial on the centre top of the fuselage behind the canopy. Unfortunately, this caused some aerodynamic interference with the fin and rudder, so it was canted to one side and moved to the side. This solved the problem with the fin but now the new position caused a rolling effect. So, they fitted a second blade aerial to the top of the fuselage canted the other way to even things up. This aerial was not connected to the radio.

Fast forward to 1963 when Henry Prince, an experienced instructor, was doing his initial conversion to the Gnat with myself in the back seat. It was a nice day and Henry was enjoying some aerobatics over the Menai Straits when there was a very loud bang. I think we sat in stunned silence for a moment before the inevitable and quite unhelpful expletives were said. So, as you would expect, we desisted with the aerobatics, slowed down, and flew gently back to overhead Valley. Visual checks from the cockpit, and close observation of the instruments, plus gentle movements of the throttle, showed no problems. Unfortunately, there were no other aircraft available for a visual check. A flypast of the tower gave no further help and so after a slow-speed check at height Henry landed on the long runway at Valley a little faster than usual. On the ground it became obvious what the problem was – the 'dummy' aerial had torn out of the fuselage skin and struck the left tailplane cutting through the leading edge and back to the main spar in which it caused a large dent. Opinion was that half the tail was close to departing from the aircraft with unknown results. It would be interesting to examine an existing Gnat to see if it had the extra unused aerial on top.

ROGER TAITE

Roger Taite

As a helicopter pilot and instructor, I found the Gnat somewhat challenging to begin with, as one might expect. However, as I got into my stride, I grew to like its handling and performance. After some three years flying it, I can safely say that it was the most enjoyable and rewarding tour of my RAF career. As all who have some time on the Gnat know full well it was not exactly viceless and could sit up and bite. Here are a couple of anecdotes to illustrate.

There was a dual exercise we had to do which covered the procedure if the airspeed looked like it was going to fall below 200kts whilst entering a vertical manoeuvre like a loop, i.e. centralise controls, close throttle and set +2 degrees on the TPI, expecting the aircraft to fall over forwards and dive away. On one occasion, with the aircraft mushing over forwards it went beyond the vertical and finished up on its back beginning to rotate in yaw and roll. This began to look suspiciously like a developing inverted-spin situation. A little back stick caused the nose to drop, and it dived away normally. Subsequent discussion with the Standards Squadron suggested, and was later proved, that the actual incidence of the tailplane did not correspond with the reading on the TPI by two degrees. This was enough to cause the inverted stall.

Another problem, which made my eyes water, was hearing a loud 'clunk' from back aft somewhere followed by an extremely loud roaring and grinding noise. The aircraft was in only a 2–3g turn. Upon releasing the stick prior to a possible ejection, the noise stopped. Any further attempt to apply any 'g' resulted in the recurrence of the noise. As there were no signs of anything amiss in the cockpit, a very gentle return and landing at Valley was carried out. Subsequent engineering investigation discovered an engine bearer had broken, thus allowing the engine to move about in the bay, transferring its not inconsiderable mechanical noise to the airframe.

MY GNAT EXPERIENCE

TINA PEACOCK-EDWARDS

Tina Peacock-Edwards

I was posted to RAF Valley in January 1974 – just after my marriage – as the first RAF(W) controller in the tower. SATCO didn't like the idea much, but my fellow controllers made me very welcome. I fear I could have been green with pink spots as long as I was competent!

It's always a good idea to know what goes on in the cockpits of the aircraft you control, and to that end I was assigned to the 'weather ship' on the morning of 21 March 1974 in Gnat Fleet No. 08, XR569 with Dave Roome (an old friend) as my pilot. Having first established that although my seat was a little low, no way was I fiddling with any little lever behind my right foot (I'd done my training, I knew exactly what went on under the seat!) we launched off into an 8/8 clear blue sky – no need to check the weather today. There followed 55 minutes of exhilarating flight over Snowdonia. I can categorically state that I have never been quite so close to sheep at any time in my life.

My memory, some 48 years later, is of a small compact bouncy aircraft with good all-round vision. I did fly it, but quite honestly, whilst handling the controls and following Dave's instructions to the letter (back a bit, left a bit) I couldn't have told you which way up I was. I later discovered I had performed a barrel roll.

My thanks to Dave for a truly memorable trip – but sadly I must report I'm still happiest with my feet firmly on the ground. At heart I'm a coward. My husband always said I wouldn't make a fighter pilot: rest easy my dear, I never ever wanted to be one, and if truth be told, there's only room for one in a family.'

TONY ELLENDER

Tony Ellender

Like others no doubt, my first instructor at Valley was Al Pollock. He sent me solo before we had done any high-level general handling, so before I had flown a Gnat above 1,000ft! The very next day Al flew the weather check in a manner which so upset the station commander that my QFI was posted – to West Raynham. Not long afterwards he flew a Hunter through Tower Bridge.

Lasting memories – at night, in the front seat, close to a cumulonimbus and I've never been better placed to see St Elmo's Fire; quite electric.

No. 85 Course's good fortune was to be at Valley when Radio Caroline first started pirate radio broadcasting from a ship moored 3.5 miles south of the Isle of Man. And the 4FTS syllabus called for a solo supersonic dive over the Irish Sea after an earlier dual demo. Simple, when solo; drop the boom on the boat. If judged to perfection the mates in the crewroom would hear the boom, positive 'feedback' so to say, and the blokes on the boat (Tony Blackburn and co.) didn't seem to mind at all.

CHAPTER 4
THE RED ARROWS

ROY SOMERVILLE

Roy Somerville

It is now nearly 48 years since my last flight in this delightful aircraft. I apologise for the lack of precise detail as I write this from Australia. The borders are closed, and my logbooks are at home in New Zealand. My 80-year-old memory will have to suffice.

I had flown the Gnat during advanced flying training, at RAF Valley in the early sixties and it was not until 1971 when I was invited to join the Red Arrows that I was able to renew my acquaintance with this aircraft.

The demands of a very short conversion and subsequent incorporation into the aerobatic team were made somewhat easier by having the beautifully responsive and manoeuvrable attributes of the Gnat. The aircraft soon became a pleasure to fly and remained so for the next four years of my two tours with the Red Arrows.

Over a couple of thousand sorties and displays, I had the usual number of minor technical problems to be expected in such a sophisticated machine. Happily, they all resolved themselves without any major mishaps. There were however two occasions that stick firmly in my memory, both being engine failures.

At the end of the winter servicing period our individual aircraft were given a thorough air test prior to the next season's training programme. I was No. 7 in the team, a position I was to occupy for three of my four years. I was due to take my aircraft up for its air test and it was usual to have another team member, if available, in the aircraft to help with recording all the details. On this occasion the team leader, Sqn Ldr Ian Dick was the other pilot and deferring to seniority he got the front seat. It was a beautiful clear winter's day, and I was looking forward to some fun flying after the air test.

Being in the front seat Ian was the pilot flying. As we were climbing up through about 25,000 feet there was a loud bang followed by the eerie silence as the

Taxiing for Valley flypast.

XP512 over North Wales in 1963. (Al Pollock)

Left: Yellowjacks (XR992 with black fin) above North Wales in July 1964. (Ray Deacon collection)

Below: Yellowjacks running in from left to right in August 1964. (Alex Wickham)

Opposite: Yellowjacks looping, August 1964. (Alex Wickham)

The 1965 Red Arrows team at Wattisham. (Bill Hickham)

Four QFI students with their instructor, Alex Wickham, at Fairford in 1966. The students are, from left to right: Mike Gray, Peter Chapman, Ken Miles and Ted Edwards.
(Alex Wickham)

XR991 nose-on view at Kemble in September 1966. (Ray Deacon)

X991 performing an over-the-loop technique over South Cerney on 2 May 1967. (Ray Deacon)

Gnat T1 XP515 55 and XP539 39 of 4 FTS, Valley in 1967. (Roger Moore via Steve Bond)

2 Squadron staff at Valley in 1973. On the ground from L to R: Roger Taite, Roger Pope, Simon Bostock, 'Crib' the dog, Rod King, Roy Gamblin, Wally Black (the boss), Roger Smith and Steve Gruner. Sitting/Standing on top of aircraft from L to R: Roy Barber, 'Tuffy' the dog, Dave Rees, Keith Marshall, and Dave Roome. (Roger Taite)

'On the wing'. Gnat formating on approach to RAF Valley. (Chris Parker)

Line-up of Indian Air Force Gnat F1 fighters. (Indian Air Force)

Gnat F1 E-1070 formating with an Indian Air Force HAL Kiran II, U703 over Farnborough in 1972. (Adrian Balch)

An apprehensive Finnish Air Force pilot about to undertake his first Gnat flight.
(Air Force Museum)

Finnish Air Force Gnat F1 fighters undergoing servicing on the snow at Jyväskylä airfield.
(Air Force Museum)

Finnish Air Force Gnat F1 fighters at Jyväskylä airfield. (Air Force Museum)

A group of Finnish Air Force pilots pose in front of the first Gnat F1 fighter delivered to the FAF, named after Count Eric Von Rosen who donated the very first aircraft (Thulin Type D) delivered to the then newly formed Finnish Air Force. Name painted on the nose of Gnat GN-101 in March 1959. (Air Force Museum)

Gnat on low-level training sortie over Wales.

Upside down, top of a loop.

No. 1 Squadron Gnats 1978. Back row from L to R: Paul Robinson, Roger Moore, Gary Burcher, Geoffrey Lamb, Roger North, Jonathan Baynton and Paddy Mullen. Front row from L to R: Dobs Dobbie, Bill Cope, Mike Keane (boss), Gee Grey, and Greg Tyrell. (Jonathan Baynton)

Red Arrows nine-ship. (Godfrey Mangion)

Red Arrows in line abreast. (via Steve Johnson)

Red Arrows promotional poster produced in 1979, the last season of Red Arrows Gnat air displays. (via Steve Johnson)

Gnats in Red Arrows, Yellowjacks and 4 FTS colours belonging to the Aviation Heritage Trust based at North Weald. Photo taken around 2019.

Gnat flies at speed down the A5 pass in North Wales, always a thrilling experience. (John MacWilliam)

engine blew out half its compressor blades. At this altitude there is plenty of time to evaluate the situation and sort out the problem. We were over the Vale of Evesham and Pershore airfield was in view about 20 miles away so that became our destination. Ian as one would expect, was flying beautifully. He made a perfect approach and landing at Pershore. My contribution was in making a Mayday call to the emergency services.

My lasting memory of this incident however was not of the flying which was what we were expected to do but of the subsequent few hours on the ground. The wing commander flying at Kemble, who was a really nice person, had driven up in his staff car to collect us as it was not too far from the base. I was again sitting in the back, probably seniority. The wing commander was quite overcome with the success of our forced landing and was a little excited. As we left the airfield on the way back, we were soon approaching a set of traffic lights. They changed to green as we approached, and he stopped. As they changed to red he drove on. This was far too much excitement for one day and I do remember something being said. The rest was uneventful.

I had elected to exercise my option to leave the RAF at my 12-year point, which coincided nicely with the end of the 1974 season, my leaving date being in early

Miss GB with the Red Arrows in July 1974. (Ray Deacon)

December. Our last public display for the year was to be at Bristol Airport where Concorde was being assembled. We flew from Kemble down to Bristol on another beautiful autumn day (what's happened to the weather these days or is it just my memory?). Ian positioned the team for our arrival in Big Nine and we pulled up over the airfield and in the vertical changed to Diamond. I was flying 7 as usual so was at the back of the formation. Just as we reached the top of the loop at around 5,000 feet there was that familiar big bang and silence as my engine blew up. Not the best place for an engine failure as there were a few thousand spectators and a commercial complex around the airfield.

To be perfectly honest you do not think too much in these sorts of situations other than the initial f***! My options were quite limited and apart from a quick radio call as the engine wound down, "Red 7 engine failure", my instincts took over. I remembered in amongst the engine failure procedures to turn the smoke off as I thought the crowd must have been thinking I could not keep up. As it turned out from inverted at 5,000 feet over the centre of the airfield it was not a bad position to be in for a forced landing. I crossed the threshold at about 160kts, pulled the brake 'chute and even managed to roll off the main runway onto a taxiway before coming to a halt.

Just as I opened the canopy a minivan appeared to pick me up. It was driven by an old friend and instructor from many years ago, who was now a senior test pilot on the Concorde engine programme. "Hello Duchess, I thought it might be you." We went for a quiet coffee. I was not really interested in watching the rest of the show. I later put in my incident report. "Engine failure on arrival at 5,000 feet, inverted. Uneventful landing." There was nothing else to say.

A couple of weeks later I was invited over to Little Rissington to see the remains of the engine where it was in pieces. Most of the compressor was gone and there was some considerable damage to the rest. I left the RAF a few weeks later. Nothing more heard. Happy memories.

DICKIE DUCKETT

I graduated from Cranwell on 30 July 1963 as a pilot officer after a three-year course that included basic flying training, and I was awarded my wings. After a spot of leave, I was posted to No. 4 Flying Training School at RAF Valley for the advanced flying course on the Gnat.

My instructor was Flt Lt Lee Jones. I soon discovered that he had previously flown the Hunter and had been one of the pilots in the Black Arrows formation aerobatic team of No. 111 Squadron in 1960 – I was certainly impressed by that.

Dickie Duckett

As the course progressed, it became clear that Lee was very keen to start a formation aerobatic team with the Gnat, which he felt would be an ideal aircraft. During its earlier into-service trials, some test pilots felt it was too sensitive for formation aerobatics, but Lee set out to prove them wrong. On some of my instructional sorties, with him as usual in the back seat, Lee would arrange to rendezvous with a couple of the other instructors over Mona, an airfield about ten miles from Valley. Using a base height of around 1,000ft, he led them through a few loops and rolls, and it was certainly exciting to watch from my position in the front cockpit. Later, Lee gained approval to form a five-aircraft team, which became the Yellowjacks, and they flew at several air displays in the summer of 1964, including Farnborough. Subsequently, the Yellowjacks morphed into the Red Arrows and became the RAF aerobatic team for 1965 with Lee as leader.

At the end of my Gnat course, after completing the Lightning course at RAF Coltishall, I was posted to No. 19(F) Squadron, initially at RAF Leconfield and then, from September 1965, at RAF Gütersloh in Germany.

In 1966, the Red Arrows, with nine aircraft led by Sqn Ldr Ray Hanna, came out to Gütersloh. One of my contemporaries from Cranwell, Doug McGregor, who had gone back to Valley as a Gnat instructor, was flying with the team, and I also knew Henry Prince. He had been one of the instructors at Valley when I was a student, and I was able to cadge a back-seat ride with him. He was the lead synchro pilot, so that certainly raised my adrenalin level. I had been encouraged to see that Doug McGregor had joined and I was interested in applying myself. There seemed to be no formal procedure, so I just mentioned my interest to Henry. A month later, I was surprised to receive a telephone call at work from Ray Hanna. He told me that he would like to have me with him for 1968, but I would first have to complete the six-month flying instructors course at the Central Flying School at RAF Little Rissington. He explained that all team pilots had to be qualified flying instructors (QFI) because the Red Arrows was not yet formally established as a separate unit – the pilots were just QFIs flying formation aerobatics in their spare time.

On 14 September, I arrived at Little Rissington and was told that the commandant of the Central Flying School wished to see me. In a brief interview, he made it clear that, although I was earmarked to join the Red Arrows, it was not

The Red Arrow pilots at Kemble on 29 March 1967. From left to right: Henry Prince, Roy Booth, Frank Hoare, Pete Evans, Derek Bell, Ray Hanna and Ernie Jones. (Ray Deacon)

automatic, and he expected me to work hard and do well on the course – I got the message. After first learning to instruct on the Jet Provost at Little Rissington, I successfully completed the Gnat instructor course at RAF Kemble at the end of January and moved down the corridor to join the Red Arrows based in the other half of the same hangar.

In 1967, the team had displayed with only seven aircraft and pilots, two of whom had left at the end of that season, so there were four new pilots for 1968: Doug Smith, Terry Kingsley, Ian Dick, and me. The other three had joined several months earlier at the end of the 1967 season, so I had a lot of catching up to do. Because I was the last new pilot to join, and there was a possibility I might not make the grade, I was designated Red 9 even though I was destined to fly in the No. 8 position in the formation. Ian and I were both 25 years old and younger and less experienced than the other pilots, and I discovered later that authority to increase the team to nine aircraft had been partly dependent on Ray Hanna accepting two young ex-Cranwell officers; we were lucky.

In those days, and probably until the late 1980s, new pilots started on the outside of the formation, with the more experienced chaps flying next to the leader. Although being on the outside of the formation was hard work and required more anticipation and larger control movements to remain in position, it was felt more important to have an experienced and stable base to the formation. As Ray Hanna said to me: "In the No. 8 slot there is no-one flying outside you, so it doesn't matter so much if your flying is a bit rough and you get out of position." That was certainly a fair comment on some of my first few formation sorties.

Learning to fly as a wingman during aerobatic manoeuvres was challenging, and on my first-ever formation loop I remember over-controlling as the speed built up on the downside of the loop. It took me a few trips to fly smoothly – the secret was to relax and feel that you were just squeezing the control column rather than moving it.

From the ground, it generally appears that the formation flying is neat and steady, but when there is a gusting wind, or thermal air currents on a hot day, there is quite a lot of movement within the formation, and it is hard work keeping position. In effect, each aircraft has its own 'bubble' within which it can move safely two or three feet without disturbing surrounding aircraft. When flying close formation, the wingmen are devoting all their concentration on holding position and are totally reliant on the leader to fly the formation safely. I need hardly add that we all had to have complete confidence and trust in each other.

The 40-degree swept-wing design of the Gnat was not only pleasing to the eye but was also helpful aerodynamically during high performance manoeuvres. If necessary, you could increase the angle of attack so that you could feel the airflow buffeting on the control surfaces, but without stalling the wings. That facility enabled you to tighten a turn, or the pull-out from a loop, significantly more than would have been possible with a straighter-winged aircraft. During one of my early formation sorties with Ray leading, he demonstrated this capability by pulling up into a loop, tightening the pull into gentle buffet on the way down and bottoming out 500ft higher than the entry height. I was able to keep my formation position despite being 'in the buffet' and it was a reassuring demonstration.

The pace of flying increased as more aircraft returned from winter servicing. Although all the aircraft were outwardly the same, there were subtle differences in their handling and performance, which became surprisingly obvious with familiarity. I was allocated XS111, one of the last Gnats off the production line. I was to fly it almost exclusively for the next two years – 555 sorties in total. Weather permitting, it was normal to do three 35-minute practice sorties a day. All training was done in the UK; there was no six-week detachment to Cyprus or Greece then, but we learned to fly in the variety of weather conditions that we were likely to experience in a normal British summer.

The Gnats used by the team had some significant differences to those used for normal training. The underwing fuel tanks had been removed to make the aircraft more manoeuvrable (and give a sleeker profile), and two small internal fuel tanks had been isolated from the fuel system to hold the diesel used to generate smoke. The overall fuel capacity was therefore reduced by about 30% to 1,800lbs, and that was a limiting factor on aircraft operation. However, a modification to the fuel system ensured that all the fuel was available for use, and the low-fuel warning light was adjusted to come on with only 250lbs remaining rather than the usual 410lbs. A further [authors' note: unauthorised!] modification was the removal of an electrical restriction (Fuse 13) on aileron movement to increase the rate of roll from 360 to 540 degrees per second. That allowed the aircraft to perform impressive twinkle rolls.

We had to learn three types of display in order to cope with different weather conditions. For a full, looping display we needed a cloud base around 4,500ft. For a rolling display we needed 2,500ft to fly barrel rolls, and for a flat display a cloud base of around 500ft was required. The aim was always to fly the best possible display. We might start off full but, if the cloud base lowered, we could change to a rolling or flat display, or vice versa if the weather improved. Thus, each type of display routine had to be designed to enable a seamless transition at various points from one to another.

The aim was to give a display that showed off the elegance and manoeuvrability of the aircraft in an exciting and skilful manner. When reversing direction back towards the crowd line, Ray flew steep wingovers rather than flatter turns – use of the vertical dimension was a key element in flying a compact display. A tight display, with positive 'g' applied most of the time, also made it easier for the wingmen to fly in steady formation. There should be some activity all the time, and one manoeuvre should flow straight into the next. Also, the display should not last too long – better to have the crowd wanting more than getting bored. In that respect, the relatively short range of our Gnats was a driving factor in deciding how long the display should be.

For major air shows we usually operated from the display airfield, but there were many occasions when a display was not over an airfield. For display sites such as motor-racing circuits and seaside resorts, we had to transit at low level from a remote operating base and, to give us a reasonable transit radius (up to 40 nm), the display had to be limited to about 16 minutes, which we felt to be about the right length. The transit range may seem very low, but I can remember a couple of occasions when one of the synchro pilots had to shut down while taxiing back to the flight line to avoid running out of fuel.

Each practice was filmed from the ground using 16-mm 'wet' film which had to be developed before viewing. In the meantime, the team manager, who watched every practice, played a very useful role in giving us a crowd's eye view of the positioning and compactness of the display. Debriefing was critical but constructive, and one learned quickly. We flew a nine-aircraft practice display for the first time on 22 February – a sortie that also marked my 1,000th flying hour. At the beginning of April, we were cleared by the AOC-in-C to 'go public', and we flew our first display on 2 April 1968 at RAF Little Rissington.

Two days later, we transited in the morning to RAF Thorney Island in order to carry out a display in the afternoon off the Brighton seafront. We broke left and right into the circuit over the airfield and, as No. 8 on the outside of the formation, I was the first to land. After touchdown it was clear that the runway was wet. The Gnat's braking parachute was not used unless pre-briefed, and by the time it became obvious that I was not slowing down quickly enough, it was too late to deploy it. The end of the runway rapidly approached, and I went into the safety barrier at about 50kts. So, there I was, sitting in my aircraft and unable to move, with eight other aircraft landing at ten-second intervals behind me. The next aircraft (Red 9) came over the stretched-out barrier net but managed to miss me, and the next (Red 4) went off the side of the runway and taxied over the grass. Those still airborne went around again and landed safely with 'chutes deployed. Later we established that the wind had changed direction in the space of a few minutes before landing so that there was a downwind component, and that it was a new runway surface with little friction.

The engineers extracted my aircraft from the barrier and worked to repair the damage, which was less than I feared. The nosewheel door was damaged and had to be removed, as was the lower radio aerial. The engineers did what they could, and Ray and I inspected it at about 1 p.m. "Are you happy to fly it?" asked Ray. I expressed some doubt, particularly as the missing nosewheel door, together with the mainwheel doors, formed the airbrakes. Ray said he would take it up for a quick air test. On return, he said it handled well, the radio was working OK with only the top aerial, but he suggested that I should not use the airbrakes. So, I flew it in the display that afternoon.

The pace of the display season increased in May with trips to Germany and Malta as well as around the UK. For long-distance transits, particularly over the sea, we sometimes had to re-attach the underwing ('slipper') fuel tanks, which increased our range to around 600nm. Normally, these would be removed before flying a display, but sometimes that was not practicable, so we flew with the tanks on but empty. The aircraft handled a little differently, and we could not do the twinkle roll, but one practice was usually sufficient preparation for a display.

The Gnat was not fitted with the navigation aids and other equipment required for flying in airways. However, military aircraft then were allowed to fly above the airway system at 30–40,000ft as operational air traffic under the control of military radars. This allowed us to fly in a straight line to our destination – a useful facility with our limited range. Another limitation on our operation was the need for an external engine-starting unit called a Palouste. So, when operating away from home, at least one of these units had to be taken with us. In the UK, this could be done in advance by road but, for overseas trips, a transport aircraft was required, which also carried the main ground crew party and other equipment and spare parts. Other technicians of various engineering trades ('The Flying Circus') flew in the back seat of the Gnats on transit flights, so that they could refuel and service the aircraft after landing – I had Cpl Dave Smith. It was a sought-after position, and each was specially selected and trained in emergency procedures. I had a different back seater every year, and each flew 90–100 transit sorties with me and, also, on several displays.

The Gnat did not have nosewheel steering, so directional control on the ground was achieved by differential braking of the mainwheels. The main undercarriage was quite narrow and made it difficult to keep the aircraft straight on the runway after touchdown if there was a significant crosswind, particularly if the runway was wet. This was well illustrated at Toulouse in France, when we had to abort our display halfway through because of the early arrival of a large storm. The runway quickly flooded, and we had to stream the braking 'chutes even though the crosswind was well over the limit to do so. I still remember vividly going down the runway in pouring rain with the aircraft swinging wildly from side to side and my speed reducing only slowly – fortunately, it was a long runway!

It was a different story later when we landed on the relatively short runway at Biggin Hill to position for the annual four-day air show. Ray Hanna was the last to land, and his braking parachute failed to deploy after touchdown on the wet surface. Those landing first always pulled over to the sides of the runway to make space for such an eventuality, and I watched as his aircraft came speeding past and into the field at the end of the runway. Fortunately, it was the easterly runway and not the westerly one, which had a steep drop-off into the valley near the end. Nevertheless, we all got rather wet and muddy pushing the aircraft out of the field in the rain.

On the third day of the air show, we flew to RAF Lakenheath to fly a display for US Armed Forces Day. When we flew back to Biggin Hill afterwards, the weather had deteriorated, and we had to carry out a radar-controlled descent and runway approach through quite heavy cloud in Diamond Nine formation. It was hard work, but we eventually broke cloud at about 300ft. We then flew a few turns in formation over the airfield before we landed. Fortunately, the weather picked up later in the afternoon, and we were able to fly a full display. There was also compensation for us in the shape of some red MGB motor cars waiting for us in the aircraft parking area.

Raymond Baxter, a great supporter of the team, was then in a senior position in PR with the British Motor Company, and he had arranged for ten red MGBs to be positioned for our use at various display venues during the year. The first was at Biggin Hill, and the cars were lined up for us as we taxied into the aircraft parking area. They had consecutive number plates – MOH 11 F to MOH 20 F – mine was number 19. The Italian aerobatic team was also at Biggin Hill and were clearly impressed by our 'wheels' even if they weren't Alfa Romeos. After the display, we were invited to a party at the Italian Embassy in central London, and Ray decided we should drive the cars there in line astern from our hotel in Bromley. I was in the ninth car with little idea of where we were going, so it was a very exciting journey, and probably riskier than anything we did in the air. I remember going through several red traffic lights in my effort to keep up with those in front, but I do not remember my drive back to our hotel after the party.

We also had the cars delivered to RAF Manston in Kent in connection with our display at an event at the Brands Hatch motor-racing circuit. After landing back at Manston, we quickly jumped into the cars and set off along the new M2 to Brands Hatch, but this time with a police car leading us, blue light flashing. It was about 60 miles, but we made it in well under an hour and did a couple of circuits of the track. "No racing," said Ray, but we didn't think that applied to our second lap, which was exciting but, amazingly, ended without incident.

We looked forward to trips abroad because we often spent a couple of days at the venue and received warm hospitality. The main air shows were also good fun because one or more of the other European teams were often present, and we got to know the pilots. A large display at Coxyde in Belgium included us and the three other European teams: Patrouille de France, Frecce Tricolori and the Belgian Diables Rouge. To mark the occasion, the Belgian team led a Box 4 of Diamond Nine formations over the airfield. It took a long time to get everyone airborne, joined up, and back safely on the ground.

The 1968 season finished in fine style at the biennial Farnborough air show which, at that time, was probably still the biggest and most prestigious air show in Europe, although the French might not agree. We displayed on four days in good weather and were well-hosted by various aerospace companies. It was Ray Hanna's final hurrah, and we welcomed Tim Nelson as the new leader for 1969. I moved from the No. 8 slot to become Red 4, and was joined by a new back seater, Junior Technician Bruce Hudson. On high-level transits in wide-battle formation, I often let him fly the aircraft, and he became quite proficient. There were two other new pilots for 1969, one of whom was Flt Lt Jerry Bowler, who I knew very well from Cranwell and Lightning days.

Our work-up training had been progressing reasonably well, despite some poor weather when, tragically, while re-joining a formation at low level during a practice sortie in late March, Jerry Bowler flew into some trees near the airfield and was killed. This was the first major accident and fatality that the Red Arrows had experienced, and it affected everyone deeply, not least the leader. A replacement pilot, Sqn Ldr Phil Dunn, was quickly selected. He was actually in the Royal Australian Air Force but was on an exchange posting with the Gnat instructor training squadron at Kemble. A very experienced pilot, he soon got up to speed as Red 9, and training continued. With the help of good weather in April we flew 55 sorties and were cleared for public display on 1 May.

A display at RAF Wildenrath in mid-June was not flown well and concluded prematurely when several of us had to break away from the formation during a loop because Tim had entered it at too low an airspeed. The deputy leader called us all together after we landed at RAF Brüggen, and it was agreed that we could not continue with Tim as leader. Ray was recalled to take over and very quickly refreshed his leading skills. Ten days later, the Queen visited the Central Flying School at RAF Little Rissington, and we put on a full display in good weather. Afterwards, Her Majesty told us how much she had enjoyed our flight.

The season progressed well with some good trips abroad. When we operated out of RAF bases, we were allowed to fly an RAF pilot in the back seat on a display, and one occasion at RAF Gütersloh sticks in my mind. The display at a German flying club had gone well, and we were flying back to Gütersloh in loose formation with the radio set to our normal display channel. Approaching Gütersloh, Ray called us to change to the local frequency. That was not a pre-set on my radio and, as my passenger was talking to me on the intercom at the time, I didn't hear the numbers. No problem, I thought: my good friend in the back seat (a Gütersloh Hunter pilot) will know — but he didn't! Fortunately, I had the booklet with all RAF station frequencies in my flying suit, so I hurriedly pulled it out and threw it back to him over my shoulder. By this time, we were getting very near to the airfield, and were moving into close formation, but I had not yet checked in on the new frequency. I knew that Ray planned to do a looping bomb burst prior to landing and, as I was in a key position in that manoeuvre, it would have to be aborted if I didn't check in very soon. Anyway, that embarrassment was averted and, despite his frequency ignorance, my passenger later went to become a very senior officer.

Later, in October, we put the tanks on and flew to Malta for a display over Valetta harbour and then on to Cyprus, via Crete, for displays at military bases and at Nicosia. Ray then said farewell again and handed over to Dennis Hazell. Dennis had not been on the team previously, but he was an experienced fighter pilot and well known to us because he ran the Gnat instructor training flight that shared our hangar at Kemble. Dennis was a strong character, and not afraid to express his views, but he was receptive to advice on his leading technique from the senior pilots, and he developed quickly in the role. He also had a lively sense of humour, which he used to good effect.

Progress in training was affected by a major accident in December 1969, when two aircraft were lost following a catastrophic engine failure in one of them during a practice sortie with five aircraft. The sortie involved pilots changing formation positions a few times to provide a new pilot, Doug Marr, with practice in different positions. We were pulling up into a loop when Doug, thinking he was still flying behind me, transmitted "Dickie you are on fire!" I had no fire warning but quickly pulled out of the formation and investigated the situation. However, the aircraft that was actually on fire, and flown by Jack Rust, had lost radio communication as a result of the damage caused by the catastrophic engine failure. Dennis Hazell, who by now could see the burning aircraft descending quickly, became increasingly concerned that the pilot had not ejected and twice ordered me to do so: "Dickie get out". Unfortunately, as I was now heading away from the airfield, I could not see the stricken aircraft and, although I had no indications that my aircraft was on fire, I was strongly influenced by the increasingly urgent calls from Red 1 and ejected. I landed close to the airfield and was quickly picked up and returned to the crewroom. It was only when Jack came in about ten minutes later that I realised what had happened. Fortunately, we suffered only minor injuries and were back flying again in a couple of weeks, but two aircraft were written off. The subsequent Board of Inquiry did not censure anyone over the accident, but it was an unwelcome and embarrassing event that was widely, but inaccurately, reported at the time.

The lost aircraft were replaced and, despite the usual mix of weather in the UK winter, the team was cleared for public display in mid-April. This was my third, and final year, and I was delighted to move from my position as Red 4 to join the synchro pair as Red 7; with Ian Dick moving up to be synchro lead. I was allocated another aircraft, XR996, which was better suited to the solo role than my trusty XS111, and a new back-seat technician – Chief Technician 'Tommy' Thomas. Flying in the back seat with the synchro pair was particularly demanding because we were often pulling up to 7g during manoeuvres, but Tommy only had to suffer that on a few occasions.

The role of the synchro pair was to fly low-level passes and other manoeuvres in front of the crowd while the main formation was re-positioning. We were cleared to run in at 35ft, the estimated height of the control tower at Kemble, but the Gnat did not have a radar altimeter, and we had to judge that height by eye. We usually flew at a height at which we felt comfortable using the ground as our reference – probably a bit lower than 35ft.

We used a display line parallel to the crowd line with our crossing point (datum) in the centre of the line, or perhaps opposite the VIP viewing stand. If the display was on an airfield, the runway would normally be the display line. When the display site was not an airfield, we plotted an imaginary runway and datum on a map of the site and picked out local landmarks, such as a wood or a pier, to help us line up. During our manoeuvres, Ian flew his tight turn, or loop, as accurately as possible, and it was my job to miss him as we crossed. To achieve a cross on datum, we had to take account of the wind speed and direction and make appropriate timing adjustments. I could also adjust my speed up or down a bit to fine tune the timing of the cross.

Probably the most demanding of our transit flights was to Iceland. We had attempted to fly there in 1968 via Stornoway in the Outer Hebrides, but poor weather in Iceland prevented us from doing so. From Stornoway it was still about 600nm to Keflavik and close to our maximum range with tanks fitted. There were no diversion options, so we needed reasonably good weather before setting off, and an actual weather report before we reached our point of no return. This time, in late August, we flew to Stornoway to position for the flight to Iceland the following day. We had with us a film crew covering our activities for Harlech TV, and I remember that Ian Dick and I spent an hour or so on a local beach explaining, with the help of diagrams in the sand, how we flew the synchro manoeuvres. Next morning, the weather was set fair, and we arrived at Keflavik without any problems. The ground crew had time to remove the tanks before displaying at Keflavik, and again at Reykjavik the following day. We then set off for Lossiemouth. All was well until, just short of the point of no return, Red 8 said he had a fuel-transfer warning light. That meant that only about half the fuel was likely to be useable, so he returned with Red 9 to Keflavik. It was a worrying moment, but they landed safely. Fortunately, the support aircraft with the ground crew was still there, and the problem was quickly fixed. Two years later, Ian Dick successfully led the team to USA via Iceland, Greenland, and northern Canada.

One of our last trips that year was to Finland, where we displayed over the waterfront at Helsinki and then at Turku. From Helsinki we were then due to fly 150nm north to display at Tampere and land there afterwards. Our Hercules support aircraft flew there a few hours ahead of us but unfortunately burst its tyres on landing and blocked the runway. Although we had the tanks on, we did not have enough fuel with them empty to do a return trip and a display – so what were we to do? We were reluctant to cancel the display, but the only alternative was to fill the slipper tanks with fuel. We calculated that they would be empty by the time we reached Tampere, so we could fly the display with full internal fuel (increasing entry speeds for manoeuvres to allow for the extra weight) and still have enough to return to Helsinki. It all worked as planned, and Tampere was duly grateful to us if not to the Hercules crew.

Another exciting year over and it was time for me to leave the team – it had been a wonderful experience. Higher authority then reminded me that I had not put my qualification as a QFI to good use, and I returned to the Lightning as an instructor, which was more appealing than moving to the back seat of a Gnat at RAF Valley. I was back in the operational world and had no idea then that four years later I would return to Kemble as Red 1 – but that's another story.

RICHIE THOMAS

Richie Thomas

There are many memorable events that occur during your flying career, some involve moments of panic, other people and places and still others the sheer exhilaration of being airborne having 'shed the surly bonds of earth'. First solos were always significant events in your progression to the front line where I flew the single-seat Hunter (for training) and the Harrier. However, one of my most vivid recollections was the first flight I had in the Gnat T1 out of RAF Valley in Anglesey with my instructor Chris Stevens. Never mind the simulator, this was the real thing. We walked out to the aircraft and took off while my brains were still in the crewroom. First thing I registered was that we were heading north-east over Anglesey on a beautiful morning, going faster than I had ever been in my life and at the front of what I would only describe as a rocket; nothing around me and no one beside me. The next minute we were low level in Wales, next minute pulling up for aerobatics, next minute a TACAN dive to enter the circuit at RAF Mona, before a final touchdown at Valley. That was it, all completed in 45 minutes, which condensed down to what seemed like seconds – how could anyone think or survive at those speeds and with such rapidly changing situations? This was the reason why I had wanted to be a pilot since I was a knee-high to a grasshopper; I was completely hooked…

After the pure excitement came the hard work learning how to fly and operate what became for me the best pure aircraft I flew in my career, including dare I say the Hunter and Harrier. Some say that the Gnat was unnecessarily overly complicated as an advanced trainer, but what it did superbly well was to prepare students for the front-line aircraft of the day, particularly the Lightning, with its classic swept-wing handling and similar flight instrumentation. The Gnat had beautifully harmonised flying controls, a quick response engine, a good power-to-weight ratio and superb aerodynamics. New terms such as 'datum shift' (the centre of gravity change as the landing gear was operated) and Hobson motor just rolled of the tongue but from those very early days a few details were rammed home to the extent that I still remember them.

First were the hydraulic failure emergency actions that had to be completed meticulously and the in right order: STUPRECC was the mnemonic, speed, trim, unlock etc. Aircraft and crew had been lost because the actions were not completed correctly. At every opportunity the hydraulics were select off by the instructor and the student's drill checked to ensure that he could handle a real failure in any situation. Similarly, great emphasis was placed on the actions following an electrics failure. Finally, my instructor, rather foolishly I thought, sent me solo. The flight was as exhilarating as could be but a blur with my main aim being a safe landing back at Valley, which I achieved successfully. Others told stories of derring-do, but I was thankful to still be of sound body and mind. The pace of the course was relentless, before an exercise was fully assimilated the next phase was on us until after 70 hours or so on the aircraft the final handling test loomed on the horizon, a critical and demanding flying test, which thankfully I passed.

My next meeting with the Gnat came after my first tour in Germany on Harriers. At the time all I wanted was to stay on the jet and hopefully take a post-graduate course, but this was not to be as I was posted to the Central Flying School to fly Gnats; to soften the blow I was told that Training Command needed front-line, fast-jet instructors, but 'why me' I asked? So, I was not in the best frame of mind when I started at RAF Little Rissington. However, very soon, certainly as soon as the flying started, everything changed and the CFS course was as enjoyable as any I had been on and flying from RAF Kemble put the icing on the cake. Flying the Gnat from the rear seat was something of an art but soon I became very comfortable tucked away in the rear cockpit. The Gnat instructor school (4 Squadron) was co-located with the Red Arrows (RAs) and at the end of the course, which I finished a few days early, I had the opportunity of training with the Reds for a couple of weeks as one of the pilots was temporary injured following a car accident. Having never thought of joining the team, formation aerobatics gave me a glimpse of what the future could hold, which was far more exciting than the thought of instructing students at RAF Valley.

I applied to join the RAs and was accepted but only after completing six months instructing at Valley. I thoroughly enjoyed the time I spent teaching and came to respect the Gnat even more. Perhaps one of the most demanding flying exercises was to demonstrate a night flapless, manual landing at the relief landing ground, RAF Mona, with no crosswind. With only the runway lights to guide you to the touchdown point, which you could not properly see, coupled with a shallow approach over the inky blackness of Anglesey, it required some bold and accurate flying. Under certain conditions some would take the sensibly cautious approach and not put themselves into the situation where such a demo was required, others did it just to prove they could! I passed on my enthusiasm for the aircraft to my only two primary students, Simon Wood and Steve Gunner both of whom cruised through the course with ease mainly because they were hand-picked, gifted aviators rather than any reflection of my instructional prowess.

The Gnat was just about the perfect aircraft for the RAs with the handling qualities I have already mentioned. One of my first jobs was to refamiliarise one of my fellow recruits, Martin (Stumpy) Stoner, back onto the Gnat as I was the most recently qualified instructor. This was a tick in the box and completely pointless as Stumpy flew the aircraft far better than I could. The flights went perfectly with nothing I could add to improve his performance. So, back into the circuit for a few roller landings. However, Stumpy was most considerate and to make me feel I was contributing to the sortie would ask questions – well a question (downwind in the circuit):

Stumpy: "Richie, what's the landing speed?"

Me: "140 knots Stumps."

Stumpy: "Right."

…downwind on the next circuit:

Stumpy: "Richie, what was that landing speed?"

Me: "140 knots Stumps."

Stumps: 'Got it.'

… and so on. I did set him homework but to no avail.

Above all the aircraft had a startling rate of roll but this could be increased with the removal of 'Fuse 13' (see page 134); this fuse enabled the ailerons to achieve full authority in the landing configuration whereas a restrictor was activated when the landing gear was raised to prevent excessive aileron authority that would put the aircraft outside its design limits. However, removal of Fuse 13 gave full aileron movement throughout the speed range which improved on the already eye-watering rate of roll. This unauthorised procedure had been used by some until during a solo aerobatic display (nothing to do with the RAs) the tail detached resulting in the loss of both crew and aircraft; Fuse 13 removal stopped forthwith.

Along with all the many attributes of the Gnat there were a couple of disadvantages, as mentioned earlier: limited fuel capacity and lack of onboard starter. The fuel limitation shaped the design of the display and eliminated what could be done if more fuel was available, but the big advantage was that the show strategy by default was compactness, action, and continuity. The first year with the Reds proved to me that the aircraft was an exceptional formation aircraft. During the second and third years I moved to the synchronised pair as number 7 then 6 cementing an already close relationship with the aircraft. Throughout two years of synchronised display flying, when the cleared height was not below 35 feet, I flew the same airframe, XR572, and together we went through all sorts of excitements, but always I could

A captain's greeting for the Red Arrows with Richie Thomas second on the left.

The final arrival at RNAS Culdrose.

rely on the aircraft to get me out of the odd challenging situation that invariably arose. Although I looked after the aircraft as well as I could in the air, I could not have survived without the dedication and professionalism of the magnificent team engineers who would do whatever was necessary to ensure that there were nine jets and a spare for each display. I consider myself privileged to have served with them. I find it difficult to single out any individual, as they were all top drawer, but Sgt Taff Lee, who was my dedicated 'circus' back seater, stuck with me through thick and thin, and was key to keeping XR572 fully serviceable for over 200 public displays, lavishing as much care and attention on the aircraft as was possible.

The final Gnat sortie was a formation transit to RNAS Culdrose where the Royal Navy were to use the aircraft for deck-handling training. After a memorable transit from Kemble, I had to say goodbye to 'my aircraft'; stupidly enough it was a rather emotional moment, but a glass of champagne on the wing and a pat on the nose marked the end of an era. I had the greatest respect for an aircraft that had given me nothing but excitement, reliability and consistency. All I could do was turn my back and walk away.

MINUS A LEG

WYNDHAM WARD

I was enjoying my first season on the Gnat; my flying circus guy in the back was George Scullion and together we enjoyed an excellent working relationship – provided I realised it was his aeroplane on loan to me to fly displays in and

Wyndham Ward

I returned it in immaculate condition. This rarely happened. I seemed to attract bird strikes. And other things…

Being short of fuel is nothing new to any of us but if you have pressing problems to sort out as well, it can be a definite health hazard. Given that George thought I was a wrecking ball with wings I still managed to sink to an all-time low on the amount of damage I caused on our way to Exeter for a display. A gear red-warning light popped up passing Yeovilton Naval Station and visual gear-down inspection revealed the right gear remained up. Not good. Only one thing for it – bounce hard off the runway and shake it down. Simple!

The boys continued to Exeter while I hung around the Yeovil circuit putting my theory to the test. I explained my little problem to Yeovilton tower and please could I have an ambulance to collect my back seater because I was ejecting him if I couldn't get my gear down. Normal stuff to these boys, they were brilliant. So much so I asked if they could put a helicopter or Hercules on their 'to do list' so I could make the display at Exeter. No problem. They were on it.

Emergency gear checklists take no time at all with a show to make and I thumped it on so hard the navy would have been proud of me. It was so brutal I almost dropped a wing but even after a teeth-shaker like that, we still had a red light on so I wasn't very optimistic. George felt much the same about the way I smashed his jet into the ground, but I tried a few more thump and go's until I was low on fuel. Arcing up to 1,000 feet I told George to eject and not bother with an after-flight inspection. He declined the offer and said he was much happier staying with me. I have to admit I wasn't surprised – I could tell he was slightly nervous the way he had been asking questions while I was toiling away. Like how many people were in China? And on my estimate of a billion, he wanted to know how come they couldn't raise a team to beat Chelsea? (a sure sign of nerves – Chelsea was never that good): but with not enough fuel to argue or take a vote I called "finals committed to land with less than 30 pounds fuel remaining." This is about 25 seconds at circuit rate, so we weren't exactly flush with the stuff.

Amazingly it worked out simply because the Gnat has outside ailerons. With a boot load of rudder on, I let the wing drop itself at slow speed keeping the stick hard over so the aileron took the brunt of all the scraping on the runway. We ended up ground-looping on the grass with George completely dazed, so I nipped up behind him, made his seat safe and hoiked him out.

Wyndham's Gnat after landing.

The doctor ran a stethoscope over him and said he was just a bit shocked – I told her it was no problem he was always like this whenever I bent his jet. Luckily, the Yeovilton hands had starred, our Hercules pitched up and bundling George inside we set off for Exeter.

The Herc boys are good at fast taxiing and they parked close to our Gnats, I hit the ground and sprinted to the boss holding my thumb up, he gave a grin and the shortest brief ever – "Wyn – Fully!"

I was tempted to ask why the briefs were so long but thought better of it. Everything went well, I enjoyed a welcome beer after a nice tight display. And George, bless him, after a few stiff whiskies to get over our jet being a mess, was as right as rain apart from nightmares about me running him out of fuel. He even forgot to give me hassle about wrecking his jet.

AS A RED PASSENGER

ERIC WARD

Eric Ward

It was in 1978 that I had the immense pleasure flying in this wonderful little aeroplane. The circumstance for so doing started a year earlier when I became involved with the Red Arrows. I was a director of a large textile company and a customer, Mike Grose, who bought great quantities of cashmere sweaters for his menswear shop in London got to know I flew and suggested I meet his brother Lloyd who had joined the Arrows. This I did and I, like others was in awe of the pilots' skill and ability in the sky

Lloyd Grose and Eric Ward

but I am afraid I, being a textile man did not think much of their dress sense so took it upon myself with friends in the trade to clothe them in the best of British. As this was not costing the service anything I soon became a 'friend in camp'.

I was privileged to fly with Lloyd lasting just under an hour, which was hugely exciting. Aesthetically, the design and shape of the Gnat looks the part with a performance to match. Strapped in, one feels very much a part of the whole. Flying at low level at such speed was to say the least, exhilarating. I flew the Gnat for ten minutes, hugely responsive and sensitive – just think what you want to do, and it happens. The flight culminated in an extremely fast, extremely low pass of the control tower at Kemble, where the single-storey building was above us!

If 'cornered' I would have to admit that in formation the Gnat nine-ship of the Red Arrows looks better, in symmetry than the Hawk – but please do not tell the existing team.

JON TYE

I was never a very enthusiastic QFI on 230 Vulcan OCU, teaching students to fly it like an airliner was not my idea of fun and whilst ruminating on my fate in the crewroom at Scampton I hatched a plan. I rang up my old mate off 176 JP course at Leeming and 4 Gnat course at Valley, Ken Tait, to see if I could drive down to Kemble for a 'jolly' with the Reds. We had both left Valley on

Jon Tye

separate ways, he to Canberras and on to CFS, me to Vulcans and CFS.

I had many such trips with Ken but this one was to prove more exciting than most. The sortie was briefed for a photographic opportunity for Arthur Gibson, an aviation photographer beloved by the Arrows. It was to include repeated roll-back manoeuvres, much disliked by those involved where the Nos. 2 and 3 would pull up and roll over and out to replace 4 and 5. These were performed at 250kts, undercarriage down and ten degrees of flap. The final part of the sortie was to be an echelon starboard break to re-join the circuit by all nine Gnats and a close stream landing with brake parachutes deployed so that Arthur could snap a picture of all nine aircraft on the runway with 'chutes deployed. This best laid plan of mice and men was not to be!

The sortie progressed as planned with Ken and I in the 5 slot. No. 3 rolling over us as we moved in to take his position and then us repeating the manoeuvre to regain our position. This was repeated for maybe half a dozen runs above the main runway for Arthur to obtain his desired shots. All quite routine. Then came the break into the circuit; the boss pulled really tight, exacerbated by a strong into-runway crosswind. Because of previous formation changes we were about No. 9 in the stream. As we went downwind Ken kept muttering to me, "Jon, we're too close in to the runway and I can't get the speed down despite engine idle, gear down and flap". He kept grumbling as we turned finals with approximately 45 degrees of bank. With about 30 degrees to go to runway heading we hit wake turbulence.

The Gnat with its marked anhedral was renowned for its dislike of wake turbulence. It rolled immediately inverted, so rapidly I can't recall whether left or right! Ken shouted, "don't eject, don't eject Jon". I had no intention of ejecting. I was already an inch shorter after surviving a big bang Martin-Baker ride at CFS five years earlier and I wasn't inclined to try the excellent Folland seat at 300ft with the top of the canopy filled by the view of a ploughed field. Fortunately for us both Ken was an absolute ace, he hit the throttle immediately and when we rolled erect we were headed 30 degrees past the runway heading and sinking like the *Titanic*. If there had been a bush on the airfield we would have hit it. The Gnat, bless it, staggered at a ridiculous angle of attack, while the Orpheus engine struggled to regain its breath. I remember it took most of the runway length to attain the airspeed necessary to climb safely away to complete what may be described as a wide bomber-type circuit while we regained our composure.

An ashen-faced Ken jumped out of the aircraft, said little to me and stormed into the boss's office to air his displeasure. In all my sorties with Ken at Kemble I was always impressed by his immense ability. He tragically lost his life when the wing failed on his Buccaneer whilst flying a Red Flag mission in the Nevada desert. A sad loss of a great friend and a superb pilot. Strangely, that failure stopped my promised posting to Honington on Buccaneers while they sorted the wing problem out.

Three things saved me that day:

a) The superb Gnat could fly in the buffet and not depart;

b) The Orpheus engine spooled up just in time;

c) Ken's natural ability.

It was several years before I dared to admit to my long-suffering wife, Jenny, the details of this particular incident.

FROM THE BACK SEAT

TOM THOMAS

"Red check in!" I sat and listened as the replies came, quick and sharp "1 – 2 – 3 – 4 – 5 – 6 – 7 – Eight's not started yet boss" the unmistakable voice of Aussie Sqn Ldr Phil Dunn (Red 9) filled the headphones "9 – 10". "Loud and clear" came the boss's reply.

Pilots practising emergency drills at Cirencester pool in 1976. (Nigel Champness)

I sat and watched the other ground crew pull chocks and Palouste starters clear of us and away towards the Argosy freight aircraft, to be loaded. I thought of the trip which was just beginning and of my luck and good fortune which had brought me onto the 'Flying Circus' side of the Red Arrows ground crew. This was indeed a job in a million! Everything after this must surely seem very humdrum and routine. This was the most thrilling experience of my life, to fly with the greatest acrobatic team in the world, to have an inside view of how it's done. I was one of the fortunate nine 'back-seat men'. We were each allotted an aircraft and flew in it with the same pilot throughout the season. We had the distinction of having our names painted on the side of the cockpit beneath that of the pilot. For this honour we suffered the doubtful pleasures of decompression checks, wet dinghy drill and aircraft escape procedure lectures, not that anyone really disliked them.

"Kemble – Red taxi?" Sqn Ldr Ray Hanna's voice cut into my drifting thoughts "Red taxi, runway zero nine, QFE one thousand and four, wind westerly five knots," Kemble tower answered with routine precision. We taxied forward, checked the brakes and swung onto the perimeter track. Waves and gestures were exchanged with the Argosy side of the ground crew. "Your strap's tight, all that gear OK Tom?" Flt Lt Terry Kingsley's voice came over the intercom just that bit clearer and louder than other R/T messages (as I was sharing his aeroplane), "All set," I assured him. "Red line up?" Sqn Ldr Hanna asked Kemble. "Red line up – take-

Ready for their next display, Red Arrows Gnats lined up on the team's dispersal at Kemble. (Tom Thomas)

off when ready". The QFE, wind direction and runway in use were repeated by Kemble. We lined up on the runway. I was sitting in the back of Red Six with Flt Lt Terry Kingsley (leading the second section of four aircraft). Ahead I could see the front five aeroplanes in vee across the runway. The tenth aircraft flown by the manager Flt Lt Pete Macintosh, with engineering officer Flt Lt George White in the back seat, took off independently afterwards.

"Up to 90, lights on go!" Sqn Ldr Hanna's short sharp routine messages continued. I watched our engine rpm build up as Terry Kingsley opened the throttle to 90% – the needle of the jet pipe temperature gauge leapt up then settled gently back. Clouds of red and blue smoke came towards us from the front section as the dye left in the diffuser pipes was drawn out and vaporised in the jet stream of the engines. "Front five – brakes off go!" Ray Hanna commanded. The front section were rolling. Terry Kingsley counted slowly then pressed the transmit button "Gypo section, brakes off go!" We surged forward straight down the centre line. The aircraft on either side of us jumped and reared as the nosewheels lifted off the runway. On our right behind Flt Lt Jack Rust sat Cpl Colin Blight, on our left, Sqn Ldr Phil Dunn with Sgt John Stuart in the back, and outboard of them was Flt Lt Ian (Widgie) Dick with Cpl Mick Harris as his rear-seat man.

I exchanged a rude sign with John Stuart and thought I could detect a grin beneath his oxygen mask. "Front five gear up go, wingover port!" the leader called. Then it was Terry Kingsley again, "Six Rotating!" and the rear section of four pulled up into a 45-degree climb. "Gear up go!" Terry called. I waited for the thump of the doors closing after the undercarriage had retracted then checked the indicator lights were out. We turned gently left and as we did so the front five in perfect vee formation came up from beneath us about a mile ahead, also turning left. The wingover continued to 3,000ft. "Two ten", the leader's voice calling the main formation's speed – "One ninety – One eighty", we slipped quietly closer, "One seventy" as the main formation turned at the top of the wingover. "One sixty" we slid into formation making the 'Diamond' complete. "All aboard!" Sqn Ldr Dunn told the boss. "Very nice" came back the reply – "Smoke on go!" The formation came out of the wingover and flew back across the airfield, nine beautiful red aircraft in 'Diamond' formation smoke streaming leaving a twisting swirling white ribbon. "Smoke off go!" the leader called and in the same transmission spoke to Kemble tower, "Red clearing, thank you Kemble". "Goodbye Red Lead, have a good trip," was Kemble's short reply.

"Red open up and relax", the boss cued the team to gently break formation. The outside men acknowledged first: "Five out – Four out – Eight out" all in rapid succession. "Red stud nine go!", the leader ordered to change radio frequency. This particular one was the team's own air-to-air frequency. "Can you see ten?" Terry asked me, meaning had Red 10 joined our loose formation. "Yes, he's with us," I confirmed. "Red check in!" the leader ordered. "Two – Three – Four – Five – Six – Seven – Eight – Nine – Ten" the voices rapidly reported, rising and falling slightly in tone. "Loud and clear," responded the boss. We now flew in two loose 'Battle' formations of five aircraft. Staying quite low we headed for Royal Naval Air Station Yeovilton. Just a short trip this one, less than 90 miles, about 16 minutes for us.

"You have it," Terry said, "keep the others in your ten o'clock." He meant I had control of the aircraft and I was to keep the front section on our left, they were about two miles ahead. This was one of the moments the 'circus' waits for, to have a go at the 'pole'. We skimmed some low fluffy clouds and banked gently around a larger mountain of 'cotton' then turned back again to maintain our correct position relative to the front section. "One at three o'clock, five miles", someone called. "Contact" was the leader's instant reply. I looked right and eventually saw it, a small light aeroplane heading toward us and then passing behind.

One of the rear section aircraft slid in close to us in tight formation. Terry put his hands on his head to indicate that he was not flying our aeroplane, the other aircraft peeled away rapidly to a safer vantage point.

Nine members of the 1968 Flying Circus pose for the camera beside a team aircraft at Kemble, (standing L to R): J/Ts Bruce Hudson, Wally Walters. Cpls Ian Bennett, Graham Thomas, Sgt Tom Thomas, J/T Mick Harris; (kneeling, L to R) Cpls Ray Thurstons, Ron Turrell, and Jeff Fletcher. (Tom Thomas, via Ray Deacon)

"Anyone got a TACAN?" the leader enquired, to enable him to check his heading (he meant had anyone a TACAN lock onto Yeovilton). "Two-oh-five, twenty-four", came a reply, giving the compass bearing and the range. "Red set up two-nine-four decimal five; two-nine-four-five." The team leader prepared the team to change radio frequency to that of Yeovilton tower. "I have control," Terry called as he pumped the throttle forward. With a surge the aeroplane slid into our slot behind and below the leader. The rest of the team followed into loose Diamond Nine. Yet no word was spoken. The discipline and anticipation of these pilots is remarkable. "Keep it loose" the leader called. "Two-nine-four-five-go!" I saw Terry lean forward to change frequency.

A few seconds later the leader called "Red check in!" Again, the replies were short and sharp, the voices rising and falling as if singing an octave of some music, "2-3-4-5-6-7-8-9-10". "Loud and clear!" the leader confirmed; then went on "Yeovilton – Yeovilton Red Arrow lead, do you read?". "Red lead – Yeovilton – I read you five by five-go ahead". A new voice in the headphones. "Yeovilton – Red Arrow lead, formation of ten aircraft at 2,000 feet five miles north-east this time," the leader informed Yeovilton "Red leader I have you identified – QFE nine nine eight, runway two seven, left hand, circuit clear," the Yeovilton controller reported. "Red lead – thank you, may we use your circuit for 15 minutes please?" the leader enquired. "Yeovilton – the circuit's all yours – no known traffic this time."

The perfect loop as described by the shadow on the sea as the 'g' comes on. (Tom Thomas, via Ray Deacon)

The leader's transmit button just clicked as his acknowledgement of Yeovilton's message. "The VIP enclosure is on the north side of the runway intersection" the leader informed the two solo aircraft, ours (six) and Flt Lt Ian Dick (seven). "We'll use the runway intersection as datum," he continued. "The GCA van and the windsock", Terry called to seven, meaning to use these points as markers for the solo's opposition manoeuvres.

"Big nine go!" the leader instructed. We (Red six) slid to our right into the No. 4 slot and Red seven had gone to the left into the No. 5 slot, making up the big nine formation. I looked left and watched the aeroplanes shining brightly and bobbing gently up and down against a blurred green background as we banked left toward Yeovilton airfield. The formation was now about three miles north-east of the airfield. The ground was getting closer now as the boss banked the formation and descended for the run in. "Thirty seconds" the leader told the team. "No colour – all white." Sqn Ldr Hanna instructed his team not to use coloured smoke for this practice.

"Smoke on go!" The airfield and its buildings flashed by about 50ft below. A brief glimpse of green turf and black tarmac runways, then "Pulling up – now!" The horizon slipped below the windscreen and down under the aircraft. The 'g' force came on forcing us down into our seats increasing our weight about four times so that I apparently weighed over 45 stone! I looked to my left to see the brilliant scarlet aeroplanes glinting in the sunshine, still rocking and bobbing gently. The formation pointed skyward trailing white smoke with an amazing background of green patchwork fields, brown stone walls, a small wood, a lake reflecting the yellow sunlight, and a beautiful blue sky with a few scattered cotton clouds. "Diamond Nine go!" The calm quiet voice of the leader ordered. "Six" – "Seven'" came the crisp replies. The split second of the command, the answer hardly mouthed and we flashed down under the number two on our left, below the leader's tail and slid smoothly back into our slot.

Other aircraft had also moved in that instant to form the 'Diamond'. We turned gently onto our backs, no 'g' force now, weightless for a few seconds; I noticed the undercarriage warning flag flicking in the airspeed indicator as our speed had dropped below that when the undercarriage should have been lowered in normal flight. The airfield, hangars, control tower, office buildings, parked aircraft and yellow-painted military vehicles all filled the canopy. Looking back over our heads I could see the smoke trail showing the path of our climb. Then we plunged downward, gathering speed, the 'g' force building as we descended, white vortices streaming from our wingtips and the altimeter unwinding madly from 4,800ft to 100ft. "Smoke off go, bending right." More instructions from the leader. We rolled into a wingover, I looked to my right, the ground seemed to be gently falling away as we climbed up into the turn. "Going down for a diamond roll," the leader called keeping the team informed of his intention, although each pilot knew the sequence inside out. We came out of the wingover descending from 3,000ft gathering speed dropping to about 200ft. "Smoke on go!" With the formation still banked the number four aircraft on the right wing seemed perilously close to the ground but Flt Lt Dickie Duckett's gaze never shifted from the No. 2 aircraft. Each member of the team has implicit faith in the leader and in each other. "Pulling up – reversing." The boss's quiet voice commanding and confident, not a word wasted. The earth seemed to rock, drop and then climb up to fill the canopy then slide down as we completed the roll. "Smoke off go!" Bending left –" Arrow go!" More sharp cool orders. "Eight" – "Nine" snapped back the equally cool replies. A pause now as we turned through 90 degrees, roughly 200ft above the airfield, holding a steady 3g turn. "Half swan go!" "Two" – "Three" clicked back the replies, sharp as any parade ground commands. "Smoke on go – playing it down." The leader told his team as he slipped off another 100ft, for the fly-by past the VIP enclosure. I peered over the starboard cockpit coaming trying to see the VIP tent, but the angle of bank was too high. I looked left and down at the grass seemingly brushing No. 5's wing tip, but both Flt Lt Euan Perreaux and his back-seat man Cpl Mick Sivell were looking up at the formation and not at all perturbed. "Datum," the leader called as we flashed over the runway intersection. "Rolling out," the steady 3g of the turn slackened for an instant then as the leader called "Pulling up!" the force increased to 4g and the formation pulled up into a loop. "Arrow go!" from the boss, "Two" – "Three" came the replies. "More pull – more power" again the boss calling. Nearly 5,000ft, on our backs, weightless again for a few moments. "Vixen go!" from the boss, then the answers – "Eight" – "Nine".

Down from the loop, the speed building from 110 knots at the top of the loop to just over 300 at the bottom, the 'g' force increasing with the speed to around 4g at the bottom. "Smoke off go!" from the leader as he pulls the formation up. "Wine glass go!" then continues into a barrel roll, at the bottom of the roll he calls "Concorde go!" The team sweep across the airfield in a low banked fly-by over the VIP enclosure. At the end of the fly-by the team change back into 'Feathered arrow', as this is rather a mouthful to say as an order and with an oxygen mask clamped to one's chin as well, the call is made as "Fred go!" The leader turns the formation back toward the airfield holding it quite low and steering for the VIP enclosure, he calls "Smoke on go!" and pulls up into a loop. Only the two extreme wingmen one each side of the formation and the two 'stem of the wine glass' aircraft smoke. "Pulling up – split go!"

The instant the command is given Terry's reply is made "Six clear!" as six and seven pull hard and climb vertically away from the formation. "Box go!" Boss Hanna now ordering the main formation to change to box, the aircraft now climbing, belly toward the crowd snap crisply from vee to box in the blink of an eye. The skill and courage to carry out these manoeuvres requires each pilot to have total faith in and 100% commitment to each other. The two aircraft from the 'stem' meanwhile had also been busy, six and seven had split from the main formation and called "Clear" then as the boss had called "box" Terry called "Six split go!" Six and seven still smoking, split from each other. From their vertical climb they pulled to the horizontal (inverted), so as the main formation changed from vee to box, I in Red six had an upside-down, split-second view of a very smart formation change, before we and seven rolled the right way up and flew away from each other. The main formation now at 90 degrees to us continued their loop, Terry looking over his left shoulder watching for Red seven turning, pulling 3 or 4g and diving gently from 3,000ft to 50ft at just under 300 knots.

This synchronisation of the two solo aircraft with each other and with the main formation is worked up over many, many practices but changes are made every time as the conditions for any two displays are never the same. The allowances for wind or cloud or airfield obstructions are continually changing. The ability to fly like this, to play it off the cuff, but to get it right every time is very special and very special to watch. To fly with these men, to share the thrill and spectacle of it all is incredible, a once in a lifetime chance, and a great honour. It takes a long time and many 'back-seat rides' to remember the details and which manoeuvre follows which, but now after three years of solo rides I seem to be able to remember most of them.

The flying now is fast and furious, the 'g' loads are never off and never constant – wonderful, I'm totally enthralled! The main formation now coming out of their loop, seven shining scarlet aircraft in perfect Vixen formation diving vertically down, "Smoke on go!" calls the leader. "Six turning" Terry calling to Ian (Widgie) Dick the other solo pilot. "Seven", Ian using his call sign to acknowledge Terry's transmission. We are turning left toward the airfield, descending rapidly. Through the top of the canopy I can see the airfield, a whole expanse of green countryside, the hangars and buildings and the runway on which we are lining up. "Six smoke on go!" Terry orders the solos. Immediately a small stream of smoke appears about four miles away coming toward us in line with the runway and like us descending toward it. On our left the main formation have reached the bottom of their loop and fly across our path toward the VIP enclosure, Sqn Ldr Hanna calls "Red – break break go!" The formation fans out into the Vixen break. We flash down the runway at 30ft beneath the main formation as they break. I look over Flt Lt Kingsley's shoulder and see seven heading toward us at a closing speed of about 700 knots (750 mph). "Six pull – now!" as Terry calls, he pulls sharply back, the aeroplane's nose lifts skywards and the 'g' force again makes itself felt; as this happens seven flashes past our left side seemingly at an angle of 45 degrees. We rocket up into a loop, a tighter loop than the normal formation one. The airfield and its buildings climb up into the canopy, we look over our heads craning our necks to see the white ribbon of smoke led by a scarlet arrow climbing toward us. Seven passes on our left slower now as we lay on our backs and slow to about 120 knots. "Holding," Terry calls and pushes the stick forward. The straps bite into my shoulders and my feet float up behind the instrument panel as negative 'g' tries to propel me from my seat. Small particles of dust float up under my visor and around me. The two briefcases under my right arm are trying to join the dust up in the canopy. "Pull now," Terry calls, his voice steady and even. The negative 'g' is released and I bump back onto my dinghy pack seat with a jar as the normal positive 'g' increases. We hurtle earthwards once more. Looking over my head I briefly glimpse seven, like us diving down streaming smoke. Our speed and 'g' load increase and we pass again at about 100ft above the ground continuing the now shallow dive down to 30ft. "Smoke off go – clearing!" Terry calls.

The ground streaks by our starboard wing tip as we bank into a tight turn. We roll out and head for a gap in some trees, then climb gently away about 45 degrees to the runway centreline and back up to 2,500ft. Terry looks over his right shoulder and sees seven making for the prearranged marker at the opposite end of the runway. "Exploded arrow go!" Ray Hanna's voice fills the earphones. I look over my left shoulder, tilting my head up and back. The seven shining specks in arrow formation heading toward the runway down its extended centreline, "Smoke on go!" the leader calls the main formation, I can see the resulting white streams. Terry calls "Six turning!" the words hardly spoken as Ian Dick's reply is snapped back "Seven!" We turn left descending again. "Smoke off go – stabilise!" The boss brings the seven-ship section straight down the centre of the runway at 100ft. Their speed is just over 400 knots as they hurtle toward us. "90" calls Terry to seven. "Roll – roll – go!" Ray Hanna calls the main formation. The seven bright red sparkling aircraft each revolve around their longitudinal axes in the blink of an eye, the roll is completed in three quarters of a second – the name of the manoeuvre 'twinkle roll' describes it admirably. "Airbrakes go – bending right!" Hanna calls as they flash by us. We are down to 50ft again. Terry calls "Roll" – a slight pause as we bank left, and then "Pull". The bank is reversed and we pull up into a tight barrel roll. Looking again over

Terry's shoulder I can see seven spiralling toward us, streaming smoke. We pass, both inverted at the apex of the roll, then down again very close to the ground. A flash of buildings, helicopters, parked vehicles, startled cattle looking skyward as we apparently brush their heads.

Then, we are climbing again, this time we stay about 500ft. We keep turning until we are behind the crowd line, I look through the left side of the windscreen. "Contact!", seven calling (he can see us). Both solos are now heading toward each other. We bank hard right through about 150 degrees, I'm looking left for seven, skidding in trying to get behind us. We reverse left, the 'g' is constant and hard. I look at the fields and trees, looking for the shadow of our aircraft hurtling across the green turf and stone houses. Then I see a second shadow. Seven's with us I tell Terry. "Echelon port go!" we hear the boss again. "Smoke on go!" We complete about a 200-degree turn so we are now heading for the airfield from behind the crowd. "Pulling up!" calls the boss – pause, then "Rolling under – now!" The main formation is on our right, coming toward us in two sections, a four and a three in echelon port. The three are line astern of the four-ship formation. They pull up into a climb and then peel under each other in succession, to carry out the twizzle. They flash past on our right. "Smoke off go!" The boss calls. We run in from behind the VIP enclosure at 50ft, one or two startled white faces peering upward. We race on at 310 knots. "Datum" calls Terry as we cross the runway intersection two aircraft in tight line astern. He counts quietly to himself then calls "Six smoke on go!"

The instance of the command we break hard right into an 80-degree bank, streaming smoke. Seven has gone left also trailing smoke. "290 holding this," Terry calls indicating his speed to Red seven. The turn is a constant 4g 270 degrees, so by maintaining 4g and 290 knots both aircraft should trace the same circle. Looking at the grass just below our right wing tip it seems to be getting a little foggy – I breathe deeply and tense the muscles in my chest, arms and legs. The fog clears as the blood is forced back to my brain. I look upward through the canopy and see a thin trail of white smoke describing an arc turning toward us, the distance is closing rapidly! At nearly 600 knots closing speed it should. Although we are on our side turning about 50ft above the ground, because of the 'g' forcing us into our seats, our brains think down is where our backsides are. I can see two white-helmeted figures in the scarlet machine rushing toward us, then they are gone underneath our windscreen. There's a shock as we fly through their smoke trail, the bank and the 'g' is suddenly released and the world suddenly turns the right way up. On the right the empty VIP tent flashes past, we hurtle down the runway at 350 knots seemingly skimming the tarmac.

Taken during one of the team's many practice sorties, this superb photograph of one of the
most exciting manoeuvres performed by the team, the Roulette, was taken from the back
seat of Terry Kingsley's aircraft by Tom Thomas. (Via Ray Deacon)

I feel a thrill as we bank left through some trees and climb gently to 2,500ft and
slow to 200 knots using the airbrakes. Terry looks left for seven who is on a course
like ours, but at the opposite end of the runway. I turn right twisting around to
look over my right shoulder my head tipped back, looking through the top of
the canopy. I see the main formation climbing up into a loop in leader's benefit
(that is line abreast with the leader's aircraft just four feet further forward than the
other six). There are no guides to help to keep four feet between wing tips in this
manoeuvre, just pure skill and judgement. I watch the formation with pride as
they reach the top of the loop. The boss calls "Arrow – go!" and the line abreast
obediently swings back into arrow. "Smoke off go!" The formation tips graciously
over the top of the loop and gathers speed heading toward the crowd.

"Smoke on go!" calls the boss. "Break – break go!" commands the boss. The
seven brilliant shining aeroplanes drift gently apart, making (to my mind) the
prettiest of all manoeuvres, the 'cascade'. We now have all nine aircraft behind
the crowd heading away from the airfield. We see one aircraft smoking – that's the
boss. Now all the aircraft have to turn back toward the airfield and keeping him in
sight, we all have to change sides of the scattered formation. How each one knows
where the others are I will never know. We and seven are turning and keeping very

low. "Pulling up" calls boss Hanna and the eight aircraft climb vertically after the leader and close on him. The altimeter winds around very quickly through 3,000 – 4,000 – 4,500ft as we slide up line astern of the boss with seven close behind us. Other aircraft climbing, slide toward us from both sides, and as we reach 4,500ft, seven calls "All aboard". The formation is complete again in the basic 'Diamond' formation.

All nine aircraft seem to float momentarily, weightless, inverted, the panorama of the Somerset countryside, Mendip Hills, with the Bristol Channel ahead of us and the star cross of the airfield runways, hangars, parked aircraft and vehicles fill the canopy. The formation slowly completes the loop and increases speed, the 'Diamond' now pointing vertically toward the earth, "Break – Break – Go!" the boss calls. "1 left – 2 left – 3 left – 4 left" the calls come back, the formation breaks into the 'bomb-burst'. We turn slightly left of the boss. All nine aircraft hurtling downward, the 'g' force increases rapidly as we pull out of the dive. We pull the nose up gently and as we reach about 1,000ft "Smoke off go!" The last command of another practice. We turn left parallel to the runway just 19 minutes from start to finish of the display.

It's been one terrific adventure, so much compressed into so short a time. The sights, the movements, changes, sounds, pressure on the body, movement of the aircraft, the adrenalin excitement, wonder, pride, so many feelings, so much life in such a short time.

We continue our left turn using airbrakes to slow down. Ahead are three aircraft, I look left across the airfield, we are travelling downwind on the right of the active runway. Over to our left on the other side of the runway is another line of five aircraft. We land alternately from left and right. As each aircraft turn finals and call "Three Greens", each in turn momentarily emits smoke to enable the aircraft next in line to identify the caller and turn into line behind him. We land and pull to the side of the runway and stop to wait for the boss to land and taxi through. Then each aircraft in numerical order turns and taxies behind. Now the 'circus's' work begins – the preparation of ten beautifully polished aeroplanes for the highlight of the Yeovilton show in three hours' time. It's a wonderful life.

THE LAST GNAT LEADER
BRIAN HOSKINS

I was born and lived in London until I decided to join one of the armed forces and went to all three recruiting offices in the city. The RAF was the only one that offered me a secure future and after a few questions about my background,

Brian Hoskins

health, and academic qualifications, I was given an application form.

I was delighted to be asked to attend the selection board at Biggin Hill and I was really surprised when I was invited to join as a pilot and report to RAF South Cerney, on 3 January 1964, for initial officer training (IOT).

I was posted to No. 2 FTS at RAF Syerston for basic flying training. I did well in all the end-of-course tests and was posted to No. 4 FTS at RAF Valley to fly the Gnat. My first sortie was on 2 July 1965 – just as Lee Jones and Ray Hanna were forming the Red Arrows with nine Gnats. I remember that first sortie so well. On the ground the Gnat was like a big go-kart and with the wings behind you it felt that you were strapping them on your back. The next 69 hours were pure joy; the controls were so light and the aircraft so responsive. Flying low level at 360kts was very exhilarating and I will never forget my first flight down the A5 pass. Ground school was comprehensive, particularly the technical aspects of the aircraft. The hydraulics and controls were complex, and we needed to understand them well. I was posted to RAF Chivenor to do the day fighter ground attack (DFGA) course on the Hunter; I really enjoyed flying this classic aircraft. At the end of the course, I was posted to No. 20 Squadron based at RAF Tengah in Singapore.

I wanted to stay on the Hunter so that I was likely to move on to one of the new aircraft coming into service: the Harrier, Jaguar, and Phantom. However, I was posted to CFS to become an instructor. The course was on the Jet Provost, but I cannot say that I enjoyed it. At that stage (1969) all the flying training schools had an aerobatic team. I was posted to the School of Refresher Training (SORF) at RAF Manby.

I managed to get into the aerobatic team, the Macaws, in 1970 and flew on the left wing. I led the team in 1971 and 1972 and flew a total of 71 displays, 46 as leader. I had hoped that being in the Macaws might help me to become a member of the Red Arrows. I applied to join the team for the 1972 season but did not get invited to interview. I had a posting back to the Hunter (45 Squadron) at RAF Wittering. I decided that after four years flying the Jet Provost, I needed to get back into the fighter world.

I had not given up the idea of joining the Red Arrows but felt that I should do a full tour at Wittering. After a difficult year in 1971 the team had two outstanding years under Ian Dick's leadership for the 1972 and 1973 seasons. The winter

A future pilot being briefed by Red Arrows pilots, Dickie Duckett and Nigel Champness.
(Nigel Champness)

training for the 1974 season was difficult because of the first fuel crisis and bad
weather and Ian was called back to lead the team. I realised that this meant that
there would have to be a new leader for 1975 and that there would be several
other changes. I knew Ian well and had flown with him on 20 Squadron in 1966. I
called him in July to see if they had done the interviews for 1975. He said they had
just been completed but asked if I was interested in joining the team. I jumped at
the chance and was selected.

I was sorry to leave 45/58 Squadrons but my ambition to join the team was very
strong. Dickie Duckett, the new leader, had five other new pilots, and the synchro
pair had both been posted. I did a short refresher course at Valley. Mel Cornwell
and Roy Barber were my instructors, and they were both going to join the team
with me. It was wonderful to be back in the Gnat. Des Sheen, who had been Red
8 for two years was selected to lead the synchro pair as Red 6 and I was surprised,
but delighted, to be Red 7. Flying line astern behind Dickie and Des was not a
problem and I really liked being at the back of the formation. Des and I had a lot to
learn; fortunately, Dickie had spent his third year on the team in the synchro pair
with Ian Dick, so was able to give us sound advice. The work-up was amazing, the
Gnat and I were in our element. Des and I worked hard to produce an exciting,

but safe, display. We had a successful year and there were only three changes going into 1976. I led the synchro pair and Mel Cornwell was Red 7. Dickie's team had another excellent year and got back to over 100 displays. I am bound to say that the two years flying the Gnat following Dickie, with Des and then Mel, providing a steady stem for the formations and good synchro pair display, was a wonderful experience.

I knew that I had to leave and hoped that it might be to the Harrier or Jaguar. So it was a real surprise when I was posted as flight commander/QFI on No. 208 Squadron flying the Buccaneer at RAF Honington. I enjoyed flying this great aircraft with a navigator in the back seat. He took care of the navigation, weapons selection and had antiquated radar and radar warning receiver to operate; I could better concentrate on flying and delivering the weapons. I would have happily stayed on the squadron but, after just two years, was selected to lead the Red Arrows. It was going to be such a great honour to lead for the last year of the Gnat and then to convert to the Hawk.

I joined them for the last month of the 1978 display season. I flew quite a few times with the current leader, Frank Hoare, and with Richard Thomas and Steve Johnson who were going to stay with me on the team. My short refresher flying course at Valley and solo aerobatic training went well. Whilst I was at Valley, I did a first flight in the Hawk with Byron Walters, who was to join the Arrows a year later.

Six of our aircraft were now in winter servicing. The early formation training went well but we had a setback when Martin Stoner (Red 5), going into his third year, announced that he needed an operation and would not be able to fly until January. The synchro pair, Richard Thomas and Steve Johnson, made good progress; the last new pilot, Neal Wharton had joined us, and we were able to make steady progress without Red 5. The aircraft were now out of winter servicing, and we flew eight aircraft together just before Christmas.

After the Christmas/New Year break, in 1979 Martin returned, and we flew our first nine-ship in early January. We flew 23 practices during that month and 24 in February – a good winter in the UK. However, the aircraft were beginning to show their age and spare parts were sparse. We flew 39 sorties in March, including a few days at RAF Valley for better weather. I discovered that my squadron commander from basic flying training, who said that I would never be a fighter or aerobatic pilot, was commanding the ground school. We had a drink together and agreed that I had been a slow learner during basic flying training.

On 2 April, the AOC-in-C watched a practice and declared us ready to display. Three days later we did our first display at RAF Leeming for the Queen Mother, the commandant-in-chief Central Flying School. On 10 April we did our first overseas display in Denmark at Aalborg, and a further nine displays during the month.

Officer commanding flying at RAF Kemble, Wing Commander Ernie Jones, a member of the team in 1967, was a QFI on the Hawk. I flew two sorties in the Hawk with him on 19/20 April and then went to Valley with him on 23 April for a simulator sortie before going solo the following day. It was extremely helpful for me to have this early look at the aircraft which was to replace the Gnat in 1980.

The display season progressed well. The engineers were working hard to find spares to keep us flying. The pilots had some problems with the brakes which were, generally, caused by the ageing anti-skid units. During the last week in May we had to transit from RAF Wittering to RAF Kemble. It was a day of showers and strong wind, but I had been briefed that it would be within crosswind limits. When we arrived at RAF Kemble it was raining and over 30kts of wind directly across the runway, well outside our crosswind limits. I decided to divert to RAF Lyneham and to land on their short runway which was facing into the wind. All was under control until Steve Johnson's brake parachute detached and he only just stopped on the runway. We decided to leave all the aircraft at RAF Lyneham and, because we had a busy week ahead, to collect them the next day after they had repaired Steve's aircraft. On the return to Kemble Steve's brake 'chute detached again, and he rolled gently into the barrier. There was little damage but, understandably, the air officer training invited me to explain this and the other incidents with the brakes.

In the middle of June, after 42 displays, we faced a real problem. Tim Curley (Red 2), in his fourth year on the team, informed me that he was unwell and that he was grounded and unlikely to fly again for some months. He was a key member of the front four and very much my right-hand man, great fun in the crewroom, and a good friend to us all. We were told that we should complete the rest of the year with seven aircraft as the easiest thing to do was to drop one from the other side of the formation. However, with Reds 4 and 8 moving forward and Red 7 moving to 8 for the first half of the display, we would have a good eight-ship display and I recommended we should fly that for the rest of the year. The air officer training was not convinced but invited me to explain the plan: he clearly believed that seven was the answer. He was also concerned that it would take too long to retrain, and we would have to cancel too many displays. It was Monday and I assured him that we would be ready for our next display on Friday. There was little change for most of us, but Neal Wharton, moving forward to Red 4, had to fly some new formation positions and manoeuvres. We flew seven practices by Thursday afternoon and were ready to display on Friday.

It was undoubtedly a shame that the second half of the Gnat's last season was with eight pilots. However, we had a very busy and successful season with a total of 116 displays. The last display was at RAF Valley on 15 September which was very appropriate as this was where the team had been founded 15 years earlier. My last sortie in the Gnat was flying back to Kemble the following day. I had flown a total of 755 hours and 301 displays. My hope, at the end of my flying training, had been met in ways I could never have imagined. The Gnat was a wonderful aircraft to fly, the all-round view from the front seat allowed you to feel that you had wings, and the aircraft took you wherever you wanted. The shape made it ideal to fly various formations, the best being the iconic Diamond Nine. Its crisp response to control inputs, and the Orpheus engine's immediate reaction to throttle movements, made it easy to stay in, or change, formation.

The only problem the Red Arrows had with the Gnat was that with just internal fuel on long-transit flights, or transits to and from displays, we were likely to be tight on fuel. I suspect that other team leaders and members have stories to tell about this. With the internal tanks full, we planned on the synchro pair having a low-level radius of action of 35–40 miles. Fortunately, in the early years there were still many small airfields available. I remember two occasions that highlight the problems this could cause: one in the synchro pair and one as leader. In June 1975, we had completed a display at Woodford and then positioned at Alconbury for one at Halton. We were planned to return to Alconbury for a display but for some reason were diverted to Upper Heyford. ATC took us on a very wide and long down-wind leg and by now Des and I were low on fuel. When they wanted us to do another pattern, we declared 'fuel priority' and landed. Then they insisted a long taxiing route; fortunately, the Gnat fuel gauges were very accurate. It began to look as though that I might not reach the parking area; I was getting so low on fuel that the engineers might have to purge the fuel lines. As we still had to do the Alconbury display I found a suitable area to park and shut down the engine for which the engineers were very grateful. They did the turnround and I joined the rest of the guys as they taxied out for the Alconbury display.

The other time was when I was leading in July 1979. Early in the afternoon we had displayed at Hockenheim out of Baden Söllingen. After refuelling we flew to Hahn for their display, at the end of which, we landed at Cologne for a display at Bretished, a small airfield about 25 miles to the south. We took off under the edge of a heavy shower of hail. The weather forecaster was not sure when the showers would be clear, so we asked Hahn to be our diversion as their display had finished. I asked the synchro pair to leave the display and head for Cologne before their last manoeuvre so that they could check the weather. As we finished Richard

Thomas informed me that the weather was not good at Cologne, so we all diverted to Hahn. On the ground, the crowd barriers were still in place and ATC wanted us to back track and follow a long, complex taxi route. I knew the synchro pair's fuel state so told the tower we could not follow their instructions but would like to park all the aircraft at the end of the runway on the operational readiness pan. They hesitated but when I told them our fuel states they agreed. The aircraft were refuelled, and we stayed there overnight. Early the next morning we returned to Kemble via Wildenrath.

The Gnat could carry two underwing fuel tanks, and a question often asked was why we did not carry them to ease the fuel/range problems. My understanding is that in the early years the pilots thought that the aircraft was less stable in formation at low speed (at the top of loops). The tanks, which extended forward ahead of the leading edges of the wings, adversely affected the sweeping shapes of the formations. I agreed, but in 1976 we were tasked to fly at Gothenburg on 16 May. As we were displaying at Biggin Hill on the two previous days, Dickie decided that we should put the tanks on so that we could fly direct. A one hour-40-minute flight in the Gnat was brilliant. We did the display with the tanks on and, to be honest, we did not encounter any problems. From the back of the Diamond Nine everyone seemed stable.

CHANGING FROM GNAT TO HAWK

I suppose that the conversion started when I went solo in the Hawk on 24 April 1979. Throughout that year the ground crew went on Hawk courses. At last, they were going to be working on a new, modern aircraft with plenty of spares, if they were required. On 16 August the team flew to Bitteswell airfield, the British Aerospace factory near Lutterworth to collect the first Hawk. We had enjoyed an excellent relationship with the manager, Albert Whitehouse, and the whole workforce for some years. They had done the annual winter servicing on the Gnat and were now preparing the Hawks, including the smoke system and painting. Following an official presentation, I led the team back to RAF Kemble in the Hawk with Ernie Jones, and the manager flew my Gnat.

We were all back together at Kemble with 12 aircraft (no winter servicing) on 12 October. I kept Richard Thomas and Steve Johnson together as the synchro pair – I believed that they would have lots of work to do to adapt their patterns for the Hawk. The formation flying was much the same but, flying a bigger aircraft, the wingmen had much greater changes of height and speed during wingovers and barrel rolls. Also, whereas the Gnat engine reacted immediately to changes of

Gnat and Hawks in October 1979.

power, there was a slight delay with the Hawk engine; everyone had to anticipate the changes more and I had to give them slightly more warning and time. We made good progress and flew nine aircraft in formation on 13 November. We took nine to Bitteswell on 17 December and showed them the various formations. Three days later we did our first full sequence watched by our AOC.

I went on to fly 2,750 hours on the Hawk, had 1,451 on the Hunter and an exhilarating 440 on the Buccaneer. However, my first impression of the Gnat in 1965 was right and I was so lucky, and feel very privileged, to have flown it for three years in the Red Arrows and to have also been the leader.

CHAPTER 5

THE GNAT FIGHTER IN FINLAND

TOM EELES

The Finnish Air Force, with its limited budget but with the potential enemy of the Soviet Union on its doorstep, needed an affordable high-performance fighter so it was very attracted to the Gnat. An order was placed for 13 Gnats, two of which were to be configured as fighter-reconnaissance aircraft and the first aircraft was delivered on 30 July 1958. In early 1957 an agreement between Folland and Valmet was signed to enable Gnats to be built in Finland under licence but, in the event, none were ever built. On 31 July 1958 Major Lauri Pekuri of the Finnish Air Force became the first Finnish pilot to achieve supersonic flight while flying a Gnat at Lake Luonetjarvi.

Major Lauri Pekuri with GN-102.

Although the Finnish Air Force was the first operational user of the Gnat F1 the aircraft was still immature, and many technical issues had not been resolved. It was not long before the first aircraft was lost in an accident on 26 August 1958 due to a technical design error in the hydraulic system. Three other Gnats were destroyed in other accidents but once the initial problems had been resolved the F1 proved to be extremely manoeuvrable and had an excellent performance when airborne. However, being technically complex it proved to be very maintenance intensive and a considerable challenge to the mainly conscript mechanics responsible for servicing. The harsh winters and hot summers in Finland also affected aircraft availability. Training new pilots was difficult without a two-seat trainer of similar performance. The Finnish Air Force used the Fouga Magister as its jet trainer, but its performance and handling did not replicate the idiosyncrasies of the Gnat. Only experienced pilots were selected to convert to the diminutive aircraft. Nevertheless, those pilots that did master this skittish little fighter made good use of it and much enjoyed the experience. The availability of spares was always an issue and so in 1972 the remaining Gnats were taken out of service, to be replaced by Saab Drakens. One Finnish Air Force Gnat F1 is displayed today in the Aviation Museum of Central Finland.

These three personal memories of flying the Gnat fighter in the Finnish Air Force have been provided by Second Lieutenant Reijo Suutala, kindly translated from Finnish by Lieutenant Colonel Jyrki Laukkanan, Lieutenant Colonel Jouko Gullsten and General Heikki Nikunen.

GNAT OPERATIONS IN FINLAND – AN OVERVIEW

JOUKO GULLSTEN

At the beginning of Gnat operations on a normal day the pilots flew the Gnat programme accepted by Finnish Air Force Headquarters (FAFHQ). After a few years of training and when the FAF had enough experienced pilots, the quick reaction alert (QRA) operation was started in 1965. The FAF had two wings which were prepared for war, the Karelian Wing (Karelian Command) with MiG-21s and the Häme Wing (Häme Command) with Gnats. During the day some pilots flew normal Gnat training flights while the others participated on alert. The alert tasks were not so interesting as the pilots had to sit and wait for possible surveillance missions, which happened very seldom. Completely different from what we see in films on Netflix when we watch World War II or the Battle of Britain in 1940.

In 1968, during the Czechoslovakian crisis the Häme Wing was to monitor the airspace in Lapland as well as in the south of Finland. The Gnats flew mainly in Lapland while the MiGs monitored the south. On one occasion the Soviets approached the border with big formations of aircraft but, however, without any real incursion taking place. In any case, this period was interesting and reminded the FAF of what could happen one day. The present situation in Eastern Europe is quite similar.

Some parts of the Gnat training programmes especially appealed to me such as air-to-air shooting with cannons and air-to-surface firings with cannons and rockets. The immediate results proved that the old adage was still true. The results were better in air-to-air shooting if you fire from as close as possible. Gnats were very steady to shoot, so the results in air-to-surface firing were very good as well. Sometimes it was difficult to carry out air-to-air firing as the first Gnat often shot the target banner off into the sea.

Gnat pilots also were expected to take part in military exercises all over Finland as an alternative to the normal routine of home-base operations. Reconnaissance flights were few, the main task being to succeed in low-level navigation and using the winter camera equipment. The Gnats also had air sampling equipment, so after Soviet nuclear tests the FAF flew sampling flights, especially in Lapland, but no positive results were ever achieved. The FAF also had several groups of Gnat aerobatic formation display teams in the 1960s. Their performances generated much hectic discussion at their home bases.

After Finland bought MiG-21s and Drakens the Gnats were often used in dissimilar air combat exercises. Dogfights were popular, the Gnats proved to be superior against the Drakens at low and high altitude. MiGs were much more challenging at high speeds and high altitudes. For example, a typical sortie profile might go as follows:

- Take-off at the same time
- Climb and fly together to the agreed altitudes
- Dogfight for a few minutes until the Draken had to land because of fuel shortage caused by using afterburner
- Gnat remained at altitude waiting for more Drakens to fight

In real life Migs and Drakens had infrared homing missiles whilst Gnats only had cannons.

In conclusion, the FAF Gnat pilots were very satisfied with their fighters and their experiences when flying them.

RIDING A WILD HORSE
REIJO SUUTALA (TRANSLATION BY JYRKI LAUKKANEN)

Jyrki Laukkanen

The Gnat was introduced into Finnish Air Force service over 60 years ago in 1958. It took our air force into a supersonic era, although only in a steep dive. Some stories have been written about the procurement of the Gnat and about some serious accidents that happened in the initial years of operation. But, the squadron service and a line pilot's point of view of flying the Gnat have got less attention. It must be remembered that, my experiences, and assessments of operating the Gnat in the early 1970s are different from those of the early years in late 1950s and early 1960s. The difficulties which were faced began soon after initiation into squadron flying with an accident to Capt Dick Karlsson in the summer of 1958. This involved the operation of the pitch-control system. After this accident more knowledge and understanding of that system was continuously added and introduced into flight training. It was argued that it was only after this and some later accidents, that the operation of pitch-control was mastered. In the beginning of the 1970s, the Gnat had been flown for over ten years and there had been two more serious accidents, and numerous near misses due to this system.

The last serious accident involving a Gnat happened in 1968. Lt Esa Rantamäki barely managed to eject from one that was making uncontrollable outside loops. The Gnat was losing a lot of altitude in each turn and crashed soon after the ejection. Due to the strong negative acceleration, the pilot lost his vision, and thus was not able to fully comprehend the situation he was in. The flight was one of the first type of training flights. The task was to practise the transition from a hydraulic-control system to a mechanical one, and vice versa. This exercise was considered necessary as a result of the Karlsson accident, which was a result of a faulty hydraulic system that put pressure on the flight-control system. The type of course attended by Lt Rantamäki was to be the last to be held for new Gnat pilots. Fortunately for me, later two more courses were organised, the first of which I attended.

This is the reason why I wanted to write about my own experiences. What made the Gnat interesting was that it was still associated with some mystique. For some pilots, it might even be a matter of awe mixed with fear. There was certainly no reason for fear, but certain critical areas had to be understood. These included the entire pitch-control system, which still involved the so-called galloping phenomenon. The name coincidentally describes this flight condition. The risk of getting into it increased at high airspeeds. The problem was the sensitivity of the pitch control. The control stick normally moved the entire stabiliser hydraulically. The control surface deflection was the same regardless of the airspeed range. This made the Gnat oversensitive at high airspeeds. Hence the nickname in the title. This wild horse taught especially the hard-handed pilots to fly. Repeated overcorrection in pitch control could result in a motion, which the word 'gallop' describes very well. The 'g' limits could be instantly exceeded. The recovery instruction was very simple. The power lever was pulled to idle, and the aircraft into a steep climb. Decreasing airspeed and easing on the stick helped to calm down the situation.

In my course, it was pointed out that the investigation of Lt Rantamäki's case provided even more information on how the pitch-control system worked in different situations. The system used so-called worm screws to memorise the position of the control surface when moving from one system to another. When changing systems, it was therefore important to keep the initial flight situation in mind. In the case of Rantamäki, while flying with mechanical control at lower speed, he returned hydraulic pressure to the stabiliser. It had been trimmed for high speed before switching to mechanical control. The stabiliser high-speed position stored in the memory did not match the position at the lower speed. As a result, the aircraft pitched down violently, when the hydraulic pressure returned the stabiliser to its high-speed trimmed position.

GN-103 in 1959 in the UK. (Folland)

MY FIRST FLIGHT

On 6 April 1970, I taxied GN-103 into position on runway 12 at Jyväskylä. All the essentials that had been taught about the aircraft were supposed to be in my head. Also, information learned through accidents. The runway was the same as where Capt Karlsson had once made a crash landing. Later, Lt Sirola had crashed at take-off to the extension of the runway on his second flight. So the historical background contributed to a dramatic setting for this exciting event. Based on the audience gathered in front of the hangar, it was obvious that information had spread in the squadron. Today is the day when the Gnat course begins flying. Over the years rumours had been spread that there is always something worth watching. It was joked in the squadron that the staff would close their office doors to come out to the airfield to follow the circus. I banished such thoughts while focusing on the take-off to come.

The oxygen-flow indicator blinked its black and white eyeball happily, indicating the tension. There is no instructor as a back-up in a single-seat fighter. All you have is what an upcoming flight will be like based on the stories by older Gnat pilots.

The leap from the previous two-seat Fouga Magister trainer is great. At the end of the runway squadron commander Maj Ville 'Vilkku' Salminen and flight leader Capt Paavo Himanen are watching in their radio vehicle. Every Gnat pilot is thinking that this is one of the most memorable experiences that life can offer. I release the brakes, push the power lever to the limit, and the aircraft shoots forward. The aircraft's desire to go is limited on the first flights, by installing a securing wire in the groove of the power lever at about 90%. In an emergency it can be passed by just pushing the throttle lever through the wire. Prior to the first flight there were two previous take-off acceleration exercises, which gave a picture of the acceleration of an aircraft with a thrust approximately equal to its basic empty weight.

The speed is immediately 100 kmph, at which point the rudder should start to work. However, something surprising is happening. The aircraft begins to turn strongly to the right, out of the runway. I push the thrust lever through the limiter wire to full power and pull the stick. The aircraft climbs just clear of the snow walls beside the runway. The first test in taming the wild horse has been passed. When the landing gear begins to retract the typical nose-up trim change requires almost full forward stick while simultaneously trimming nose down. It has been said that without any control action the Gnat will loop. A climb angle of 30-40 degrees is soon achieved.

In front of the windscreen there is only blue while the earth's surface is rapidly falling behind. The rest of the flight went according to plan, as well as the second flight flown immediately after the first one. On the second take-off I was prepared for the tendency to turn to the right. In my first take-off the squadron commander was already apprehensive after seeing the Gnat turning off the runway. He joked later that he already had requested a mechanic to be positioned in hangar number three. The third flight of GN-103 that day was flown by the squadron deputy commander. After that flight GN-103 was towed directly to the service hangar from which it was delivered for my flight in the morning. Investigations revealed that the so-called trim plates located on the outer edges of the jet nozzle were installed in the wrong place. Their purpose is to compensate for the turn tendency caused by the engine especially at low airspeeds and high-power settings.

GETTING TO KNOW MY WILD HORSE

The training on type progressed according to the programme without major complications. Special attention was paid to the exercises that included use of the back-up functions of the pitch-control system. Basic aerobatics were included soon after the first few flights. Aileron rolls proved to be quite easy, the control stick to the side and the aircraft rolls. Vertical manoeuvring was also easy thanks to a considerable power reserve. The exception was 'g' force, which was of a different order and longer duration than we were used to.

One amusing detail came to my mind from my first aerobatic flight. In the beginning the loops became Immelmans. Due to the gyroscopic forces of the engine, the control stick had to be held fully deflected to the right on top of the loop. No matter how I tried to resist, the aircraft tried to roll level on top of the loop. We discussed this on the ground with my flight instructor, but we could not find an explanation. Being a short man, I had to raise the seat higher than normal and finally an explanation was found. The control stick hit my knee and had no room to deflect fully sideways. My destiny after that was to sit a little straighter to see out through the gunsight.

THE GNAT SQUADRON'S MISSION

One of the main goals of our training was to make us qualified for quick reaction alert duty as soon as possible. There was a shortage of Gnat pilots, and the aircraft was very well suited for this purpose due to its fast field readiness. The pilot could spend his time in the coffee room, for example, but with the alarm buzzer ringing, the aircraft was in the sky in five minutes. The take-off instructions may have been given to the aircraft during start-up, or in the air as soon as the radio had warmed up.

Thus, after a rather intensive period of training, it was known that a small group of pilots would be on alert duty. Recalling the role and significance of the Gnat squadron at the turn of the 1970s, I would like to say that its most important task was to perform quick reaction alert duty alternately with Rissala's MiG-21F-13 squadron. So there was a ready need for our aircraft and we were a welcome addition to the QRA team.

At Luonetjärvi, the MiG-21F-13 squadron of the Häme Wing was not responsible for QRA duty except in exceptional cases. The MiG-21F-13 was not particularly suitable for the purpose because quick readiness required sitting in the cockpit. Add to this the requirement to wear a pressure suit, sitting in the cockpit in the summer heat was uncomfortable at the best of times. On-call times were short and needed more pilots, while the Gnat pilot in the coffee room was on call all day alone.

FIGHTER TRAINING

The QRA service naturally required a moderate instrument flight routine. The aircraft type was badly equipped for this purpose. Qualifications to operate in class 2 weather minimums could not be maintained. Flying on instruments and especially the on approaches were practised too few times. The only IMC navigation instrument was one ADF, and that too was difficult to tune from the side panel. Normally in an NDB approach, an outer NDB beacon was tuned in, and after passing it, the final approach was flown with a back indication of this beacon. It was preferred to focus on flying rather than trying to tune the locator. Pilots with only little experience were not recommended to make a go-around in IMC due to the strong pitch-trim change as described earlier. To get the most out of the aircraft, it was necessary to familiarise oneself with its flight characteristics and performance. That took a lot of studying, and physics was tested. There were no g-suits available to the pilots, although the aircraft system allowed their use. In dogfight exercises trying to get the pipper on an opponent, those pilots with best g-tolerance were usually most successful. Each pilot certainly developed his own way of operating. I myself did a gymnastics programme to train my abdominal muscles every evening. Generally, the larger the number of muscles able to be held at the same time in tension, the better one withstood long-term 'g' forces. The artificial control stick feel was created by a spring load. During long dogfight exercises, continuous pulling against the spring required getting experience. Our squadron sergeant major had acquired a so-called Bullworker rod on his wall. The purpose was to improve the bicep muscles of the squadron pilots between flights.

FIRING THE GUNS

The Gnat had been involved in a shooting accident years earlier. As a result the weapons had been banned from firing. Captain Jorma 'Jomppe' Mustakallio, had received a grenade chip into his thigh after a projectile had exploded in the mouthpiece of the cannon. Indeed, the gun barrels protruded from the outer edges of the air intakes, somewhat flush with the pilot's thighs. We do not know who lifted the ban but one beautiful day a message came that firing would start again.

Shooting patterns from years ago were excavated, and training was initiated in a hurry. On the technical side, the mouthpieces of the cannons were examined, new ones were even made if necessary, and test shooting of the weapons was initiated. Pilots practised air-to-air shooting patterns with available Gnats. The old pilots recalled how the shooting patterns were supposed to go. A Fouga flew as a target plane. I was thinking about the pattern in which the shooting would take place from a rather tight turn. As a result I tried a less tight firing position, which would give the gunsight time to calm down. However, the older officers overruled me. Officers always know best!

Armament practice camps were set up, and there was an expectation in the air filled with excitement. After all, it had been some time since the previous firings,

Loading the gun of a Gnat at Oulu. (Via Jyrki Laukkanen)

and there was no clear picture of the accuracy of the weapons. In the squadron the shooting started naturally in a hierarchical order, with younger pilots just monitoring the first results. We noticed that the accuracy was not very promising. I was the last one to shoot, and I was already pretty sure that my idea of shooting in a less tight turn was good. The gyro gunsight system has not enough time to compute the advance needed for aiming after a wingover and the following tight turn. After the first shooting round was done, the results were viewed with some embarrassment.

Those who noticed about my indiscipline at the time, one after another, were eager to talk with me. However, the squadron commander took the reins, and the next firing round was shot from a slightly revised pattern. The cannons proved to be accurate and effective. The intensity of the recoil in a small aircraft seemed surprising. The effect was the same as if you had opened the airbrakes. In addition, the aircraft's shaking prevented the firing of long-aimed bursts. A story went around that some engineer had calculated that the aircraft could be completely stopped by a long series of bursts. The procedure was arranged so that the Fougas were the first to start shooting, and finally came two Gnats. This was because the Gnat's cannon fire usually either cut the tow wire or dropped the tow target into the sea. Naturally, there was a competition as to whoever had the most target droppings into the sea.

Shooting camp. (Ilmavoimat)

EFFECTIVE ARMAMENT

Confidence in the functioning of the weapons system had been gained. The most important weapon system of a fighter was at that time cannons, and their suitability for the Gnat was confirmed. Later, there was still an opportunity to test the rockets. This was related to an applied practice firing camp held in the Rovajärvi shooting area in 1971.

The transition of the Gnat squadron to history was already in process. Yet, five Gnats had been refurbished for the camp. They were flown in formation above cloud from Jyväskylä to Rovaniemi. A planned dashing arrival did not go as intended. The weather at Rovaniemi was quite poor due to a snowstorm. The intention was to vector the formation below the cloud cover by radar, from which to break the formation for one-ship landings. The radar operator didn't have his best day, let alone knowledge of the Gnat type at all. The formation was successfully scattered, after which the radio call signs were already messed up.

The situation was made even worse when one after another Gnat reported a flashing low-fuel warning light. Eventually everybody found themselves safely on the runway and ready to fire the cannons. The solemn closing ceremony of the camp included a low-level attack in the firing range. The armament of a four-ship Gnat formation was a full load of rockets. They were fired in a single shot after an aggressive dive and low-level pull-up. It was an impressive sight, although the hit accuracy may have been modest. The rockets were particularly sensitive to aircraft oscillations, and in that situation the Gnats did not even try to get into the best firing position.

RECCE VERSIONS

The Finnish Air Force acquired 13 Gnats, two of which were so-called photo-reconnaissance versions. They were the last delivered aircraft, GN-112 and GN-113. This version was equipped with oblique cameras that were able to photograph low-level stereo coverage, which made image interpretation easier. The actual processing of the photos was assigned to another branch of the service.

One related photo-reconnaissance exercise was held back. The photographic centre trained some artillery officers, who wanted to ascertain pilots' navigational accuracy. They seemed to have some kind of preconception about it. A small islet from the Åland archipelago had been chosen as the target, which had to be photographed at a height of 50 metres at a speed of 700kmph. The squadron saved its reputation when the rock found in the pictures was the same shape as on the map.

SONIC BOOMS

As the Gnat was the first aircraft in Finnish service to reach sonic speed, supersonic flights were the last flights in the training syllabus. They were awaited with anticipation in the squadron, because after these flights those paying for the associated club sauna evening would be known. The supersonic flight was carried out by climbing to the altitude of 13,500 metres north of the base, from where the aircraft was turned towards the base at a 45-degree dive angle with full power. The recovery was made at a height of 10,000 metres. The cone from which the boom was heard was quite narrow. I had to repeat my first dive because the boom went over the base and was not heard. During the operation, care had to be taken not to point the boom towards the Vihtavuori explosive factory. They were reportedly sensitive to the tinkle of windows. The boom performed with drop tanks was billed separately at the club sauna. With the drop tanks, it was much harder for the Gnat to reach even Mach 1.0. It felt like pushing a balloon under water. The aerodynamic drag began to be felt in a completely different way as airspeed approached the speed of sound, while the aircraft began to vibrate and become more unstable. The sonic boom was generated below the Mach 1.0 reading, because the local airspeed on the curved surfaces of the aircraft reached Mach 1.0. The greatest significance of the supersonic dive was for practice but with no operational use.

CONCLUSIONS

The overall significance of the Gnat as a fighter remained quite questionable as the main use was radiation measurement flights. Those flights were routinely performed once a month, but in the statistics on the use of the aircraft their significance was negligible. The flights themselves were interesting. Air particle samples were taken into an underwing pod while flying above the tropopause at 13,000 metres. The pods were then sent for examination under laboratory conditions.

There were many shortcomings in flight training. However, these were corrected as knowledge and understanding grew. The technical shortcomings that occurred were corrected with more than 300 modifications made in Finland. This describes the level and work motivation of technical personnel in our air force. Although the list of aircraft shortcomings is long, it was a top-class fighter in terms of performance and the manoeuvring characteristics at the time. When Senior Lt Jouko Gullsten flew the last aircraft to the museum in 1972, another colourful page was turned in our aviation history. This happened when the first Draken fighters were already flying in the sky of Jyväskylä. At the time, there were still pilots who had flown all our jet trainer and fighter types. So there was a basis for comparison. They felt the

Gnat had the best manoeuvring performance at low and medium altitudes. This was even noticed in practice. Although the flight hours had come to an end, the aircraft transferred to the museum had remained competitive to the last.

HEIKKI NIKUNEN

I was born on 12 April 1939 in Lahti, Southern Finland, and for some reason as a little boy I was already very excited about flying. I even planned to build wings and fly with them, but luckily my realism was developing a little faster than my constructing ability. I was very keen on aviation literature and learned that the Finnish Air Force was founded on 6 March 1918 and had begun to train fighter tactics in the loose, broad section and finger-four method as early as 1935. Furthermore, training in the accuracy of aerial gunnery had been emphasised heavily. I also read everything about our war pilots who were one of the very decisive factors when our defence forces repulsed Stalin's occupation attempts in the Winter War and in the Continuation War. From the strategic attacks of Stalin during 1944 the only one which failed was the one against Finland. According to the Grub Street publication *Aces High*, Finland has the world record in the number of fighter aces in proportion to the population.

Pilots and Gnats of 21 Squadron, Häme Wing, Finnish Air Force Jyväskylä. (Bristol Siddeley)

As a teenager I joined Lahti Aviation Club and completed a sailplane course. Following a variety of courses at Air War School, I was lucky to get the privilege to choose my first squadron, and at that time our hottest fighters were Gnats, so my choice, of course, was Fighter Squadron 21 (from July 1962 Fighter Squadron 11) flying Gnats in Luonetjärvi Air Force Base. Our jet planes in cadet course had been Fouga CM 170 Magisters, and now the next step was the de Havilland DH 100 Vampire Mk.52. We flew about 135 Vampire hours in seven months and then it was time to move on. Both Fouga and Vampire had rather conventional performances with thrust/weight ratios of 0.26 and 0.33 respectively. That meant quite controlled acceleration during take-off and use of potential energy of altitude during aerobatics. The Gnat in clean configuration had the thrust/weight ratio of 0.69 and that meant quite a different take-off acceleration and also almost total freedom in aerobatics.

At that time there were no trainers and simulators, so Gnat flying was real solo from the very first take-off. We used a kind of 'narrative human simulator' when older pilots described the chronological tempo of the events during take-off: apply the brakes and open the throttle – when the brakes begin to slip release them and increase the rpm to the maximum – at 220 km/h (120 knots) raise the nosewheel and fly off with stick almost fully back – apply the brakes, select wheels up – return the stick smoothly forward to counteract the nose-up trim change – when the stick is in the neutral position retrim the tailplane from -6 to about -2 to climb away. It was quite handy to sit in an armchair and repeat in your mind and with your movements each stage of the take-off in the right rhythm. In every respect the preceding technical, functional and operational training was both very detailed and exhaustive.

Before the first take-off we had an acceleration exercise in the form of interrupted take-off. We youngsters were wondering why it was necessary, why not to continue right away up in the sky? Well, that rehearsal proved to be really valuable. When you opened the throttle your head dashed against the ejection-seat head rest and everything happened so quickly that you were only just able to pull the throttle back at the right speed of 200 km/h (108 knots). So now you knew that before take-off you sit tight, put your head firmly to the ejection-seat head rest and be ready to perform all the take-off steps quickly and accurately.

I flew my first Gnat sortie on 4 July 1962. It was a fine sunny summer day. The older pilots told us to aim our climb into the sun. The midsummer sun was high in the sky and I was thinking that the climb cannot be that steep. Runway 13 was in use and I taxied to the northern end of it. After thorough checks and take-off clearance from the tower I opened the throttle, released the brakes and then it was going in full swing! Training had been detailed and effective, so the take-off was smooth and the flight path steady. When I climbed at 740 km/h (400 knots) the sun was in the upper corner of my windshield. So the guys were right, I was going up at an amazing angle. When I started the turn to my training area I of course used instinctively the Vampire stick force and was at lightning speed at about 90 degrees bank. The rate of roll without external stores was 300 degrees/sec. so you could do a real quick move to the excessive bank and the correction back to some 45 degrees bank.

The programme of the first flight included tests of manoeuvrability at different speeds and attitudes and at the approach and landing speeds with undercarriage and flaps down. Flying the Gnat gave the wonderful feeling of almost unlimited manoeuvrability, there was no need to dive to increase speed, you just pushed the throttle forward. All in all, one got the feeling, that the wings spread out of your own sides and the fighter did anything you wanted.

Later a new method was adopted for the first take-off. Due to the 2050kp of the Bristol Siddeley Orpheus engine the first take-off could be done well with a reduced power setting and so with more moderate acceleration. Anyway, I am very happy to have had the chance of experiencing that unforgettable flash to the sky! The Orpheus was a very reliable and effective engine which responded quickly and precisely to the throttle movements. There was a distinct difference between the axial supercharger of the Orpheus and the radial one of the de Havilland Goblin 35. When you pushed the throttle forward in the Vampire, the rpm started to increase and continued higher than you planned and when you then pulled it back a little bit it started to decrease, and again, lower than you planned. Flying the Gnat you could make the landing by setting the tailplane to -8, keeping the control stick in a permanent position and making the necessary control adjustments by the throttle. The flying programme included the use of various systems like simulating a hydraulic failure and electric trimmer motor failure. It was quite astonishing how heavy the controls became without the power of hydraulic pressure. Then there were all those basic procedures and quite a lot of aerobatics.

The Gnat was ideal for dogfighting and it was easily beating the later Mach 2 fighters if they made the error to begin a dogfight instead of using energy tactics. The Gnat's weapons system was quite good for the dogfight but it lacked the radar and missiles for the all-weather interception missions.

In the 1950s our air force had started to make plans for new fighters and the candidates were Folland Gnat, Hawker Hunter and Dassault Mystère IV. Maj Lauri Pekuri test flew those three types in June 1956. He evaluated the Gnat as by far the best in climb and manoeuvrability. Also, the price of the Gnat was only half that of the Hawker Hunter. The acquisition agreement on 12 Gnat fighters was done on 17

GN-113 at Oulu in September 1964 (via Jyrki Laukkanan)

October 1956 and also a preliminary plan for the licence manufacture of 20 Gnats by Valmet was agreed on 28 February 1957 (but later abandoned). The first two Gnats, GN-101 and GN-102, landed at Luonetjärvi Air Force Base on 30 July 1958. On 26 August 1958 GN-102 was damaged beyond repair in the landing accident which was caused by a design error in the tailplane/Hobson control system. The control system was repaired by several modifications and the lost plane was replaced with a test plane of the RAF which was purchased at half-price. It got the marking GN-113 and was modified with a Vinten nose camera for reconnaissance missions.

The Gnat was the first fighter in Finland which could in level flight exceed the speed of 1,000km/h (540 knots) and it was very popular with pilots because of its agility and climb performance. One pilot died in a take-off accident because of trimming error. For technical personnel Gnat caused a lot of extra work because of many modifications. Our air force had 13 Gnats with markings GN 101-113 during 1958–1972. The last flight was flown on 24 October 1972. Some memories of the Gnat come back when flying our current jet trainer BAE Hawk Mk.51. It also has quite sharp teeth in the dogfight.

My last duty was air force commander and in 1992 I got the 'once in a lifetime' mission to decide the type of our new fighter after an extensive and detailed competition. I selected F-18 C/D Hornet and it says something about the Gnat that after 6,300 flight hours and 72 aircraft types (including sailplanes and civilian aircraft) the two fighters which come first in my mind are the Gnat and Hornet.

CHAPTER 6

THE GNAT FIGHTER IN INDIA

TOM EELES

In much the same way as Finland, India showed great interest in the Gnat fighter and in September 1956 signed a contract with Folland for the licence production of the aircraft and its Orpheus turbojet in India. The first 13 aircraft for the Indian Air Force were assembled by Folland in their factory at Hamble, in Hampshire. There followed sub-assemblies and partly completed aircraft built in England until Hindustan Aircraft took over, first, final assembly, then full aircraft production. The first flight of an Indian Air Force Gnat took place in England on 11 January 1958. It was then air freighted to India in a Fairchild Packet transport and accepted by the Indian Air Force on 30 January 1958. The first Indian Air Force squadron, No. 23, converted from Vampires to Gnats on 18 March 1960, using six Gnats built by Folland. The last Gnat built in India was delivered on 31 January 1974.

An artist's impression of a Gnat shooting down a Sabre during the Battle of Boyra in 1971.

Just as the Finns had discovered, the Indian Air Force found out quickly that the fighter was an extremely difficult aircraft to handle in the early stages of training. The Indian Air Force did not acquire a trainer version, but it did have the Hawker Hunter in service which had a broadly similar performance. Trainee Gnat pilots were selected from Hunter squadrons and flew dual checks in Hunter trainers before being released on to the Gnat. The Gnat fighter never had the trim datum-shift system fitted to the RAF's trainer version, so tyro pilots found that, as the Gnat accelerated rapidly after take-off, the extreme nose-up change of trim that occurred on landing-gear retraction was very difficult to control until experience was gained. However, once confidence was achieved, pilots exploited the agility of the tiny fighter to the maximum.

It was not long before the Indian Air Force Gnats were involved in live combat. During the 1965 conflict with Pakistan, Gnats were credited with having shot down seven Pakistani Sabres. Unfortunately, one Gnat, flown by Sqn Ldr Brij Pal Singh Sikand, suffered total electrical failure, became separated from the remainder of his formation and forced-landed at an abandoned Pakistani airfield. The Gnat was captured by the Pakistanis, along with the pilot, and it is displayed today in the Pakistan Air Force Museum as a war trophy. The Indian Gnat squadrons saw action again in the war against Pakistan of 1971. The most notable action was the Battle of Boyra over what is now Bangladesh. The Indian Air Force Gnats shot down two Pakistani Sabres and badly damaged another. Another notable air combat took place over Srinagar where an Indian pilot held his own against six Sabres shooting down two in the process, before being shot down himself. He was awarded India's highest gallantry award posthumously. The Gnat proved to be a frustrating opponent to the larger, heavier Sabre, often considered to be the best dogfighter of that era. The Gnat pilots made best use of the vertical in combat, where the Sabre was a disadvantage. Being so small it was difficult to see, and its light weight gave it great agility. The Indians soon bestowed the name 'Sabre Slayer' on their diminutive fighters.

The Indian Air Force was impressed by the aircraft's performance in these two wars but, just as the Finns had discovered, it had many unresolved technical issues. The hydraulics were unreliable, the guns often failed in flight and the longitudinal control system left much to be desired. The Gnat was also always short of fuel. To address these issues, the Indian Air Force issued a requirement for an improved Gnat in 1972, initially to be optimised as an interceptor but then expanding to include ground-attack missions. This became known as the Ajeet, meaning Unconquerable.

THE HAL AJEET

Following the issue of the Indian Air Force's requirement for an improved version of the Gnat, the Hindustan Aircraft Limited (HAL) design bureau completed in 1974 the design of a Mk. 2 version of the Gnat known as Ajeet. This version of the aircraft had better performance characteristics and equipment, including improved communications and navigation systems, more reliable longitudinal control, and increased combat capability. The last-named characteristic was achieved by a re-designed fuel system, dispensing with the underwing drop tanks in favour of integral wing tanks, so permitting additional underwing armament to be carried. The last two Gnat Mk. 1 aircraft on HAL's production line were converted as prototypes for the Ajeet. The first of these was flown on 5 March 1975 and the second on 5 November 1975. First flight of a production Ajeet was made on 30 September 1976. Armament consisted of two 30mm Aden cannon in the intake fairings (as in the Gnat), and four underwing pylons that could carry bombs, rockets or drop tanks on the outer pylons. A two-seat trainer version was also developed but never entered service. HAL built a total of 175 Gnats, and 89 Ajeets, production ceasing in 1991.

The Ajeet.

HOW I (ALMOST) MISSED THE WAR
SUBRAMANIAM RAGHAVENDRAN

Subramaniam Raghavendran

I had commanded No. 23 Squadron from April 1959 till end of 1961. During that time we had converted onto the transonic Gnat aircraft from the subsonic Vampire and the squadron had earned a reputation as a highly professional one which had learned to fully exploit the amazing performance of the Gnat in climb, manoeuvrability and very small profile. We had won the front gun trophy in the annual armament meet, much to everybody's surprise, including our own! The Gnat is a very jumpy aircraft, far from a steady platform like the Hunter, Vampire and Toofani [Dassault Ouragan]. But we managed to shock everybody. The only other nation to use the Gnat in the fighter role was Finland, which had a squadron of it for a short time. I was posted as one of the staff officers in the then only operational command in the Indian Air Force, appropriately called Operational Command. I was in charge of the operational training of the fighters in the command. My life there deserves another story.

In 1963, I got an opportunity to go to Iraq as a flying instructor for two years. When that tenure ended, in their usual services way, the air force didn't tell me where I was posted until I had left foreign shores. I landed in Bombay, as it was then, and managed to get a call through to Wg Cdr J. B. Lal, the P1 in Air Headquarters (officer in charge of posting of officers up to the rank of wing commander) and asked him where I was posted. Wg Cdr Lal nonchalantly told me that I was posted to Ambala to command No. 23 Squadron again, after a break of four years.

I had left the squadron in Ambala in 1961, having commanded it as a squadron leader. The rank of the CO of operational squadrons in the IAF had been upgraded to wing commander. I believe I am the only person to have commanded the same squadron twice. This was in late July 1965.

Having taken over command, from Wg Cdr Bhupinder 'Bhindi' Singh, I left on 45 days' leave to collect my wife and second daughter from Bombay, where they were arriving from abroad and to bring our first daughter from Madras, where she had been sent a few months earlier to get into the school system. I had flown a couple of sorties on the Gnat before I left but not any operational training sorties, as I wanted to get back from leave and do some serious flying.

The political situation with Pakistan, when I left Ambala, seemed OK but started to deteriorate by the day almost immediately. I was reading about it in the newspapers that Pakistan had made incursions in the Akhnur sector. Then I read that four Vampire aircraft that had been on a mission to support the army in that area had been shot down. I knew my leave was about to be over and sure enough the recall telegram reached me two weeks after my leave started. I rushed back with my wife and second daughter. We had no house as yet and so I got some accommodation in the Sirhind Club.

During the short time I was away, a flight from my squadron under Sqn Ldr (later Air Marshal) B. S. Sikand had been sent to Halwara first and then on to Pathankot in a matter of days. This was in response to the four Vampires having been shot down by the Pakistani Air Force. Some pilots, including Sqn Ldr (later Air Marshal) Johnny Greene and others, from the other Gnat squadron, which was not yet fully operational had been sent along also. Open war had not been declared but by the time I returned, two Sabres had been shot down in the Akhnur sector by Sqn Ldr (later Wing Commander) Trevor Keelor, and Flt Lt (later Air Commodore) V. S. 'Pat' Pathania from my squadron. About the day I arrived, I think, Sikand and his formation had gone on a sweep and got separated. Sikand got lost and taking Pasrur airfield in Pakistan (just across the border) to be one of our disused airfields, made a landing there and got captured by the Pakistanis. Enough to make one's head whirl.

I had to join my squadron in Pathankot immediately and take the lead, but I hadn't done any combat training in the Gnat nor used the gun sight for four years. And we were going to fight for real and not make-believe. I quickly did a couple of sorties, practising pulling high 'g' but there was nobody to interact with. Except for Rozario, who had just joined the squadron and had not yet started flying the Gnat, there was nobody in my squadron left behind, with whom I could practice combat. Also, all training missions were prohibited, to conserve the hours for operations. Most important of all, if I told the station commander that I needed to do some training flying with some pilots available in the other Gnat squadron on the base, he would promptly decide that this was not the place or that there was insufficient time to undertake so many training sorties to get back my skills. He would, in all likelihood, tell command and air headquarters that I should be taken off command. I was not about to take that chance. Fighter pilots train all their lives to be able to fly in a war, or better still, lead a squadron in war and I was not going to miss this one.

So, off I went to Pathankot to fight a war. But the Gnat was an amazing aircraft. As people will tell you, pilots who were average would come to the Gnat squadrons and go out as above the average because the aircraft made you more alert and brought out the best in you to exploit its capabilities fully. Senior pilots who used to be sceptical about our tales of performance and combat manoeuvring changed their mind when they flew the Gnat. One was my good friend Omi Taneja who flew it later on and told me: "Rags, what you said about the Gnat was true. It took me some time to catch my breath after take-off!"

I had more hours on the Gnat and other fighters than most people. The couple of sorties in the Gnat that I managed to get in before going to Pathankot, with 'g' suit on and pulling 8g brought back most of my confidence. The pressure of the 'g' suit on the abdomen and the legs made me feel that I was back in full control. Also I had not been off flying altogether. I had been instructing the previous two years on Vampire and Jet Provost aircraft to trainee pilots and keeping up my flying skills. I quickly recapped the sighting system and the gun-firing system, including putting the 'gun dip' switch 'on' during an operational mission. This was a switch you must put on above a certain height if you were to fire the guns. The guns were located in the lip of the air intakes of the engine and if the engine was operating at high power, it would surge and pack up when the turbulence from the shells leaving the barrels affected the airflow. To prevent this, the engine was automatically throttled back as the guns fired.

So, when I arrived in Pathankot, I was reasonably confident but apprehensive. I could not afford to fail in performance or professionalism. I could not indicate any lack of resoluteness in tone or body language that I felt that I was not equal to the task. If I failed in performance, I would die, and if I failed in professionalism as a combat leader, my squadron would fail.

I realised how true it was when some wise person said that an individual who does not know fear is not courageous, but one who has known fear and gone ahead to perform up to his full capabilities in battle is the courageous one. I certainly needed it. Nobody was aware of the odds that I was working against. My parent base commander, Gp Capt David Bouche, was out of the loop and it didn't strike him that I hadn't had a chance to train; and the base commander at Pathankot took it for granted that I was 'fully in the groove'. My only fear was that I may not perform as well as I was capable of, due to being out of practice. There was a Mystère squadron commander who was not up to the task and was removed after a few days of war.

One of the supreme imperatives of combat flying is that you must have utmost faith in the capabilities of your wingman and trust that you would look out for each other. This is where the term 'guarding your tail' was coined. I had not flown with anybody in the squadron and the only person who had been in the squadron during my previous tenure was Flt Lt 'Pat' Pathania. He had been a young but dependable flying officer when I had left the squadron and was now a senior flight lieutenant and designated leader of elements in his own rights. But I told him that whenever I flew on a mission, he was to be my No. 2. This was to be only on missions across the border, not on the endless combat air patrols that we flew over the airfield after 5 September 1965, when Pakistan Air Force Sabres attacked Pathankot.

Our job was twofold. One was the CAP missions, and the other was to escort the ground-attack fighters and the Canberra bombers, when they carried out daytime raids on Pakistan. All the escorting that we did was to targets other than airfields, army formations or targets like railway yards etc. One reason that we didn't escort the fighters to airfields was that we didn't have the range to accompany them that far at low level. The Canberras attacked the airfields by night, anyway. The two Mystère squadrons (Nos. 3 and 31) had the benefit of my squadron to escort their missions but the squadrons operating from Adampur didn't have this luxury until later in the war.

The Hunter squadrons went out from Ambala unescorted because the Hunter was considered capable of looking after itself. It was not too widely known that the Hunter could manoeuvre as well as the Gnat, if it was 'clean' – that is without drop tanks and bombs. If the pilot was to use 'two notches' of flaps – 15 degrees, it was unbeatable. But the squadrons never trained for this kind of combat and all training was done with tanks on. The standard call from the leader of any formation, Hunters or otherwise, when enemy fighters are sighted should have been 'drop stores' and take on the opposition. The corollary to it is that if you have started high 'g' manoeuvre, the tanks and bombs may not jettison as the load on the holding clamps would prevent them from opening to release the stores. I believe that many of the Hunters that we lost during the war were manoeuvring with their tanks on. Without doubt Pakistani fighters would have been their ORP aircraft in 'clean' configuration. We lost some very good, senior Hunter pilots in the war.

The CAP missions were no great problem. We would be on a roster and go round and round the airfield, on either side, covering each other and looking around, getting cricks in the neck, reversing the orbits to give relief to the muscles on the other side. We also expected to get warning from our ground observers, radars and lookouts in the air traffic tower. It is unfortunate that we didn't start this until after the PAF strike.

The missions across the border escorting the fighters and Canberras were a different matter. We expected to meet opposition. The success of the mission and the survival of the escorted aircraft was our responsibility. We had to think of the performance of the Sabres and Starfighters that Pakistan had. The Starfighters were supersonic, and we were only transonic, in a dive. The Sabres and Starfighters could carry Sidewinder air-to-air missiles. We discussed all this amongst ourselves and even talked to the MiG-21 squadron commander, Wg Cdr (later Air Marshal) Malcolm 'Mally' Wollen, since they also carried comparable missiles.

Two things were clear to us. We were supremely confident of our ability to outmanoeuvre both types of aircraft. The Sidewinder missile could not be launched if the 'g' force at the time of launch was 2g or more. Also, it was very erratic close to the ground, say less than 2,000ft and when the target was in line with the sun. So, we worked out our tactics. As we reached the target area, the escort Gnats would get into a tight spiral at about 4,000–5,000ft and look out for the enemy aircraft. We would fly at the throttle setting that we had arrived on target with, to keep up with the Mystères at 420 knots or increase to that setting when we arrived with the Canberras. We were not worried about what the strike aircraft were doing and concentrated on *not* getting hypnotised by their weapon delivery etc. Sometimes we did take a quick glance to see tanks being attacked etc. Since our strike fighters from Pathankot were never assigned to an airfield attack, we did not get any 'guaranteed' opposition. But we scanned all-round the target for any enemy aircraft approaching as well as above. The intention was that, if any enemy aircraft was spotted, the strike formation would be alerted to leave the target area and we would take them on.

Most missions were escorted by two Gnats and we would plan to be on opposite sides of the orbit so that we could cover each other's tails. Our tactics would be to take on the enemy aircraft in close combat. If one of us was in a tight spot, the manoeuvre to escape any missile-armed enemy was to point the nose towards the sun and open full throttle. No aircraft could keep up with the Gnat climb, with a power/weight ratio of 1. Even if they stuck behind for a short time, the missile would not be able to track the small exhaust of the Gnat with the sun ahead. The alternative was to dive down to low level where the missile, again, would not be effective. Unfortunately for our tally of Sabres, we didn't meet enemy aircraft on any missions, except for 'Kala' Sandhu towards the end of the war. This was especially so in my case – there went my hopes of decorations.

Many Mystère and Canberra squadron commanders got an MVC or VrC award essentially for courageous leadership on missions during the war, but we Gnat pilots had to shoot down a Sabre to get an award. The only exception was Sqn Ldr Johnny Greene, whom I personally recommended for a VrC for continuous good leadership while attached to my squadron and I fought with the powers that be to accept this exception. I believe his is the only case of a VrC being awarded other than for a specific act of bravery. But whenever Gnats met Sabres, the latter always got shot down or ran away – throughout the war not one Gnat from my squadron was shot down but many Sabres were. In later years when our officers met Pakistani officers abroad, on courses or at air show events, they all admitted that they were terrified of the Gnat.

We had some exciting times during the escort work. The only fighters that we escorted were the Mystères from Pathankot. They flew really, really low, especially while coming from the targets. We were concentrating on pivoting our heads all round to look for enemy aircraft. We had no chance of navigating by map. Going to the target was not so bad as never was any formation bounced on the way in. Since we were swivelling our heads on top, the Mystères had to tell us when they left the target, and we would latch on to them and escort them back. But we had far less fuel capacity than them and could not fly all the way back at treetop level. Once we were safe inside our territory, we had to pull up to a height where our fuel consumption would reduce, and we could get back home. The agreement was that the formation leader would tell us how far and what direction base was. It didn't always work out, either the formation leader was not sure of his position, having exited in a hurry from the target on a heading other than planned or when we left the Mystère formation, the visibility from higher up, due to the haze, would prevent us from identifying known landmarks. A number of times we landed back with no fuel even for an overshoot! Thank God we had no losses due to fuel starvation, other than Sikand's aircraft.

But it wasn't always a routine matter of taking off with the Mystères from Pathankot. More often than not, they would go to Ambala after their mission. Then, we would have to rendezvous with them on their way to the target for their mission next day. This took quite a bit of doing. The timing had to be perfect as nobody had the fuel to orbit around and join up. When the command tried it the first time, the orders came to us to be at a specific landmark at a precise time, to the second. We were there precisely, sighted them well in time and were turning to join them when one of the pilots noticed us and excitedly started shouting "Bogeys, bogeys to starboard". Command had forgotten to tell them that they were getting escorts. We quickly told them, fortunately we were on the right channel, that we were the escorts. There was great relief in the voice of the Mystère leader when he said "Roger, Roger". Next time onwards, we arranged the rendezvous between the squadrons and it worked out well.

With the Canberras the problem was different, especially with the bombers and not so much the intruders. Their idea of low flying was about 1,000 feet! We had to be like shepherd dogs, breaking R/T silence and literally screaming at them to 'get down'. This was especially so while returning from a mission, we could never be sure that enemy aircraft were not following us and they would easily spot the large bombers when they were not really low.

We had a natty way of joining up with them for escorting. They would give a coded call two minutes before reaching overhead Pathankot. We would scramble from ORP and lift off just in time to come up on either side of the formation as they flew past the runway.

Our endless CAP sorties from half an hour before dawn to half an hour after dusk were painful. Both physically and mentally. Our endurance time was about one hour and so you can work out how much effort went into it. Not once were we attacked but we were at high tension throughout. After half the sortie was over, we would reverse the orbit to give relief to our neck and arm muscles and to an extent our butts! We found a new problem while doing the CAPs. The Hobson unit that controlled the movements of the slab tail would freeze if we kept on orbiting with more or less the same position of the elevator. We had been everlastingly having a problem with this unit over the years and had recently lost some aircraft due to its malfunction. So, when we found this problem, all we could do was to periodically porpoise the aircraft to circulate the hydraulics.

There was a mission when Sqn Ldr Johnny Greene and Flt Lt Pat Pathania had Sabres in their sights, but both their guns jammed and would not fire. So we worked out a system whereby the first two CAP missions would fire a few rounds into the Chakki River, along the perimeter of the airfield, to 'clear' the guns. Then all the aircraft likely to get into combat would be cleared for the day. It was war and who bothered about getting permissions and checking out things. We learned only after the operations that we had seriously interfered with the life of people in the vicinity. The river bed was the open-air lavatory for hundreds of people in the area. Can you imagine 30mm explosive cannon shells going off near you when you are contemplating the skies above and relieving yourself? I am not sure whether it helped in their 'evacuation' or not, but they certainly got out of the area in a hurry. Thank God we didn't cause any casualties. Of course, we had always fired the guns in the open and sandy part of the riverbed and would have seen if anybody had been there. Had we opened fire indiscriminately in the brush along the banks, the results would have been catastrophic.

Though we wanted to carry out 'sweeps' and bring up Pakistani fighters and take them on, we could not as we were told to keep all the aircraft for ORP duties, CAPs and escort missions. As the war progressed, even the escort missions became fewer and fewer. So, endless combat air patrols over the base became the main task. The war was over soon, and the Tashkent Declaration followed where the Indian government gave back Haji Pir Pass, an incredibly stupid thing to do.

It was decided that Pathankot would be the permanent base for No. 23 Squadron. It seems to have been my fate, ever since my marriage that I only had to go to a unit and it was moved elsewhere. No. 23 had peacefully existed in Ambala, where I left it four years earlier, after moving it to Palam and Ambala. But the moment I joined it again, not only does it move but gets into a war!

The squadron had one more historical event to undertake before I handed it over. In 1966, the government decided that it would no longer adopt the unwritten principle it had followed of not operating any fighter aircraft from the Srinagar Valley. So, we were the first fighter squadron, after 1948, to be sent to Srinagar to show the flag for a few weeks. That was in 1966 and we had a very enjoyable time, just flying around, no ORP, and picnicking. The outing lasted three weeks.

By the middle of 1967, I was getting flying fatigue. I had done 17 years of non-stop flying, had more hours than most people of my age and seniority, had 21 postings/moves, and had been given only 13 months of leave in all this time. On the two occasions that I had asked for and been granted 45 days leave, I was recalled within two/three weeks. The first time was when I went to get married, and I was recalled after three weeks because the squadron (No. 4) had been ordered to move to the boondocks of Adampur. The second time was when I had just returned from Iraq and had gone to collect my family (who were arriving later) from Mumbai, and to meet my mother and other family members whom we had not seen for two years. I was recalled in two weeks to go to war.

THE LAST DOGFIGHT OVER SRINAGAR
G.M. DAVID

It had been a quiet day. The daily raid had not taken place and the sun was low on the horizon. A dusk scramble was ordered, and Sqn Ldr V. S. Pathania VrC and Flt Lt B. N. Bopaiyya got airborne to set up a CAP overhead. Since it continued to be quiet and the sun was setting they were ordered to burn fuel and land. At this point four Sabres were spotted high over the field rolling in for a steep glide attack along Runway 31. Pathania, who was over Runway 13 dumbbell, tightened his turn into the attackers and established contact with the Nos. 1 and 2 who were established in the dive. The L60 guns who were 'tied', opened fire on their own at all and sundry. Bopaiyya, who was over Runway 31 dumbbell, was ordered into a hard turn by Pathania to keep his tail clear and was told that he would be picking up Nos. 3 and 4 sliding into the bombing run below him. Pathania and Bopaiyya establishing contact, dived through the exploding shells and went for their respective targets. Pathania dived through the flak and got on the tail of the No. 2 midway down the runway who promptly threw a hard turn to the left and ducked into the valley south-west of the runway to keep his energy levels high. In the turn after about 270 degrees and facing us at the 31ORP, Pathania got into position less than 200yds behind and he gave a quarter second burst of 30mm cannon.

We saw puffs of smoke from the Sabre who further tightened his turn, jettisoned his drop tanks, and went into an impossibly tight turn. Pathania did a yo-yo, got into position a second time and gave a second short burst. His guns jammed. Throughout all this, the L60s were firing away merrily at Pathania, Bopaiyya and the Sabres. Bopaiyya in the meantime who latched onto the No. 4 attacker had dived through the L60 fire and was last seen pursuing him towards the south-west. Pathania coolly began to give a running commentary on R/T. He said that his guns had jammed and that he would not allow the target to have the fuel to make it back to his base. The Sabre who was by now trailing smoke rolled out towards Pir Panjal to get away. Pathania slipped out from his six o'clock position and slid out to his right. The Sabre, on spotting him, promptly threw a hard turn into Pathania to dislodge him from his tail and rolled out towards the west. Pathania kept him doing hard turns for some time till he himself began to run low on fuel, when he broke off. Pathania reported that the Sabre was smoking heavily and unable to maintain speed. Bopaiyya who was unable catch up with the receding

An artist's impression of a F-86 Sabre being shot at by a Gnat.

Sabres, also returned overhead low on fuel. The army subsequently reported an aircraft crossing Pir Panjal smoking heavily. We are certain he must have ejected after crossing into Pakistan.

One funny bit through all this was that the No. 4 Sabre, who probably had his armament switch selection wrong, dropped his tanks instead of his bombs. Realising his error on pull-out he dropped his bombs in level flight. It was an amazing site as the bombs struck the runway too shallow and skipped. Having the same velocity as the mother aircraft we saw them lazily rise and begin to catch up with it. They curved up to about 100 feet below him before starting a lazy descent. They lobbed outside the airfield boundary and exploded. We don't think that guy ever realised how close his own bombs had come to him.

Now came the mother of all recoveries. The two Gnats had to be got back and the runway had been hit. Wg Cdr Raina our CO, cool as ever, inspected the runway, plotting the craters. He instructed the aircraft to land on the left lane, shift to the right lane 1,200yds up the runway and then shift back to the left lane after 2,000yds. It was dusk by now. There was no time to lay the goose necks. He just parked his jeep abeam the first crater and to indicate the beginning of the clear patch for touchdown. He talked them down coolly on the mobile R/T set to a safe touchdown. Pathania and Bopaiyya both switched lanes as briefed and landed safely on a cratered runway in semi-darkness without landing or runway lighting.

A lot has been said about the Gnat Mk. 1. But little has been reported about the only Param vir Chakra (VrC) which was awarded to Fg Off N. S. Sekhon flying a Gnat in Srinagar on 14 December 1971. I was posted to No. 18 Squadron and we were on detachment to Srinagar during the 1971 War with Pakistan (Operation Cactus Lily). On that cold winter morning I was with Fg Off Y. Singh on CAP duty at the underground base ops. The following is the sequence of events that took place on 14 December 1971 at dawn.

The pilots on two minutes readiness of Standby 2 as it is known in air defence parlance were Flt Lt G. S. Ghumman 'G Man' and Fg Off N. S. Sekhon 'Brother'. The air raid took place at dawn. There was no warning of the impending attack. The first warning came from the ops posted in the near vicinity of the airfield. It was the ops in Awantipura airfield who warned of the attack. The attackers came in from the south-east doing a run in towards Wular Lake along Runway 31, with the escape route towards Baramula with a 30-degree left course correction.

We were in the station base ops dugout when the warning came. The station commander Gp Capt Sanadi, the OC Flying Wg Cdr Oberoi and we were present along with the rest of the complement when the attack took place. The scramble was ordered and we rushed out from the underground to the CAP control which was right above the dugout. The ops ATC was a few paces ahead. As Yogi (Fg Off Y. Singh) and I got into position in the CAP control all hell had broken loose. The L60 ack ack batteries had opened fire in an easterly direction. The L60 Regiment No. 2 I/c was with us. We could hear the sound of the Gnats on the ORP starting up. We yelled to have the scramble cancelled since we had spotted the attackers in line astern formation aligning themselves with Runway 31 to do a medium-glide bombing attack from about 10,000ft above. We again tried to have the scramble cancelled but due to communication failure, it was not possible. The scrambling Gnats were on ATC frequency and, the CAP control was on Air Force Guard frequency. The duty ATC officer had not reached his position and there was no way to cancel the scramble even though it had been ordered by the station commander. Fg Off Y. Singh tried to get to the ATC (which was in front) to cancel the scramble.

G Man and Sekhon had started up, carried out their RT checks, moved out of the blast pens and were ready to roll. They could not be contacted as Y. Singh had not yet managed to get into the ops ATC and grab the microphone. Precious seconds were ticking by. The attackers were now identified as four F-86 Sabres and the Nos. 1 and 2 were beginning to roll into the dive with Nos. 3 and 4 in trail all spaced about 2,000yds behind each other. We could only watch this as spectators. G Man after calling the ATC a few times decided to roll. The scramble was on. The Sabres were in the dive. Brother began his roll 20 seconds behind as per the procedure. The No. 1 Sabre was close to his bomb-release point. Sekhon was 1,000yds down the runway when the leader's bombs struck it just ahead of the ORP. Sekhon was still on the ground on his take-off run-in line with us 2,000yds up when the second set of bombs from the No. 2 Sabre impacted 1,000yds behind him on the runway. At this time the No. 1 had flown over Sekhon as he was unsticking and hitting his gear up. G Man in the meantime, as per the procedure, had unstuck, done a hard turn left and ducked into the valley immediately south of the airfield to gain speed and pull up to get into opposite circles to Sekhon to set up CAP as quickly as possible. The visibility was very poor and less than 1,000 yards in shallow fog and haze and turning into the sun did not help G Man.

By this time Sekhon was airborne and with the gear going up when the No. 2 Sabre whizzed over his head. Sekhon was 3,000yds up the runway and accelerating when No. 3's bombs hit 100yds behind him. His RT call at this time was, "I have two b******s ahead of me I will not let them go". He gave chase to these two Sabres. G Man in the meantime had changed over to the CAP frequency and was on the east end of the field. The Nos. 3 and 4 attackers were in the getaway mode past the other end of the runway and fast receding at max getaway speed. There was no way G Man could have established visual contact. In fact, by this time the

Nos. 1 and 2 Sabres on realising that they had a Gnat on their tails had gone into a hard right turn about 10nms north-east of the field with Sekhon holding the turn. The crew on the late shift of 8 a.m. were on their way to the airfield when they saw the three aircraft milling around. The bus stopped on the roadside and Flt Lt Manchi Captain who was on that bus saw two Sabres in a hard right turn with one Gnat holding the turn, all 200 yards behind each other. There was a burst of 30mm cannon fire, and he saw the trailing Sabre jettison its tanks and go into a last-ditch kind of manoeuvre. They disappeared behind the treeline.

Back at CAP control G Man was sent in the last seen direction of the combat. From the CAP control all we could see was the occasional glint of aircraft manoeuvring in the distance. The poor visibility prevented G Man from acquiring visual contact with the aircraft in combat. In the meantime, Nos. 3 and 4 Sabres had done a getaway toward the south-west ranges of Pir Panjal. From the CAP control we heard a high-speed whine. It was the escorts who had not been spotted by us. Sekhon made his next transmission, "I have one guy in front of me, there is someone getting behind me". We heard one more burst of 30mm cannon fire followed by a long three to four seconds of 0.5-mm machine-gun fire. This was followed by Sekhon's last transmission, "I think I am hit. G Man come". Sekhon's Gnat had been hit and he ejected at low altitude. The parachute opened but had not fully deployed due to the low altitude. His rear fuselage and stabiliser had 37 0.5mm bullet holes in it.

Two things stand out about the man. He was not one given to drinking. But every night he would have one large brandy at the bar and panic that the war was nearly over and the enemy never seemed to be around when he was airborne. The second was that the war would be over before he could shoot one of the raiders. His faith in the Gnat was supreme and he firmly believed that it had the manoeuvre capability to get him out of any situation.

THE ONE THAT GOT AWAY!
MANNA MURDESHWAR

On 4 September 1965 we were gung-ho! Our months of training had been tested and now we had faced our first air battle. Not only had we come out of it unscathed, but we had a war hero amongst us, to boot.

Pathankot was agog with excitement, and we knew we had all hopes and eyes riveted on us as we taxied out for yet another foray. The Gnat had proven its mettle and within just a day we'd began to acquire an 'iconic status'. Enough indeed, to put the swagger into us.

Our 23 Squadron detachment of seven aircraft and seven pilots (the eighth was still 'missing') were ordered to patrol the area and counter any enemy aircraft threatening our objectives. Our leader was Johnny Greene. I was his No. 2. AJS No. 3 and Pat No. 4. We set course for the Chamb–Jaurian Sector in a loose, low-level tactical formation, which Johnny led, barely skimming the treetops.

Mid-way to the battle area, while we were still trailing 'clouds of glory'. I spotted Sabres on our left diabolically attacking our troops with devilish precision. They attacked singly, forming a left-hand circuit pattern like the ones we adopted during practice at the firing ranges. They rained down fire and smoke on our tenuously entrenched troops and spotting their gleeful sport I conveyed their presence to Johnny on the R/T.

Since AJS and Pat were on our right and in a better position to get behind the Sabres, upon instructions they just rolled over us and trailed the malignant Sabre jets. Johnny and I followed suit. From my position, I could see that each of us was behind a Sabre. I had a position of vantage since I had done a high wingover and rolled behind the Sabre that had just pulled up from a dastardly attack. My descending speed helped me to get within 400yds of its tail. With my gunsight 'on' and the 'diamonds pipped' I pulled the trigger. "This was for real, Man!" This was no practice sortie!

Imagine my incredulous frustration when, after firing just one bullet, my gun stopped. "C'mon! C'mon baby, don't give up on me now!" I coaxed. But it had done just that – it had given up. Cursing my luck and scanning the sky for stray Sabres and vainglorious Gnats, I peeled off to base – valiant, vitiated, vulnerable, but not vanquished.

Once on the ground, and subsequent to our debrief, I learnt that although Johnny and AJS had got behind their respective Sabres, their film revealed a high angle of attack which had afforded the Sabres a chance to escape. Pat was the only one who had been fortunate enough to shoot down his targeted Sabre and win himself a VrC! My film was labelled 'exemplary' and I was told to claim the kill since the army had certified they had found a wreckage. "A kill, with only one bullet fired?" It seemed too preposterous even in these permissive booty-bestowing times and I reluctantly let my conscience forgo this 'skull' which I could have added to my belt.

VELU GOOFS UP

P.M. VELANKAR VM

During the 1971 war I was in 22 Squadron, and we were operating from Dumdum. The squadron had been flying detachments and had a major

P. M. Velankar

portion of the unit operating from Dumdum since September–October 1971.

Squadron aircraft crossed the international border to attack various ground targets or as an escort to Hunters for the first time on 4 December 1971. A good number of sorties were carried out by almost all the pilots of the squadron.

I did not cross the border that day but was detailed to carry out CAP sorties over Dumdum. I did three or four sorties with different No. 2s. it was the same story the next day. Even after requesting the flight commander to let me go on a ground-attack sortie, I was informed that the CO did not want to send me across the border. My relations with the CO were not the most cordial. He thought I was a good for nothing useless pilot. On my part the feeling was mutual.

So once again I did four CAP sorties. The same thing happened on the third day as well. Doing CAP sorties every day, for three days, had its effects. Things had become so bad that even after flying was over for the day my head kept snapping and swivelling from left to right as if still looking around for the bogies. It was OK so far as it went but caused a lot of trouble in the evening when I could not put the glass to my lips as my head kept swivelling! For the first couple of sips I had literally to hold it still with my left hand and take a sip from the glass in the right. Things used to improve after a couple of drinks and were back to normal by the time my usual quota was consumed!

On the fourth day, the sun did not rise from the west, but I had a feeling that things would be different. However, on the first sortie, I was again detailed for a CAP. Boondi took a four-aircraft formation for a ground attack on river-borne targets at a placed called Satkhira. The time was around 10.30 or 11.00 when I was told that the CO wanted me. He told me, as I was keen to do a strike sortie, to take a two-aircraft formation to Satkhira and to get airborne as soon as possible. Vinod Batheja was detailed as No. 2. Apparently I had my flight commander to thank.

This being my first-ever sortie in enemy territory and as a leader to boot, I was extremely excited and rushed to prepare the map and the normal planning for the sortie. I wanted desperately for everything to go smoothly with no f***-ups! As usual when you are in a hurry, things are out of reach. A frantic search for the map, the pencils, protractor and ruler was yielding slow results. In between people were telling me to hurry up as the CO was enquiring whether I had got airborne or was still on the ground. Finally, I found all I needed and I had just drawn the line joining Dumdum to Satkhira and measured the distance which appeared neither too little nor too much. Calculation of distances, timings and fuel consumption were next in line and still to be done when I was told that if I was not airborne within 15 minutes some other targets were planned and then I could forget about the strike and keep swivelling my neck over Dumdum airfield.

All this while Batheja was hovering around and like a good No. 2 was neither a hindrance nor help. But now he piped up: "Velu, it is fine I have been to that place in the morning with Boondi and everything was OK, no sweat." So I replied, "OK Bats let us go, briefing as per the SOP" and we proceeded to the aircraft.

It took less than 18 minutes between my being told to go for the sortie and setting off for the aircraft. Start-up, taxi and take-off and reaching the target at a height of 800 to 1,000ft was smooth and normal. The weather was fine with good visibility and thin 8/8 cloud cover at medium altitude. Our targets were ships/mechanised boats plying on the river in the Satkhira area. There were quite a few of them and fairly big in size too. I told Bats to get in position and go for the targets.

One has trained every day to take on the enemy, that and only that is the purpose of all your training, hard work, in fact of your life and very existence. Very few of us are lucky to really achieve and fulfil to any degree the raison d'etre of their being. I feel we were two of those lucky few. No words can describe how one really feels at times like this.

We carried out two passes. I asked for a fuel check and requested Bats to join up for our return. He gave me the fuel state, just borderline, but also said, "Velu there, there at two o'clock about three miles is a big ship". I made contact, could not resist such a good target, and agreed for just one more pass. We got carried away and did one more pass. The ship was doomed. We set course for Dumdum at 500 to 1,000ft. I saw the fuel state and started easing up. We climbed up to 5,000 then 6,000ft and levelled out as there was thin cloud layer above that. Now Bats gave a call of Bingo. I was taken aback; we were still some distance from the base. I checked with the SU if they had joy on us and to give us pigeons to base. They had joy and we got the pigeons. We were a few miles from Jessore airfield. But I did not feel happy as Bats was Bingo minus and wanted to land at Jessore. I told him to shut up and maintain position and we started climbing. We got through the cloud layer and kept climbing to level out at around 16,000ft as there was another cloud layer above that and much darker and thicker. We set the rpm for range flying and continued towards base. By now Bats was yelling about his fuel state and was wanting to land at Jessore or he may not reach the base. I told him to shut up once again and to maintain his position. I was getting worried, I thought, if I did not take back the formation with my No. 2 intact, I would never again cross the border. In fact, the way things were between me and the powers that be, I might not even fly again.

I called up the SU and reported: "This is Vodka 1, steering so and so, at FL 160, estimate so and so miles from base." SU promptly came on and said: "Vodka 1 have joy on you your pigeon's so and so". The pigeons tallied with my report and gave me a little bit of relief. I recognised the voice of the controller, it was Bagchi, a thorough professional and a very good controller. I dropped all the formalities and said, "Bagchi, this is Velu, my No. 2 is low on fuel, we are on top of 8/8s and have no contact with the ground, can you please take us and position us so that we can make a direct approach and landing and also commence descent in such a way that the whole thing is done at the least power setting, a sort of GCA if you can do that." Being a professional he came back promptly and told me to stand by. Within no time he started controlling us giving new courses to steer. We continued, started our descent when told to do so, entered cloud and carried on following directions till such time he said, "Runway should be in front of you, report contact". I reported contact thanked Bagchi and told him we were changing over to tower. Bagchi had done a wonderful job.

Runway in use and touchdown point was just ahead, and we were ideally positioned for direct approach and landing. And all this while once we had commenced descent, we were flying at the least power setting. (Mercifully except for asking if he could eject once or twice Bats had kept silent, which was good as it did not disturb my prayers!) I confirmed that Bats had the runway in contact, told him to land first and went round after he had rounded off and was about to touch down. By now for the last minute or so my own Bingo light was also on. I heard Bats asking if he could switch off at the end of the runway. I told him *not* to do anything of the kind and switch off only after reaching the dispersal. To this day I am grateful to Bagchi for bringing us back safely, which may not have been possible considering the s*** we were in.

After landing on the tarmac I saw that Bats was just getting out of the aircraft. I switched off, jumped out and briskly caught up with him, nearly catching him by the scruff of the neck and shouted: "Damn it Bats you had said, 'yes, absolutely sure everything ok', "so why the hell did we land up in such s***?"

He said everything was OK except that we had followed a high–low–high profile! The mistake was mine for leading a strike formation without proper planning. I told Bats in a threatening voice if he ever told anyone of the closest shave which we had, I would kill him. I also kept quiet about the whole thing. RS Mehtamour EO later gave me the refuelling figures. I have a feeling that the last few minutes before Bats had reached the tarmac and switched off, his engine was running on fuel fumes *and* my prayers. Since that time I became a firm believer in the power of prayer. Later I carried out quite a few sorties, happily without any f***-ups and to the satisfaction of all.

FIRE WARNING ON TAKE-OFF

This incident took place when I was posted to 22 Squadron. One day I was detailed to carry out an air test on an aircraft after completion of one of the 100 hours servicing cycles from the R&SS (Repair and Servicing Section).

All my checks were normal and everything was expected until I had unstuck and got airborne the fire-warning light came on. Barely off the ground and with aircraft accelerating normally but speed well below 150kts, ejection was not an option. There was also no question of throttling back, checking the wake for smoke etc. The jet pipe temperature (JPT) was within limits.

Writing and reading this takes time but in reality, as soon as I saw the fire-warning light, I had transmitted the emergency and asked the ATC to check if they could see any fire or smoke coming out of my aircraft. As usual, not anticipating such a call from an aircraft that had just unstuck, no one from the ATC including the duty pilot understood the call and I had the mortification to hear the ATC asking me to repeat. I again told them that my fire-warning light was on and to check my aircraft for signs of any fire. What I got back was, "Your transmission not clear, come again". I repeated the call and as everything felt normal, except for the fire-warning light which was shining brightly, informed the ATC that I was turning downwind for an immediate landing. Incidentally, another aircraft had lined up after me and even though now I cannot recollect the identity of that pilot, he was on the ball and was the first one to tell me that there was no smoke or fire visible on the aircraft. A couple of other aircraft were in the circuit and by now the ATC also confirmed that it appeared that there was no fire and that no smoke was visible on my aircraft.

A 'tear-ass' curved approach and normal landing was carried out. The warning light was on even during the landing run, it was again confirmed by the ATC and a couple of aircraft that everything seemed normal and there was no sign of any fire. So I taxied back to the R&SS. Seeing the aircraft returning so fast, the EO, Flt Lt R. S. Mehata, others and SNCOs came to receive the aircraft. I called the engine fellow and frantically pointed to the warning light which was still burning brightly. There was no change in his expression as he nodded his head and gave me the thumbs-up sign. Now, what did he mean by giving me thumbs up – the bloody fire-warning light was on, had scared the s*** out of me and here was this fellow nonchalantly giving me thumbs up! I scowled and again frantically pointed to the brightly burning light. The process of nodding his head giving me a thumbs-up sign was repeated but this time with the sign for me to cut the engine. The whole thing had taken place in just about 45 seconds. It was definitely less than a minute in any case. By now the flight commander, the CO and the whole of the squadron pilots knew of the emergency and my returning to the R&SS. I entered the snag in F-700, and explained the same to the engine tradesmen. I walked back to the squadron, expecting a pat on the back and a 'good show' for keeping a cool head and professional handling of the emergency from the flight commander.

However, I found that all the squadron pilots were in the crewroom waiting to be addressed by the squadron commander. I was unceremoniously ushered into the room and told to find a seat. At this point in time, I cannot recollect the exact words of the CO, but the substance of it was that I was a bloody fool who did not know my aircraft. As everyone knows the fuel tanks are virtually wrapped around the engine and in case of any fire, because of the construction, before anyone can say 'Jack Robinson', the aircraft would simply *explode*. The wisest thing to do in the Gnat, in case of the fire-warning light coming on was to *eject* immediately or else one was a goner in an exploding aircraft. I was very lucky and must thank god for being alive to continue my rum drinking days etc. The talk continued in a similar vein for quite some time. It was solid bamboo and I was suitably chastised.

Within a month or so of this incident, Vinod Batheja while flying on a medium- to high-level sortie, reported fire-warning light on and ejected. Every Gnat pilot will own up to missing a couple of heartbeats looking at the shining fire-warning lights due to the sun's reflection thinking that it was on. To this day I believe that but for that particular talk, he would have taken proper emergency action and landed back safely.

R. M. 'Mike' Oliver, Folland test pilot writes:

I was interested to read Velankar's account of his experience. Fire-warning systems are capable of tormenting innocent pilots in a quite shameless manner. On an early flight in the first Gnat trainer, I fell victim to their macabre sense of humour. On the trainer, the system was different from that on the fighter in that there were primary and secondary warning panels. If a primary warning was triggered, alarm bells sounded in the headset and warning lights on the top of the coaming started flashing. You then had to look at the primary warning panel to see which of the fire, hyd, oxy etc. words were lit up. On this early flight of the aircraft, I was at about 20,000 feet when the dangers, as we called them, sounded and the warning lights started flashing. I looked at the primary warning panel and found nothing was showing, so I checked everything, cancelled the clangers, called air traffic and headed for Chilbolton. A couple of minutes later the clangers sounded again, but still nothing on the panel, so once more I checked everything and cancelled them. Just when Chilbolton came in sight they sounded yet again, and this time 'fire' was illuminated on the primary warning panel. I informed air traffic, told them to keep their binoculars on me and landed safely. When I went down to flight development to debrief, I heard giggles coming from the film-reading girls and discovered that they had just come to the point on the voice recorder when I exclaimed in a rather agitated voice, "Oh no, bloody hell, not fire, please couldn't you make it something else".

HOW NOT TO IMPRESS YOUR GIRLFRIEND

ADI GHANDHI

Adi Ghandhi

I remember one day Matty (later my wife of 50 years) was to come for a visit to the squadron for breakfast, so I decided to show her my prowess by a little beat-up of the airfield. Having gone through what we felt was such intensive training we thought we knew everything, but one learns the hard way, *if* one survives these stupid moments of bravado. Well I was airborne when she arrived and Kelly a course mate took her up to the ATC from where she would see my antics better. I came down in a swoop at high speed for starters and whizzed past the ATC. I was indeed so low that I could see her standing on the parapet outside. This was poor airmanship because when you are at such dangerously low levels you should be concentrating on your height and not your girlfriend on the ground. I guess I was determined to keep her back from her plans to go abroad and had to impress her enough that I meant what I said, how stupid can you be at that age? So, then it was a low run followed by a loop next and since I had not done low-level aeros ever I was quite surprised how close the ground looked when I was vertically down finishing it off. Scared? Yes, but I was not giving up. Silly? Yes, but who realised it at the time.

The ATC and the COO were by now wondering who authorised this beat-up of the airfield, so I was asked to land back. Not yet registering that I was now in serious trouble, I did one last low run this time intending to do a roll near the ATC before peeling off for a circuit and landing. I came in low and fast, but not knowing what to do I was in level flight. I whipped on bank for a fast roll. Yikes, as I reached about 130–150 degrees bank I saw the ground so close that I nearly lost control of my bowels. I whipped the aircraft out of the roll so quickly that I went over the other side and frightened myself again. These low-level aerobatics were not that easy, I realised, because by now my knees were doing a serious imitation of the 'watusi'. My head was spinning, and I had to steady myself with some serious willpower to be able to finish the circuit and land. I taxied back to the dispersal and after switching off I just could not get out of the aircraft.

The ground crew were wondering what the matter was but kept silent. The engineering officer came along and gave me the good news that the CO wanted to see me. This was the summons to my early departure from fighter flying. I managed to get out of the aircraft and on shaky legs walked to the CO's office. Fortunately for me the flight commander was officiating and, as I entered, he saw my face ashen and my legs wobbly and realised I had already punished myself enough. He broke into that wry smile of his and asked me what I thought I was doing. No answer, best policy when in serious trouble. Then a rebuke, "you idiot what you did was suicidal, you nearly killed yourself", again silence. "The next time you want to do something like this please ask and if I feel you are up to it, I will brief you on how to do it", he said, "Now get out of my sight". I did with the greatest of alacrity since I had found my knees again by now, especially knowing that I was not to be thrown out of flying.

I walked into the crewroom still shaky but with this big smile on my face when I saw her standing there. She was impressed but did not like the fact that I had been so dangerously low. The guys were dying to find out what had happened with the flight commander, but they had to wait till I dropped her back at the hospital and came back to the squadron. "What kind of a roll was that?" "Don't even ask me," I said, "the ground appeared so close, I saw my grave". Promptly I was given two or three healthy kicks with the toe end of the flying boots. You see all aircraft tend to barrel a little when you roll. That is why you try and fly at a speed that is as close to your 'zero' angle of attack to minimise the barrel. A point roll needs an artist's brush to keep the nose pointed at the same place on the horizon. I will forever remember that lesson and never ever tried to be smarter than I was, God himself had given me this one chance. So many experienced guys have gone down doing this low-level roll, even test pilots, and where did I get off trying one without even a briefing or any experience at all? A lesson learnt for the rest of my life, but then the air force constantly taught me lessons throughout my career, just maybe not such dangerous ones.

Two other incidents on the Gnat fleet are indicative of the early years of our training and how we were still growing as an air force and in the bargain doing some things that today one could never think of doing without serious consequences. The first one is hilarious but not to the senior officer who went through the experience. The Gnat as you can see is a small aircraft and low slung with even the undercarriages embedded in the fuselage. The cockpit side wall was about four to four and a half feet high and though there was a small ladder to get in our egos forced us to jump up onto the side on our arms and then stick a leg in and get in. Getting out too was similar, just a jump off the side of the cockpit.

We had this senior officer who was a squadron leader then. He was a tall guy around 6" 2' and one would think he may have been able to just put his leg over and get in, but no he couldn't. He was on duty one day and there was a scramble ordered and as usual every pilot tries his hardest to get airborne as fast as he can so that the mission can react to the intruder soonest. This duty meant staying available at the beginning of the runway with all switches ready for the start and the helmet fixed up so that all one had to do was run and get in, fire up the aircraft and shoot off into the sky as ordered. These duties were normally for half a day and started half an hour before sunrise and finished half an hour after sunset.

So a scramble was ordered and he ran hell for leather towards his aircraft, and in his eagerness yanked himself right over the aircraft and down the other side missing the whole cockpit. Hurt, and shaken but resolved he did manage to get airborne soon after a quick run around the aircraft. He came back after the mission hurting somewhat but with a caustic smile on his face as if to say, "OK, OK I know, I know". He did get ribbed about it at the bar later, but it was all in good spirits and of course after imbibing a few too.

The Gnat was a great air defence aircraft because it had a starting cycle of just 50 seconds after the air started blowing. It was an air-blown start that had the turbine rotating before ignition took place. It was therefore one of the fastest aircraft off the ground during a scramble. Most other aircraft took about two to three minutes for the process. In fact the Gnat scramble was slowed down only by the pilot readiness time of strapping himself in and closing the canopy. So one day it happened that a foreign visitor, or was it a team of DAs, was to come and of course post 1965 the Sabre killer was grabbing all the attention.

To impress them on the kind of readiness we could deploy it was decided to give them a demo scramble from the ORP. One of the flight commanders (loved by all the young pilots) was nominated to do the demo. He was all set and the team landed up at the ORP and was told what was about to be demonstrated. So all the visitors looked at this diminutive little package of explosive activity that he was and smiled at him. Then the station commander went and whispered something in his ear, got a perplexed look from the pilot and then a stoic manner while he waited for the scramble order. As soon as it came, he ran to the aircraft, jumped in and was off on the roll so fast we were all wondering how he had managed it. He got off the ground in much less than two minutes. That was amazing by any standards, and we were all keen to find out how he had done it. Apparently, the station commander had whispered that he wanted to see a sub two-minute scramble if possible. The flight commander, being the good officer that he was did it, but how? He was so angry at the suggestion itself that he did not strap up and got airborne sitting free in his ejection seat. This was not an example to be set to us younger lot and so this came out only after a few days. What if something had happened and he needed to eject? He would have been thrown out of the aircraft without his parachute strapped on and would have been in a freefall situation which would have been fatal. Everyone was so hyped up after the first war that for any of us who had been in that, there was this feeling of invincibility which was very dangerous indeed.

Another story with reference to the same flight commander bears telling. In the station where we were, it had a huge tarmac runway with the flight offices located along the edge with a storm drain that was all that divided the two. So, one day a Gnat was brought out after servicing onto the flight line for its final test run. Normally the aircraft is well secured with chocks and then an experienced tradesman is asked to do the ground run where the engine rpm is increased gradually to 100%. Well on this day it happened to be the first trial run by this young ground crew man. The aircraft was run up gradually and the rpm raised to 100%. Now this increase was normally done very gradually. But this new young guy decided to do it much faster. This along with the fact that the chocks were not well secured caused a strange incident. The aircraft jumped the chocks and now the guy panicked. He forgot to throttle back immediately. The aircraft then headed straight for the flight offices. Had it not been for the storm drain that slowed him down there would have been a major disaster. As it is he did jump the drain and crashed into the flight commander's office. Fortunately, he just broke into the wall and did not go much further. But imagine the surprise of our flight commander when he saw one of his Gnats in his office. Subsequently ground runs on the main tarmac were stopped and taken onto the cross runway for safety's sake.

FESTIVAL OF LIGHTS
ASHOK CHIBBAR

The Indian festival of lights or Diwali is celebrated with great pomp and show all over India. And all people of various faiths participate. It is a time for great joy and

Ashok Chibbar

happiness as it signifies the triumph of good over evil, epitomised by the victory of Lord Rama over Ravana. Homes are decorated with fancy lights, and crackers are exploded to enhance the levels of happiness. Well, many years ago, I 'celebrated' this festival in a very different manner while flying a Gnat.

The Hawks were then operating from a base in the east, north of the mighty Brahmaputra River. Post the 1971 war there had been some changes in the squadron line, notably the arrival of 'Mountaineer' Chou and the inimitable 'Crow' De. Both these gentlemen were poles apart in their demeanour, with Chou being a smiling and generally quiet guy. Both came in as the senior and junior flight commanders respectively. Crow being the more vocal, and, having been posted in from a squadron, which had been once commanded by the legendary Johnny Greene, took over the role of armament training officer.

Crow would spend endless hours in giving lectures (nay sermons) on the virtues of the gyro gunsight (GGS) fitted on the Gnat. He would call us 'primitive' since we had been used to employing the 'fixed cross' for armament delivery. Slowly but surely, he made valiant attempts to change our mindset. To his credit, he succeeded to some extent. But often, the Gnat would disagree with his sermons and, invariably, ensure that the GGS would not work satisfactorily forcing us to go back to the 'primitive' fixed cross. After a year of good flying and training hard the test of our capabilities in the form of Squadron Combat Efficiency Meet Eastern Air Command or the SCEMEAC 1973 loomed over our heads.

The month was November and the squadron got down to brass tacks of weapon delivery and cine evasive exercises. Live weapon delivery in the form of machine guns (front guns) and T-10 rocket projectiles (R/P) was conducted over the air-to-ground firing range located at Dulongmukh which was at the foothills of the Himalayan Range close to the Subansiri River. Having practised regularly, I was part of the squadron's four-aircraft rocket projectile team.

It was 13 November 1973 and Crow was the leader, Malkani the No. 2, the CO (Indru) No. 3 and I was the No. 4. The formation took off at ten-second intervals and joined up in tactical formation soon after. We were armed with two T-10 R/Ps each. After a short navigation at low level we were to fire the R/Ps at the designated target at Dulongmukh Range. The navigation to the initial point (IP) was uneventful and Crow gave a crisp call of "attack formation go" and "switches left". This meant we were to trail behind at 1,000 yards behind each other, put on the armament switches and the attack would be on the target to our left.

Each one of us fired our first rocket and lined up for the second attack. As I fired my second rocket and pulled out of the dive, I noticed that the Bingo light had come on. This indicated I had only 250lbs of fuel. The nearest air force airfield was Jorhat and for that I needed at least 500lbs! I gave a call to Crow: "Flamingo 1 from 4. Bingo light on, landing at Lilabari."

Lilabari was an unused civil airfield about 5,000–6,000 feet in length. There was no air traffic control nor any runway lights. But that was my only option except, of course, to eject. Crow responded with "Can't hear you. Flamingo channel Echo go". Return to base was to be at medium level, individually, since fuel was at a premium. With dusk setting in, I turned towards Lilabari, not very far from my position. Taking a grave chance, Indru, the CO and my subsection leader, turned back to assist me.

Then came Diwali. Along with the Bingo light, the generator failure light came on, then the low-fuel pressure light, and then the invertor 'doll's eye' turned white. When I lowered the landing gear to see the three red lights glaring at me, the hydraulic-failure light came on. Along with the hydraulic failure there was an audio-warning mechanism. When one cancelled the audio warning an amber light would glow. So now another light came on! Since the hydraulic failure meant I must 'split the tail' (act of disconnecting the elevator from the 'all-moving' tailplane) another light came on. The cockpit was now fully lit up. Except for the fire-warning light and the oil pressure doll's eye, which remained black. Only the crackers were missing!

Sensing my nervousness at landing at Lilabari, the Gnat decided to show some mercy. Slowly, the hydraulic pressure built up and the system's warning light went off. The landing gear came down with a thud and three green lights stared at me. And then, as if by some miracle, one by one all lights including the Bingo light went off.

When I announced this to the CO, he asked me if I could manage to reach Jorhat. I said I would try. I gingerly turned the aircraft. I had to cross the Brahmaputra to reach the airfield at Jorhat. So, I added a couple of thousand feet to my altitude just in case I had to eject. The CO returned to base while I converged on to Jorhat. Just short of crossing the river, Diwali started again, in the same sequence! But, by now I was confident that the 'failures' were due to some electrical malfunction and continued to make an uneventful landing at Jorhat.

That evening, dressed in my anti-g suit I was the 'guest of honour' at the officers' mess with pilots of a Hunter squadron hosting me to a round of drinks.

CHAPTER 7
TEST AND RESEARCH

FLYING THE GNAT AS TEST PILOTS AT RAE BEDFORD

DENNIS STANGROOM

I arrived as OC Flight Systems Squadron RAE Bedford in October 1979 and first flew Gnat 513, a conventional two-seater, on 31 October 1979. It was used for continuation training (CT) and in conversion to the single-seat Gnat XP505 for those, like me, who had not flown the Gnat in training.

During early April 1980 both Gnats were taken to Gibraltar for a trial requested by the Royal Navy. HMS *Broadsword* was a Type 22 guide missile frigate. The

The single-seat Gnat XP505.

requirement was for a target, similar to that presented by a cruise missile, to test the Seawolf short-range defensive missile system. I have no idea what the original brief was, but the profiles ended up with repetitive runs at 50ft asl, 490kts with a 6g turn short of the ship. The RN sailed away happy with the result.

Gnat 513 did not appear in my logbook again after I delivered it to Boscombe Down on 21 April 1980. It seems to have been replaced with Hunter T8 321. However, I continued to fly Gnat 505, occasionally on CT, but mainly collecting data on turbulence during low-level flight. There was also a trial, avoided by pilots whatever their background, that sounded like fun, but turned out to be a grim test of the stomach. It was called 'parameter identification'. The boffins discovered they could extract data of interest on aerodynamic derivatives from the unique system fitted to 505. Rapid rolling throughout the flight envelope appeared to be straightforward until 'g' was added to the formula. Forty-five minutes was spent aiming at the corner points of the envelope whilst often failing but filling in many of the others. When the trials officer had enough data, or maybe enough complaints, the relief in the crewroom was palpable. I also flew the aircraft on a Rapier missile trial with similar requirements to that of the Seawolf. In all I flew some 65 hours.

RAE Hawk, Gnat and Hunter flying together in formation.

I flew the last flight on 28 April 1983 in formation with a Hawk T Mk. 1 and Hunter T8. It has since moved around various museums and last I heard it was in storage.

I still think of the Gnat as one of my favourites. The cockpit fitted like a glove, although rather too much so when wearing an immersion suit. In the latter case, the inability to achieve adequate aileron during crosswind landings occasionally made for interesting touchdowns. To fly it well required a good deal of pilot compensation and the longitudinal control system, at least on 505, had significant backlash. Nevertheless, I found it great fun to aerobat, demanding in high-altitude formation and at low level a pure pleasure. Much of the trials low flying was done at 100ft agl, in a variety of terrain all over the UK and not once was there a low-flying complaint. More importantly, even the birds found it impossible to hit.

ROGER BEAZLEY

Roger Beazley

Following basic RAF flying training I had the privilege of being selected for the fast-jet stream and went off to RAF Valley for advanced flying training on the Folland Gnat. The thought was exciting and early flying was both challenging and enjoyable; I was fortunate to have a very experienced fast-jet instructor ex-Hunter FR10, the low-level reconnaissance version. In consequence my low-level navigation training [both dual and solo] was particularly exciting and the Gnat was perfect for that part of the 80-hour course along with preparation for my Hunter course.

Unfortunately, not all went well for others during my five months in North Wales. There was a double fatality caused by an imperfect landing in manual flying (i.e. simulating a hydraulic failure, therefore in manual with limited control effectiveness). One of my course colleagues and his instructor were required to eject with the Gnat out of control in what was assumed to be a spin. Another course colleague lost his canopy whilst cruising at high level which took him very much by surprise and another lost his nosewheel either during landing or take-off – I can't remember – I suspect he very much does! I was lucky in that I suffered no such incidents although during the course I had to divert twice due to Valley's runway being blocked by others – once to Mona just down the road on Anglesey and the other to Shawbury somewhat further away in Shropshire.

Trials flight Gnat.

It was some 16 years before I checked out again on the Gnat but in the meantime had a couple of informal rides, one with the Red Arrows in Belgium thanks to Dickie Duckett and Ray Hanna and one jolly trip in Scotland with the author of this very book.

During my early test pilot career at Boscombe Down I found myself tasked to fly one of the Red Arrows' Gnats which apparently had briefly lost control during a single training sortie. The problem was that the NCO engineer in the back had ejected although the pilot had subsequently recovered and landed safely. Clearly there was an investigation, and I was tasked to check the aeroplane for its lateral and directional control qualities; the Red Arrow pilots were not impressed when this 'outsider' turned up. I was, however, lucky in two respects: firstly, I knew a couple of the Reds who made things easier for me and, secondly, during the flight test (with a non-display pilot current on the Gnat in the back seat) I found that under prolonged 'g' force, one of the flaps had a tendency to ride up. The Reds displayed with ten degrees of down flap so that was enough for me although I never learnt whether that was the cause of the original brief loss of control. Whatever, I departed from the Red's crewroom with a restrained grin of satisfaction on my face.

In March 1982 I arrived at the Royal Aircraft Establishment Bedford to take over as commander flying which included two flight test squadrons, along with the airfield, air traffic and meteorology services with supporting facilities of an officers' mess and married quarters. My professional boss was based at Farnborough some 85 miles away with a locally based senior civil servant scientist heading up the research facilities at the two local sites, my day-to-day administrative and tasking

Roger Beazley (seventh from right with kneepads) with the RAE team.

boss. I knew it was going to be a big job and I suspected it would not allow much flying for me – this last sentence proved to be incorrect.

Flight Systems Squadron (FSS) was the real research outfit with some very interesting work on Harrier, BAC 111, HS 748 and a DH125 Dominie. It also operated a Folland Gnat XP505. Radar Research Squadron (RRS) focused on development rather than research and operated a range of Canberras as well as two Viscounts, a Nimrod, Meteor and Buccaneer. My initial flying concentrated on supporting the BAC 111 and HS 748 projects and the Canberras on which I was current on arrival having been refreshed on the type prior to arriving at Bedford. It was three months before I checked out on the Gnat. The two-seat Gnat having departed but with my somewhat dated training on the type I was content to regain my currency solo, XP505 having been modified for solo operations with the rear seat being filled with scientific kit. It was a Gnat that had never served in the RAF's training role.

My initial trials flights with 505 were on turbulence work flying low level (but not below 100ft) around North Wales – clearly great fun and as Dennis mentioned above apparently with no complaints. I was also introduced to parameter-identification flights which Dennis mentioned – very sick-making and I maintained a suspicion that for such flights I was regularly selected. Other 'turbulence' flights in 505 included sorties through the wake of other aeroplanes – not easy to get it right unless the 'target' aircraft was streaming smoke. Other trips outside the turbulence work included using the Gnat for certain radar calibration work and,

Gnat T.1 XP505 RAE Bedford on a farewell visit to Valley on 28 March 1983. Its last flight was 29 April 1983. (Steve Bond)

following a RAF mid-air Phantom v Crop Sprayer, trying to identify a suitable anti-collision strobe light which could be specified as a safety feature.

There was no doubt that my 35 hours of research flying in 505 at RAE Bedford was certainly varied, enjoyable and, in a number of cases, unique.

Some years later, in a rather larger aeroplane, taxiing in at Valley the nav looked over my shoulder and said – "Gosh, look at all those paraffin darts" – over the years that expression has stuck with me, it is most appropriate.

CHAPTER 8

CIVILIAN GNATS

RIDING THE POCKET ROCKET

STAN HODGKINS

The 'g' eases off as I approach the top of the loop and my 'turning trousers' relax a bit – head back to pick up the display line as soon as possible – 4,600 feet, 150 knots, that's OK to pull through. As we start on the way down, I throttle back and glance quickly at the hydraulic pressure gauge – it's at two o' clock – where it should be (2,900 psi). That means that the flying controls are in good health. The last thing you need in the Gnat is a hydraulic failure at the top of a loop – we would need to STUPRECC, and quick.

Ask any pilot who was lucky enough to have trained on this delightful, slippery, sexy, little pocket-rocket what they remember about it and you will invariably get a fast, Pavlovian response of this drill, which was obviously permanently engraved in our memories. As long as it is carried out promptly and methodically there is no problem, but there is certainly no time for pussyfooting around with a checklist when the hydraulics failed.

Probably the other vivid recollection for most pilots would be the quantum leap in performance after basic training in the Jet Provost Mk. 4. It was easily the biggest jump in the progression from JP 3 to Lightning. In fact, as I remember, from Gnat to Hunter was a slight disappointment from a sheer performance point of view, although there were many qualities yet to appreciate in the beautiful Hawker jet. Four thirty-millimetre Aden cannon for a start.

From a technical viewpoint the Gnat was an extremely clever and original design, throughout you can see the idea of items and equipment serving dual and sometimes multiple purposes. Some of course, for instance the inboard ailerons, which drooped in lieu of flaps, were lost in the 'development' of the trainer version, but most were retained. The most obvious dual feature is the undercarriage which has a 'halfway' position to serve as an extremely effective airbrake, thus saving a multiplicity of hydraulic jacks, pipery, selectors and of course most importantly in the quest for performance – space and weight. Even detail design was similar, for instance the standby altimeter serves as the cabin altimeter in normal operation

Stan Hodgkins

and the hydraulic pressure gauge also indicates the air pressure available for undercarriage lowering in emergency.

In the 1990s Kennet Aviation at Cranfield operated two Gnats, Tim Manna's G-TIMM and G-BVPP. G-TIMM, although painted as XM693, the third production aircraft, is really XP504 in disguise. Although it was at Valley when I did my AFTS course in 1968, for one reason or other I never did fly it at that time. G-BVPP was painted in early Red Arrows colours with the serial XR996. It is in fact XP534 which I did fly just once in March 1969. Both aircraft flew some 3,000 hours during their time at Valley, mostly with some aspiring jet-jockey perspiring in the front cockpit while he struggled valiantly to keep his mind ahead of the fickle little machine. I remember trying to set up the TACAN offset (like an area nav waypoint) whilst on instruments in thick cloud – I'd look away from the panel to the right-hand console to crank the wretched little wheel thing and when I looked back we were almost upside down. Talk about light on the ailerons!

My own memories of those days are quite vivid. My first instructor, Mike Smith was an ex-Lightning pilot, and therefore to me, a god. I must say however that for a fighter pilot he was extremely patient. On my first flight in the Gnat, we charged off down a flooded runway 32 at Valley like a ferret on heat. Sitting in the front with my bum about a foot off the ground the impression of speed was incredible. Of course, the man in the back was doing all the flying and talking at the same time as QFIs do. We lifted off in a shower of spray, there were amazing rumblings from below as the gear tucked itself away and we shot straight into a 200-foot cloud base. Almost immediately there was a blast of air in my face as the pressurisation came on and my ears popped violently. By now the ASI was well on its way towards 300 knots and we were well and truly India Michael Charlie (IMC). At about 350 knots he cranked on 45 degrees of bank and selected 3g – this I learned later was the standard instrument departure from Valley. As a former Sea Vixen observer, it seemed to me more like a toss-bombing manoeuvre. We straightened out on the climb-out heading at 360 knots with the VSI against the stop and the altimeter winding rapidly clockwise. A minute or two later we punched through the cloud tops at 15,000ft into brilliant sunshine. I loved it.

Kemble civilian Gnat.

The rest of that familiarisation flight many years ago is hazy but those first few minutes made a *big* impression. Things happened very quickly, and you obviously had to be on the ball to cope. We all wondered if we would be able to make the grade. Anyway, most of us did and looking back it was a terrific trainer that prepared us well for the heavy metal we were to fly on the front line. I must admit though, that I never dreamed that I would ever be lucky enough to strap one on again. When I did it all came back like yesterday.

So, "What's it like, Mister?"

Approaching this pretty little jet, sitting slightly nose up on its neat but narrow landing gear, one is struck of course by its small size but also by its purposeful appearance. It does look as if it would not suffer fools gladly. Of course, that is true of all aircraft but especially true of this one. It is a typical jet of the sixties: fast, complex and unforgiving, so just sharpen up, old man.

Out with the flip cards and do the walk-round – straightforward. Pull down the step on the side of the intake, one heave and you're up – no ladder needed. Check the rear seat – seat safe, harness correctly stowed using the restraint bars housed in the nose, no loose articles, switches set. Check the front seat and jump in. The seats were specially designed for the Gnat by Folland and have no safety pins, just a lever below the headrest which sticks uncomfortably in the back of your neck when the seat is 'safe'.

In the front seat the sitting position is just about perfect, which makes a pleasant change from some other British machinery of the same era. The seat is well reclined and very comfortable despite the hard glass-fibre seat pack containing the life raft and survival pack. The stick and throttle are exactly where they should be, and the rudder pedals are out of sight below the panel. A quick adjustment and the whole thing fits like a glove. The cockpit has an undated look about it (well to an old geezer like me), a sign of good, well-thought-out design. Dominating the main instrument panel is the OR946 IFIS, a large, unambiguous attitude indicator and compass/navigation display side by side. This was the standard British instrument display of the time, also used in the Buccaneer and Lightning. All other controls and indicators are neatly and logically laid out with a standard warning panel on the right of the main panel and a row of cautionary warning captions centrally above. Although it's tight the overall impression is one of neatness and efficiency.

Strapping in is again no-nonsense with a combined safety and parachute harness and the unique, combined oxygen/RT connector. The idea behind this feature is that if the oxygen should become disconnected in flight RT will also be lost, thereby alerting the pilot immediately and preventing the onset of hypoxia.

Cockpit checks are left to right in true air force fashion. HP on, hit the gang-bar and we're ready to start. The Palouste air-starter (small jet engine to start larger jet engine using bleed air) alongside is already running and Pete gives me the thumbs up. I raise my right thumb and then jab it down like the weatherman on TV changing pictures. At the same time I press the relight button on the throttle with my left thumb. The Palouste howls like a banshee, the air-starter hose has a violent erection and the Bristol-Siddeley Orpheus spins up behind me with a rumble. The engine lights up and the jet pipe temperature rises rapidly. At 300°C I release the relight button and flip up my right thumb. The Palouste calms down, the hose collapses and we're in business thrust-wise. As the engine accelerates to idle rpm of 38%–40% the systems come online. Hydraulics 2,500–3,000 psi, AC, DC, Fuel captions out and I start the after-start checks. These are routine with flaps, radios, controls plus a very important one – trim. This is a vital check to test the serviceability of the tailplane system and is somewhat less than straightforward. They used to say that half the course at Valley was learning the Gnat pitch-control system and the other half was everything else.

Now back to the fun bit. On completion of the extensive trim check I am ready to taxi. "Mike Mike, clear to holding point Foxtrot, Runway 04, QNH 1006" says Cranfield, and off we go. A little bit of power, a dab on the brakes to check them, she nods against the soft nose oleo and rolls forward. The brakes are powerful and progressive but have a very slight delay in operation which sounds awkward but isn't. Even with full fuel (full external slipper tanks) the aircraft will continue to accelerate at idle rpm so gentle braking is constantly needed to avoid a speeding ticket! By the time I get to Foxtrot the pre-take-off checks are done, and they clear me onto the runway for immediate departure.

Lining up on the centreline I take a mental note of the 'picture'. The Gnat sits very close to the ground, and it is all too easy to flare too high on landing. Set 90% rpm, brakes holding – just – let them go – and we're off like a dirty shirt. Full power – 100%, the acceleration is brisk to say the least.

A quick check of the engine instruments as they stabilise, a touch of brake to keep straight until the rudder becomes effective at about 70 knots and the ASI comes off the stop. At 100 knots I ease the stick back to just 'crack' the nosewheel clear of the runway and hold the correct take-off attitude. There are two undesirable possibilities if you get this wrong. Raise the nose too high and there is a real risk of a tailstrike, make coarse pitch inputs and the dreaded PIO (pilot induced oscillation) can result. This did cause one or two nasty incidents during RAF service and is to be avoided. As the airspeed increases and the tailplane becomes more effective it is quite a delicate business holding the take-off attitude, doubly so on an undulating runway such as Cranfield. Unstick is not clean, especially with full slipper tanks, but at 160 knots we are safely airborne, and I push the gear/airbrake lever fully forward and up it comes with the usual thumps and clunks. Two notches of flap (20 degrees) were set for take-off, and these are raised at about 200 knots. Next, the pressurisation is switched on by bringing the two levers on the starboard cockpit wall (one hot, one cold) together in the position for the desired cockpit temperature – very neat.

As the speed builds up one is quickly aware that this aeroplane needs flying. In roll it has neutral stability, if not a touch of negative. This means that to hold a given angle of bank requires constant aileron inputs – this is a shock at first but soon becomes automatic. Needless to say, the ailerons are light and very effective with a rate of roll of up to 200 degrees per second. Above 150 knots an airspeed switch operates and restricts aileron travel from 28 degrees to 16 degrees. This is to prevent higher rates of roll inducing yaw-roll coupling and possible fin failure which did occur in service. Pitch control is slightly heavier and holding an attitude is easy. The manual rudder is moderately heavy in comparison with the powered controls but light enough and effective.

The recommended climbing speed is 350 knots, climbing attitude is ten degrees nose up and less than five minutes after brakes off we are levelling off at 25,000 feet over the fens. About 1,000 feet anticipation is needed for a smooth level off. This is a good spot for a bit of general handling as it is clear airspace and there are excellent ground features to lock onto, like the Wash and the twin Bedford canals. London Military also give an excellent radar service, which is a great help.

At 25,000 feet the aircraft is even lighter on the ailerons and the response in roll is increased. It is easy to over control in pitch and to hit the pre-stall buffet in tight turns. The aeroplane has classic swept-wing characteristics; for best turning performance it should be flown in the light buffet, sometimes referred to as the 'nibble' in the trade. This is always strange to pilots accustomed to straight-winged aircraft and it can seem as though the machine is about to stall or spin. For a max-rate turn full power is applied and the aircraft rapidly rolled into the turn – after a good lookout of course. Back pressure is then applied on the stick until either the 7g limit is reached or until the light buffet is felt. This will depend on the speed of entry into the turn (IAS). If the 'g' limit is reached first the aircraft is held in a level turn until the nibble is felt as the airspeed reduces. The nose is then allowed to drop so that a descending 7g turn, on the buffet, is held. If one pulls too hard the buffet becomes progressively heavier, drag increases dramatically, the rate of turn reduces and the speed washes off. This is how the foolish fighter pilot throws away energy and the bad guy slides into his 'six o' clock'. Tell me about it, we've all been there.

During training the aircraft was flown routinely up to 45,000 feet – that took 20 minutes, the last 5,000 feet taking practically half that time. Climbing the Gnat to high level it was easy to see where the tropopause was on the day. When the temperature stopped reducing, the rate of climb would suddenly halve. In no other aircraft I have flown was this so obvious as it was in the Gnat – the Orpheus must be very temperature sensitive. If the aircraft was dived from 45,000 feet with full power a clean, dent-free Gnat could practically reach Mach 1.3 at about 30,000 feet so that students could get their first experience of supersonic flight.

For cruise, 85% is right for any altitude and this gives range speed – 360kts at sea level, 330kts at 10,000ft and about 300kts IAS at 20,000ft. Operating on a permit-to-fly it's VFR/VMC of course and FL 245 is the usual limit for ferrying between air shows. In practice this gives a cruise TAS of approximately 400kts at that level. With a fuel capacity of 2,800lbs including slipper tanks and a fuel flow of 23lbs/min, we have a range of about 450nms, which is adequate for around the UK. However, fuel can get tight when airspace restrictions force transit around or below controlled airspace. At 2,000ft fuel burn is up at 42lbs/min, TAS is less, and range is significantly reduced. It is an interesting thought that back in the sixties the 'Reds' as they are referred to these days, toured North America. I crossed the 'pond' a couple of times in the Buccaneer with the comfort of a Victor tanker, two engines and a navigator, but it must have felt very lonely in one of those little red jets over all that cold water.

Having completed the climb and recorded the time to height and engine instrument readings, most of the air test is done at around FL 100, so it's throttle back, airbrakes out, then half roll and pull through. The airbrakes (gear halfway down) are extremely effective and produce very little trim change but heavy buffet and a lot of noise. A minute or so later we are levelling out and it's time to check the operation of the undercarriage and flaps.

First the airbrakes are selected and when the airspeed is less than the 250-knot limit the lever is moved to the fully aft position to lower the undercarriage. Initially there is a nose-down change of trim, then nose up when the datum shift operates.

This is a mechanical linkage between the starboard undercarriage leg and the tailplane actuator which progressively moves the tailplane through three and a half degrees to counteract the nose-down trim change when the undercarriage is lowered. It should be monitored on every selection for obvious reasons. Lowering takes approximately eight seconds and retraction seven seconds. On retraction the trim change is negligible. There are five stages of flap settings, ten to 50 degrees operated by a lever above the throttle which moves down and back. Flap limitation speeds are 300 knots between up and 20 degrees and 200 knots between 20 and

50 degrees. Selecting ten flap gives a moderate nose-down trim change and slight nose-down change with subsequent selections. Forty and 50 degrees of flap also produce airframe buffet which can conceal pre-stall buffet – this should be borne in mind on final approach.

So far, the aircraft has been flown normally, i.e. with power controls operating. Now we must check out handling in the dreaded *manual*. On the starboard console there are two little levers, side by side. One is the LP fuel cock, which we leave well alone in flight, and the other is the power controls on/off cock. With this we can switch off the power controls and leave the other hydraulic services operating. There is also one of these in the back seat so that the instructor can give you a hydraulic failure any time he likes. This is where the STUPRECC drill comes in.

The first three letters stand for speed, trim and unlock. That's the important bit. Without going too deeply into the subject, all we are trying to do is to make sure that when the hydraulic pressure runs out, the tailplane is in the correct position. If we mess this up we might not have enough tailplane/elevator authority to land. For real, the first indication of a genuine hydraulic failure would be the flashing lights and the clangers of the central-warning system. The well-trained Gnat pilot then just can't help himself – he checks that the speed is below 450kts/Mach 0.9, he trims the tail to the ideal sector and unlocks the elevator using the sliding selector just below the flap lever. Power controls are selected off and the hydraulics are exhausted by carefully waggling the stick in the approved manner. Standby trim is selected onto the stick top and the beast brought home for a flapless landing. There should be enough pressure in the accumulator to lower the gear or it can be blown down using the air in the aileron accumulator. Handling in manual is interesting; the ailerons are all there and somewhat heavy, but pitch control is different. The tiny elevators produce little effect with large stick movement and basic control is with the standby electric trim. This must sound weird to most GA pilots, but you do get used to it. Landing in manual should be from a straight-in approach, adding ten knots to the normal threshold speed and onto a long runway, streaming the drag 'chute on touchdown. One continuous application of brake is used to conserve hydraulic pressure.

Aerobatics in the Gnat are a real pleasure. The only non-standard feature is that rudder must not be used during manoeuvres so that a true slow roll is not possible. Also rolling is only permitted through 360 degrees. Successive rolls can be performed but after each 360 degrees the roll must be arrested, and sideslip eliminated. These restrictions are a precaution against yaw-roll coupling which can put unacceptable loads on the fin. For air display flying I set ten degrees of flap and loops are commenced at 350kts using a 5g pull-up. For rolling manoeuvres about 250 to 300kts is fine. The final fast run is about 480kts, clean, with an upward roll left then right.

One of the nicest things about flying a fast jet is going home. The 'run-in-and-break' is of course the most efficient way to get a piece of fighter machinery back on the ground – it's not just a jet-jock show-off manoeuvre. It is also quite a tricky thing to do at a busy GA airfield like Cranfield, without rotting off the locals. The aim is to whistle down the dead side (ATC kindly grounds the helis for a few minutes) at about 40kts, 200ft, and snap into a 4–5g upward break, throttle closed, airbrakes out. At the 180, we should be about 280kts, 1,000ft. When the speed reduces to 250, the gear is lowered, three greens obtained, and 20 degrees of flap selected. Just past the downwind end of the runway – 200kts, 40 degrees of flap, and we pitch into the finals turn. Power is added as necessary, about 70%, to maintain about 160 knots until roll out and the final stage of flap lowered. Speed is then bled off to achieve a threshold speed of around 130 knots, depending on weight. The ideal approach is very flat and one's bum is very close to the ground on touchdown. Ground contact is very positive and feels *fast!* The Maxaret anti-skid brakes are powerful but, in a crosswind, there is a tendency for the aircraft to rock from side to side if braking is unequal, due to the narrow-track undercarriage. This however feels much worse than it is and can be cured by simply taking the feet momentarily off the brake pedals. If needed the brake 'chute can be streamed and provides a small amount of deceleration, although in the RAF it was considered to be just a training aid.

Here I was then, at the top of this loop – no business being here at my age – in this Folland fun machine, pulling and grunting with the best. Get on with it you old fool! We pull through, crowd right and with about 30 degrees nose down I roll left, power on into a level 4g turn back towards the crowd for a Derry turn. Check, push, roll under and pull. Barrel up into a big wingover left, seeing the smoke trail appearing over my left shoulder. Flap up, full poke – dive for crowd centre, unloading and going like a train on the last pass. The little machine seems to know that it was built for this. We touch 480 knots at 100 feet opposite the VIP tent – stick back – and it's up, up and away – roll left, roll right. What a treat, what a jet!

THE SPORT OF KINGS
MARK FITZGERALD

It all began in September 1995. It was Freshers Week in Cambridge, where I had just started life as an Economics undergraduate at Trinity College. As was customary for all new students, I went along to the Freshers Fair where a sign caught my eye that

Mark Fitzgerald

changed the path of my life forever. It read: 'Learn to Fly for Free'. Like any other student who was short of cash yet had high ambitions in life, this seemed an intriguing proposition. It was there that I was introduced to Cambridge University Air Squadron (CUAS) and the concept of flying for the RAF. I had never even considered the possibility of flying military aircraft but having been told that I could fly for free with an option to leave upon graduation, it almost seemed too good to be true. I was sold.

My love for flying began as a young child always wanting to visit the captain in the cockpit whilst flying abroad on holiday. Embarrassingly perhaps, this even continued well into my early 20s until 9/11 put a stop to it. I remember approaches in 747s into Kai Tak in Hong Kong and London Heathrow, having convinced the captains that I should be allowed to sit in the jump-seat as a result of having been taught to fly by the finest instructors in the world. The RAF prides itself in providing the very best instruction – I was lucky enough to have accumulated over 100 hours on the mighty Bulldog as well as a trip in a Jaguar – which opened my eyes to flying fast jets. That back-seat flight in the Jaguar had me totally hooked. Had an RAF recruitment officer told me to sign the next 12 years of my life away upon landing back that day at RAF Coltishall, I would have signed on the dotted line there and then. As it happens, I subsequently decided to pass on an RAF commission upon my graduation, but I made myself a promise. Somehow, somewhere, and in some way, I would one day fly military aircraft. I thoroughly intended to keep this promise.

A brief stint working in the City was followed by a total change of career. I decided to start up my own tech business in 2000 with my next-door neighbour. The company was relatively successful, to the point whereby ten years later I exited the business, helping me fund my passion for flying. But it was in my mid-twenties that I discovered North Weald airfield. My very best friend, Kev Whyman (also ex-CUAS), had joined a Jet Provost syndicate there. It was quite inexpensive to join the group with the cost of flying the JP not being too dissimilar to renting a light aircraft from a flying club. These economics were surprising to me. What most people don't realise is that certain ex-miliary aircraft are relatively cheap to buy, as their resale market is very limited. It was all surprisingly accessible.

Enter Tony Haig-Thomas (THT). A former RAF fighter pilot. He'd flown most fast jets of his era, with his fondest time taking place in Aden driving Hunters.

A genuinely no-nonsense individual. He had little time for political correctness. During the decades either side of the millennium, he was single-handedly responsible for teaching virtually all UK civilian pilots how to fly a military jet – the JP. He was a brilliant instructor, combining his air force training skills with an incredible conviction that flying jets was easy, but you just needed to possess the right attitude. Not only did he teach me to fly the JP. He also introduced me to display flying. Under his stewardship, both Kev Whyman and I became JP display pilots on the air-show circuit. Initially with solo displays, we managed to perform at air shows across the UK and Europe. This was followed soon by a JP formation display. I have extremely fond memories of our time together flying to various destinations around the UK and the continent, but there was a jet both Kev and I really aspired to fly. It was the Folland Gnat.

Often parked next to the JPs we'd fly at North Weald was a Folland Gnat (G-BVPP). It was owned by two individuals, one of whom happened to run our JP syndicate – Mark Grimshaw. Although he'd never flown in the RAF, Mark had an RAF family background. His father was one of the pilots in the 22-ship Hunter formation loop back in the 1950s. It's a record that still stands today. Whilst flying back from the Yeovilton air show in 2004, Mark's Gnat experienced a flame-out on finals at North Weald. He managed to land the jet in a field just outside the airfield boundary and walk away from it along with his passenger (a future Gnat pilot– Oliver Wheeldon). The jet was a write-off, but Kev and I sensed an opportunity. We convinced Mark that we should start a new syndicate by acquiring a Folland Gnat between the three of us. By the summer of 2005 we were the proud owners of G-RORI (XR538) which had been based at Kemble. A significant new chapter was about to begin in our flying careers.

Flying the Gnat is a step-up. The jet needs to be shown respect, otherwise it will bite you. Even though I never flew with him in the Gnat, I remember THT telling me "It's a slippery old thing". Although wonderful to handle and ridiculously light on the controls, you really need to understand the unique idiosyncrasies it possesses, and always be 'ahead of the aircraft'. This is where I was extremely lucky to have been taught by one of the world's most accomplished test pilots – Peter 'Willy' Hackett. At the time, Willy was the RAF project test pilot on the Typhoon, with a list of accolades most test pilots would envy, including the development of the VAAC (experimental fly-by-wire Harrier) and subsequently the Joint Strike Fighter (JSF) F-35 Lightning II.

Kev and I followed the full RAF Gnat training syllabus, with the only exclusions being instrument flight (as UK permit-to-fly aircraft can only be flown in day VFR conditions), weapons training (sadly we're not allowed to fire missiles as civilians) and for the time being, formation flight (given we only had one Gnat at our disposal). Although Willy performed the majority of our training, some instructional flight was also provided by Mark Grimshaw, who from what I could tell was the first genuine civilian to become a Gnat instructor in the UK.

It was a proud day at Kemble in August 2005, where having bashed the circuit all weekend, Willy finally let both Kev and myself go solo. The brief was clear – take-off with internal fuel only, depart to the north for ten minutes of general handling, recover for five circuits to an overshoot (so as to preserve the tyre-wear), and land on the last one. No PFLs. If you have an engine failure, eject. No PFLs (underlined this time). I actually really enjoyed PFLs, primarily on account of the fact that I was good at them and with a gliding speed of 180kts, you always had to be on your game. However, with the closure of so many airfields over the years and the fact that we typically have to fly below controlled airspace, the chances of you actually being able to glide to a suitable landing site in the UK following an engine failure are unfortunately pretty slim.

Post first-solo training persisted for both of us on the Gnat until we completed our final handling test, whilst continuing JP formation display flying throughout.

The Gnat display team. From left to right: Kev Whyman, Chris Heames and Mark Fitzgerald.

However, our sights were now set on a solo Gnat display, which up until that point were mostly being performed by Mark Grimshaw, who had displayed the Gnat for several years already. Willy was being sent out to the US as the RAF's test pilot on the JSF, so we needed someone to fill Willy's boots for the next few years. This is when we met Chris 'Heamsey' Heames – an old-school RAF fighter pilot who had flown pretty much everything and amassed over 13,500 'hands-on' fast-jet flight hours, having turned down every single desk job he'd ever been offered. He knew the UK like the back of his hand. Wherever we flew together there wouldn't be a moment where there wasn't a ground feature which he'd recognise from memory and navigate from. Heamsey did not need GPS. He didn't need a map either. When transiting around the UK in the Gnat at nearly 400kts at relatively low level, it was a useful skill to have.

Heamsey was instrumental in teaching both Kev and I how to display the Gnat. He believed that the key to safely displaying a swept-wing jet at low level was energy management, whilst keeping the display 'tight'. Staying close to the crowd is important in the Gnat given its small size. Fortunately, it possesses a pretty good turning radius when slowing down and selecting one or two stages of flap, so it's often a better spectacle to slow down a little when performing reversals or turning manoeuvres. The Reds were famous for always flying with one stage of flap throughout their display, and this was a tip we'd often use ourselves. However, there is nothing more exhilarating than parking the throttle fully forward with a clean aircraft whilst low-level running-in towards the crowd.

I remember a few years later displaying solo at the Cleethorpes Air Show on the estuary of the Humber in north-east Lincolnshire. I had been on frequency with London Mil who had earlier given me a transit there at FL 140. They told me to contact them at the end of the display at FL 140 to transit me back to North Weald. Where airspace permitted, I would end my solo Gnat display with a vertical departure. I had seen Mark Grimshaw do it before. It literally looked like a rocket going into space, as by the time you were above FL 100, the Gnat was too small to be seen. I called "final pass" at the end of the display whilst 100ft above the water running towards the crowd with clear blue skies above. Full throttle. Airspeed was well above 500kts, and I ensured my pull-up was timed perfectly to avoid busting the crowd-line. As soon as I hit the vertical, and performed one vertical roll, I could see my altimeter racing away towards FL 100. I called "display complete" and changed frequency sharply to London Mil. I checked in with my call-sign, now above FL 100 still perfectly vertical, albeit with the airspeed decaying. Now approaching FL 140, I gently pulled back on the control column pointing the aircraft southbound and found myself flying inverted at FL 140 level towards home. "G-RORI with you level at FL 140", I said whilst still upside down. A magical end to a display in the Gnat pocket rocket.

As much as I loved displaying the Gnat solo, there was one desire I couldn't let rest. We needed to find another Gnat to really advance the cause and be able to provide a Gnat synchro pair display. There was always something quite special seeing the synchro pair element of any Reds display, especially when watching archive footage of the Reds flying the Gnat. Fortunately, an opportunity presented itself. Welcome Stephen Partridge-Hicks (aka 'Maverick/Mav'). A very successful city banker who co-owned a Gnat, along with his close friend Tim 'Moose' Manna. Moose was a former US Navy pilot, who had lived in the UK for many years and restored countless historic ex-military aircraft (both piston and jet). In my opinion, he deserved a medal for everything he had done to keep historic aircraft flying in the UK, but rather surprisingly to me at the time, he didn't fly most of the aircraft he restored. It was an interesting concept to me – spending vast amounts of your own money to restore an aircraft you'll probably never fly in, instead letting others do so and display them for the benefit of the public on the air-show circuit. Tim had a huge hangar at North Weald filled with historic aircraft. As the years went by, it was noticeable how the composition of aircraft was shifting from virtually all turbine, to virtually all (warbird) piston. I asked Tim why the change? He said, "Mark, tastes change with age". He had slowly started to fall in love with Seafires, Sea Furies, Skyraiders, Gannets and the like, whilst gradually selling his collection of jets to create space for these elder warbirds. The half of the Gnat that bore his name (G-TIMM) was seemingly an open target. Kev, Mark and I weren't going to let it out of our sights.

A deal was struck with Tim. Maverick joined our team, thereby adding G-TIMM to our collection. Unlike G-RORI which was painted in the 4FTS red and white colours from its training role at RAF Valley, G-TIMM was painted in the Red Arrows all-red coat. A fitting paint scheme plus a colourful new member joining our team of pilots. Mav loved his flying, at one point being the UK aerobatics champion. However, he had never flown his Gnat, as it wasn't in an airworthy condition. We were about to fix that.

After some gentle persuasion and agreement of a commercial deal, Tim's engineering organisation managed to get G-TIMM airworthy once again. No sooner had it done so, we were asked to perform a Gnat pairs display in Marrakech. Mark, Kev and I looked at this opportunity in bemusement. Having all now flown a fair number of hours in the Gnat, we realised the complexity of what was being asked. Given the extremely short range of the Gnat, this would be a mission involving multiple stops across Europe, landing at civilian airfields entirely ill-equipped to deal with a Gnat, bureaucracy headaches with ferry permits for non-EASA aircraft types, and a myriad of things that could go wrong. But there was something about this challenge that made us determined to deliver, and planning began.

The first stop was Jersey, followed by Bordeaux for the night. This would be followed by Valladolid in central Spain, Gibraltar for an evening and a final flight to Marrakech. Choosing suitable airfields wasn't as seamless as it may sound. The greatest practical design flaw the Gnat inherited was the lack of a starter generator. How the aircraft went into service without one, I really don't know. You need a low-pressure air starter (Palouste) to channel a high flow rate of compressed air into the engine to get it started/self-sustain itself. Nowadays however, such a unit is hard to find at most non-military airfields. Even if found, much of the time they are unserviceable. Any such long-range missions therefore require a significant amount of planning, phoning ahead and reading between the lines of broken English suggesting that all will be OK. It usually won't. After three days of various issues along the way, we somehow made it with both jets to Marrakech. Things however were about to get very difficult for us. After all, we were now in Africa with two military jets (as civilians) and a lot of locals asking what we were doing there.

They say that in Africa everything is possible. Whilst that might be the case in some circumstances, my experience is that bureaucracy and little fiefdoms create a quite different reality. After three days of negotiating with the various powers that be at the airport, we were finally allowed to display the jets subject to an arduous list of limitations, essentially turning our aerobatics display into a flypast. It hadn't helped that the display site was next to a royal palace. In the end we managed to launch both aircraft and landed back at Marrakech. It was mission accomplished, but not the mission we had envisaged.

After all the fraught negotiations with the airport staff, the mood had changed. We began to fear that these jets would perhaps be stuck in Morocco forever. By then I, quite frankly, just wanted to get out of Morocco and not come back anytime soon. However, our problems were far from over. We had sent a whole array of ground-support equipment to Marrakech prior to our arrival. This included spare tyres, oils, wheel pumps, and various other consumables. Hugely unhelpful, airport security wouldn't let any of it on to the airfield. Furthermore, they would only accept fuel purchased with cash in local currency. We went to the cash machines in the airport and took out a boot load of cash, only to subsequently find out that they won't accept it unless we have the receipt from the cash machine to prove where we got it.

We therefore ended up with twice the local currency needed to pay for the fuel. But the big problem was getting a clearance to fly back to Gibraltar. Mark had spent nearly two hours negotiating with air traffic in the control tower that we need to depart. I think they wanted an unofficial monetary payment to allow us to leave. Eventually a more junior person there took pity on Mark and discreetly whispered to him, "pick up that phone there and speak to someone in Casablanca to get you a clearance". It worked. We couldn't depart that airport fast enough having effectively lived in there for the last three days. The moment we took off brought with it a feeling of escaping on the last flight out of Saigon. I can't think of many moments when I've been more relieved than when we touched down in Gibraltar. That Great Escape was greatly celebrated on the Rock that night.

You would have thought that we would have learnt from our experience and stuck to flying in UK skies alone. However, we were getting invites for our pairs display from across Europe. We'd often display in countries we could reach in one hop, namely the likes of Belgium, the Netherlands, France, and Ireland, however a request came in one day to display at Al-Ain in the UAE. I remember at the time I was extremely busy with my tech business, so I made it clear I was going to miss this one. But Mark had different ideas. He was determined to make this happen on account of growing up in the Middle East while his father was stationed there flying Hunters. He made it his personal mission to deliver on this air show commitment and roped in Willy to fly down with him in the other jet. As before, this mission required multiple stops, and sadly a costly incident occurred on the way.

Having landed in Egypt, Willy's jet (G-TIMM) was low on hydraulic oil. The Gnat uses OM-15, a mineral-based fluid. Having been assured by one of the aircraft engineering companies on the airfield that they had OM-15 in stock and subsequently selling it to us, it eventually transpired this hydraulic fluid was not OM-15. It was Skydrol, a synthetic-based fluid, and one which the Gnat really doesn't like. Soon after taking off, Willy's Gnat experienced a full hydraulic failure. As a team we practise hydraulic failures all the time, given the Gnat's unique longitudinal-control system and how it handles such a failure. 'Flying in manual' as it's known, is a far cry from the joyfully nimble flight controls one usually experiences. You find you're suddenly flying in what seems like a super-tanker at sea, with very limited and sluggish manoeuvrability. We were all incredibly well versed in the STUPRECC emergency drill, whereby you start controlling the aircraft in a similar mindset to how you'd fly an airliner, with a much wider gentler circuit giving yourself a long final approach. Unsurprisingly, Willy landed the jet back safely in Egypt, but the subsequent engineering mission and cost to recover that aircraft to the UK was significant. Although Mark made it to Al-Ain with his jet (G-RORI) and managed to fulfil his display ambitions there, the eventual recovery of G-TIMM left the team with many financial scars.

It was around this time that a new aviation charity had been formed, called Vulcan to the Sky. It had managed to raise millions of pounds in lottery funding and donations from the public to restore a Vulcan to flight. We thought this was a great model to copy, especially if we could get the public to help support the Gnat in a similar manner. I took the lead in forming a new charity called the Heritage Aircraft Trust, whose primary purpose was to restore the aircraft to flight and help educate the public about the Gnat, thereby inspiring next generations into aviation and our armed services as well. Our whole team was incredibly passionate about keeping our nation's aviation heritage alive and we were determined to create an organisation to help preserve the future of the Gnat for years to come.

However, the Gnat requires significant specialist engineering support, and to properly achieve our goals, we decided it was vital to create our own engineering organisation to focus solely on the aircraft. Fortunately, we had a very important individual join our team, Pete Walker. Pete had a distinguished engineering career in the RAF, serving on a variety of aircraft including the likes of the Jaguar and the Hercules. But it was his time teaching engineering to recruits at the RAF Engineering School at Halton (1SOTT) which saw him amass vast amounts of knowledge on the Gnat. It is fair to say that there is no-one living today who knows more about engineering on the Gnat than Pete, and we knew we needed to get him on board as our chief engineer. Pete also had an incredibly good relationship with the CAA, as he'd been involved in getting the very first Gnat in private hands on to the UK permit-to-fly register back in the 1980s, as well as many other ex-military types. Fortunately, under Pete's direction, the Heritage Aircraft Trust engineering organisation was born. This was an incredibly important moment for the future of the charity, as our engineering destiny was finally in our own hands.

No sooner had we achieved the above, we were already thinking about adding a third jet to our team. Oliver Wheeldon (who had several years earlier walked away from a forced landing with Mark in a Gnat) wanted to join the team. We told him he could if he brought a Gnat with him. At the time, there was one going for sale that was based at Kemble (G-MOUR). Formerly owned by Dave Gilmour of Pink Floyd fame, this Gnat was painted in the original Yellowjacks paint scheme. Oli rose to the challenge and months later G-MOUR arrived at North Weald on a low-loader to the bemusement of many motorists on the M4 and M25. The engineering team got to work to kick off the restoration and the following year G-MOUR was ready to fly.

Three Gnats in various liveries with a Hawk.

From a flying perspective, we had always wanted a third jet, to properly be able to call ourselves 'The Gnat Display Team'. Seeing three Gnats in a Vic formation is something special and added a multitude of new sequence possibilities and formation manoeuvres we could include in our display. It was also poignant to represent the history of the Yellowjacks with G-MOUR's yellow paint scheme, by having it lead a formation flanked by a jet in Reds' colours, and the other in 4FTS colours. We now had the complete RAF story in one formation.

By the time G-MOUR was ready for flight, Mark had to leave the team. He was offered a job in the US, and it looked like he was going to move out there permanently. This caused an organisational change within the team. I had already become an authorised instructor on the Gnat, having completed the instructor course, and been signed off by Willy. The life of a Gnat instructor is much tougher than in most aircraft types, as you have significantly obscured forward visibility because of the student's ejection-seat head box right in front of you. You need to learn quickly to fly with your head always tilted to the left or right in order to see anything forward of the aircraft. This is particularly important with new students learning to land the jet.

I remember being told that Gnat instructors at RAF Valley would always pray for crosswinds to assist their visibility on short finals. Also, with one's helmet touching either the far left or far right side of the canopy, it made it hard to see the air-speed indicator, which as an instructor was the primary instrument to ensure that your student wasn't going to get you into trouble on finals. Fortunately, someone at Folland had also decided to install a second ASI on top of the port-side coaming of the rear-seat cockpit, thereby allowing the instructor to keep their ASI scan to a minimum, ready to take over the controls should a student get it all wrong. A very useful addition, probably brought in as a modification during the service life of the aircraft following some mishaps with students at Valley. Also, sitting in the back of the jet was an extremely tight fit even for the smallest of pilots, so at 6" I was never particularly comfortable sitting in the rear seat. Mark, who was far larger in build than I, seemed to possess Houdini-like skills to somehow get into the jet. I now had to fill his shoes following his departure, and one of my first acts as chief pilot was to send Maverick on his first solo. A nail-biting moment for any new instructor or chief pilot, but Maverick performed it admirably.

With the third jet online and Mark not being around, we decided that Heamsey was the right chap to lead our new three-ship formation display. We would usually use 'RedGnat' as our formation call-sign, with Kev as RedGnat 2 and myself at RedGnat 3. Building up our three-ship display was probably the most rewarding flying I've ever had in the Gnat. The display had a mix of everything – an aerobatics formation segment, followed by a synchro-pair element interspersed with individual manoeuvres, with the formation re-joining for a departure finale. Tailchasing was also part of the syllabus, which everyone enjoyed. "Never let a good tailchase turn into a dogfight" was always briefed, although I always chuckled at the alternative saying: "Never let a good dogfight turn into a tailchase." This all truly was the Sport of Kings.

2014 was the most remarkable year for our team. It happened to coincide with the 50th anniversary of the Reds, who contacted us and asked if we could perform some flypasts with them. This was a genuine schoolboy dream come true for me. The first flypast was due to take place at the RAF Waddington Air Show. The brief was for the nine Reds to fly in a Vic formation, with a three-ship tucked-in led by a Hunter and two Gnats either side, creating a giant triangle in the sky. Heamsey loved flying the Hunter and would lead the three jets north of Waddington to join with the Reds, allowing the now 12-ship formation to run in together. The Reds were departing from Scampton, whilst we were already positioned at Waddington. We gave ourselves plenty of time to get airborne, find the Reds, join in a turning orbit away from the airfield, and then run-in on time nicely tucked-in with the rest of the formation. I don't know who was controlling ATC at Waddington that day, but they made us hold at the end of the runway for over 25 minutes.

Heamsey was on the radio reminding them we needed to meet the Reds, but bizarrely they wouldn't let us launch between the display acts on before us. When Heamsey let them know that we were due to meet the Reds in less than five minutes and we were still on the ground, finally a clearance was given. There was no hanging about on our part, and as soon as we were airborne, we turned sharply north to intercept the Reds. By now there was no time at all to perform a gentle turning join and settle ourselves into position, as the Reds had already positioned for a straight-in approach for the flypast, and they declined a suggestion of an orbit. Heamsey established what I can only describe as the most perfect overtake speed and approach vector from an incredibly awkward angle and somehow got us all into position just as the whole formation approached the airfield boundary. Fifteen seconds later the Reds climbed away whilst our three-ship continued straight and level. I really couldn't believe we had made it. The subsequent photos from the ground looked amazing and Heamsey had absolutely nailed it. Albeit brief, my dream of flying with the Reds had finally come true.

One week later our second flypast with the Reds was due at RIAT in Fairford. We had been asked to perform a pairs display at Kemble the day before as the Reds Association were having a gathering there. These were all the original Red Arrows veterans who had flown with Gnats and in some cases were also part of the original Yellowjacks. They were led by Henry Prince. A true gentleman. Henry Prince and Ray Hanna are probably the two most famous Red Arrows of the Gnat era, and I finally had the opportunity to meet one of them. Henry had also been part of the Yellowjacks and thereafter became a member of the founding Red Arrows team. It had been agreed that the following day I would take Henry flying in the back of a Gnat from Kemble to RIAT. This was a true honour for me and a flight I will never forget. When you know you genuinely bring joy to someone else, it is a very uplifting feeling. It had been a long time since Henry last flew in a Gnat, and it was obvious given his age that this would be his last. By the time we landed at RIAT, Henry had tears in his eyes. I was struggling to keep mine at bay.

That day was a busy one. We had to get the jets ready for a late-afternoon flight with the Reds. This time it was just two Gnats the Reds wanted. I was to fly in G-MOUR, with Kev in G-TIMM. Again, the nine Reds were to fly in their customary Vic formation, but with Kev and myself tucked-in in line astern off Red 1, creating an arrow-like shape in the sky. This was an entirely different experience to what had happened the week before. We leisurely joined the Reds west of Fairford, with Kev leading our line-astern join perfectly. We then spent 25 minutes coasting around the clear Gloucestershire skies with the Reds, performing various formation manoeuvres and formation changes. It was one of these moments in my

With the Red Arrows at RIAT.

life which I just didn't want to end. As the sun was setting, all I could think about was how privileged I was to be in this ridiculously lucky position. However, all good things come to an end, and as we flew down the display line at RIAT with all the VIPs watching ahead of the gala dinner there that evening, the Reds broke off into a loop, whilst Kev and I continued straight and level. Formation flying simply doesn't get better than that.

Kev and I attended that RIAT Gala dinner afterwards, where we were even personally thanked by the chief of the Air Staff for our help. However, this had been a team effort. We had worked for half a decade to build a really strong engineering team, who travelled with us everywhere we displayed. Preparing a Gnat for flight is not a quick 'kick the tyres and light the fires' process. To do it properly takes around two man hours. Although we had been taught all the pre-flight actions needed, we had taken the operational decision several years earlier that our pilots would focus on the flying itself and leave this important element to our engineering team. Also, as with all aircraft, snags emerge and to have your own Gnat-focused engineers on hand to fix any issues is worth its weight in gold. Kevin Broughall, James Mohr, Nigel Fall and Connor Holland were all genuinely instrumental in our team's success.

That summer was a busy display season for us, including an unforgettable request to perform a formation flypast with the Vulcan. It was to take place at

Dunsfold and we had been asked by the air show organisers to provide all three jets. Although some other display teams had performed flypasts with the Vulcan, I noticed that virtually all would do so by formating on the Vulcan. I wanted our team to do something different and proposed a unique formation composition, which I'm pretty sure had never been attempted before with a Vulcan and three Gnats. I proposed that the Vulcan would formate on our Yellow Gnat, and then be flanked either side by our other two Gnats.

Martin Withers was an experienced RAF pilot, famous for dropping the first bomb from the Vulcan on Port Stanley at the beginning of the Falklands war. He was delighted with the idea and the plan was set. Over the skies west of Dunsfold Martin's Vulcan joined Heamsey's Yellow Gnat in line astern, whilst Kev and I formated on the Vulcan in echelon right and echelon left respectively. I had no idea how large the Vulcan really was until I saw it airborne with my own eyes a few metres away. I will never forget the moment when the Vulcan turned into a left-hand orbit towards me whilst I was close-in in echelon left. For a split second, its vast delta-wing suddenly obscured the entirety of what I could see in my canopy, and all 77 tons of metal alloy were now heading in my direction. It really made one ensure to never leave those all-important formation references – not even for the twinkling of an eye.

Sadly, from the highs of 2014, came the exceptionally painful lows of 2015, after which things would never quite be the same again. It was the middle of the air show season and we had been asked to display at Oulton Park in Cheshire as part of the 'Carfest' event. Kev was due to fly in his favourite jet (G-TIMM), whilst I flew in mine (G-RORI). Having prepositioned both jets nearby at Hawarden earlier in the week, Kev was to lead our pairs display. As usual, we began the display with a variety of formation aerobatics, after which we split into two units, allowing us to perform an opposition pass. This was followed by individual solo manoeuvres. Due to the cloud base that day, I had performed a wingover in front of the crowd, running-in on the 45-degree line, and exiting on the other. Now with my back to the crowd and me repositioning on to the display line, Kev was to perform two twinkle rolls. A twinkle roll is simply an aileron roll, performed by slightly raising the nose of the aircraft from straight and level flight, and rolling hard (usually to the left) for 360 degrees. The Gnat has an impressive roll-rate of nearly 400 degrees per second at speed. This makes the twinkle roll a relatively straightforward aerobatic manoeuvre, that's complete almost before it started. Since my jet was over two miles away and pointing in the other direction at the time, I didn't see what happened. As I turned the corner to run in for my next manoeuvre, I noticed a huge plume of black smoke around one mile north of the

The Gnat display team flying with a Vulcan.

display site. I could tell something was wrong, and following failed attempts to radio Kev, I asked the display director if he'd seen a deployed parachute. As he confirmed my greatest fear, I flew over the top of the bellowing black smoke and could see the orange fireball emanating from its centre. It was and remains, by far, the worst moment of my life.

I have watched the video of the crash many hundreds of times, and still don't understand how this accident happened. Inexplicably, during the second twinkle roll, the jet's roll is reversed two-thirds of the way through, it's nose pitches abruptly towards the ground whilst nearly inverted and departs crashing into trees. Kev and I were best friends for nearly 20 years. Best men at each other's weddings. We both shared a passion for flying from our days in Cambridge together studying Economics, and unlike myself, Kev had even properly joined the RAF to fly fast jets. We both had very similar hours on the Gnat and I calculated from my own logbook that Kev will have almost certainly flown over 1,000 twinkle rolls in the Gnat over that last decade. He was current on the jet, generally fit and someone who would take his display flying incredibly seriously. Having been intricately involved with the AAIB investigation and seeing all its findings, it didn't really provide any answer as to what caused the crash to happen. Specifically, what would make a display pilot try to reverse an aileron roll when the manoeuvre was nearly complete, in a jet that was fully serviceable? My opinion was that there was some distraction that Kev experienced in the cockpit at just the wrong moment. Perhaps a loose article or a visual illusion of some sort. Sadly, we will never know the answer.

After the tragedy, I continued to display the Gnat, and the following year was glad to perform a missing-man formation at the Carfest event in memory of Kev. Additionally, we were asked to perform another flypast with the Vulcan during its last few days of flight before permanent retirement. This took place at Church Fenton, where during the final pass with the Vulcan, we performed a modified missing-man formation. I believe I am the very last person in the world to have flown in formation with a Vulcan. I suspect I will likely remain so.

When looking around the world at what remains of the Gnat T1 fleet, the USA was the main benefactor outside of the UK. On several occasions Oli and I went out to the US to meet fellow Gnat owners. John Mulvey, based in Colorado, still today has the largest collection of Gnat spares in the world, as well as several airframes. The most notable US owner was Tom Foley (who I never met but Pete Walker had dealings with). He was famous back in the 1990s for his 'million-dollar Gnat' having upgraded everything that was possible on the aircraft, even adding an autopilot. However, the main use of Gnats in the US was for a totally different reason, namely in the filming of 'Hot Shots 2' (a spoof of 'Top Gun'). We spoke to several owners and pilots who had taken part in the filming. Many lives (and Gnats) had been lost, primarily on account of flying with inert ejection seats and being asked to fly inverted at incredibly low level for long distances.

The Americans have a slightly different view of flying swept-wing jets. Whilst in the UK it would be unimaginable to fly without live seats, that is the norm in America. They are also able to make as many modifications to the aircraft as they want, whereas that is a far taller regulatory order here. Although all permit-to-fly jet aircraft in the UK have been modified for gaseous oxygen and modern radios/transponders, the ones in the US have typically gone further. They include installation of avionics to fly under IFR and starter-generator installations, which in my opinion are all excellent modifications to make operation of the Gnat safer and more manageable. What we noticed however, is that most of the current Gnat owners in the US are getting on in years and have personally stopped flying them for a long time. There seems to be little interest in younger generations. I think it's fair to say that the Gnat never really caught the imagination of buyers and pilots out there, whereas the Czech-made Aero Vodochody L-39 Albatros has a thriving community. Perhaps it's the fact that the L-39 is larger and easier to fly, although I can assure any L-39 pilot that you can't even begin to compare the two aircraft when it comes to sheer performance and manoeuvrability.

Whilst in the US, there was an opportunity that arose for the charity to buy one of the T1 Gnats used in the filming of 'Hot Shots', and given the incredibly competitive price offered, it was purchased and sent back home to the UK for the charity to restore as a future project. We had also found our next recruit. Edwin Brenninkmeyer. I don't think I've ever met anyone who loves flying as much as Edwin. Although he had no military background, his list of aviation accolades

Gnat at North Weald in 2021.

was almost as long as he is tall, at nearly 6" 6'. We were extremely concerned about Edwin's ability to eject safely from a Gnat, but having performed several seat pulls with him strapped-in, it was determined that he was cleared to fly in the front seat, but not from the rear seat. Once this pretty important fact was determined, we had yet another alluring plan. During our US travels we had been put in touch with an owner of the ex-Indian Air Force Gnat F1. We realised that this could be our chance to complete the Folland story and restore a Gnat single-seat fighter. A few months later the Gnat F1 was transported by sea in a shipping container. The restoration project began, with the intention of making this the only flying Gnat F1 in the world. At the time of writing, the charity hopes to get this aircraft (G-SLYR) airworthy soon. This really will be an iconic achievement once we succeed, and quite a sight to see a formation of Gnats led by a Gnat F1 fighter.

Over the last couple of decades our team have devoted significant time and personal resource to maintain ex-military aircraft in flight. We are great believers in the importance of keeping these unique and majestic aircraft flying for centuries to come. Rather like birds, these aircraft were born to fly and not sit in museums. Further, younger generations are more interested in seeing flying aircraft, so any intent to inspire them into aviation is far more relevant with air displays than traditional museums.

To that end, our charity continues to hunt for like-minded individuals to join our team of trustees, either as pilots, or as individuals who would enjoy the challenge and involvement of restoring an iconic aircraft. It is vital we keep our nation's aviation heritage alive, and we hope others will join us in what is an incredibly rewarding life experience.

LAST WORD

Can Petter's diminutive pocket rocket, the Gnat, be considered to have been a success? Revolutionary in concept, it was a delight to fly and technically complex, but when it went wrong, a regular occurrence, it posed significant challenges to its pilots, particularly student pilots, and to those who worked hard to keep it serviceable. Many were lost in accidents. Despite all these challenges, those who mastered it loved it. In the hands of the Indian Air Force the fighter proved to be an outstanding combat aircraft in both air-to-air and air-to-ground operations despite its limited endurance. Conceived as an advanced trainer designed to prepare pilots for advanced fast-jet aircraft such as the Lightning, the trainer not only produced many highly capable front-line pilots for the RAF, but also delighted the crowds at air displays and earned a reputation second to none as a display aircraft in the hands of the RAF aerobatic team the Red Arrows. The fact that a number are still flying more than 60 years after it was designed by Petter is a testament to its longevity, and to its designer's foresight. With a total of 449 Gnats built, including the Indian Ajeet version and 105 trainers, the Gnat can rightly claim to have been a very successful design that has outlived many of its contemporaries.

Perhaps the very last word should be left to Ray Hanna, that outstanding display pilot and Red Arrows leader of great distinction. Apparently, when once asked what he thought was the best lead-in aircraft for the Gnat, he is rumoured to have replied, "The Lightning".

GLOSSARY OF TERMS

AC	Aircraft
AEROS	Aerobatics
AFS	Advanced Flying School
AIR CDRE	Air Commodore
AIFG	Advanced Instrument Flying Grading
AOC	Air Officer Commanding
AOC-in-C	Air Officer Commanding in Chief
ATC	Air Traffic Control
BIFG	Basic Instrument Flying Grading
CFS	Central Flying School
CIRE	Command Instrument Rating Examiner
CU	Cumulus
DEMO	Demonstration
DFC	Distinguished Flying Cross
DME	Distance Measurement Equipment
FAA	Federal Aviation Authority
FAM	Familiarisation
FHT	Final Handling Test
FLT CDR	Flight Commander
FLT	Flight
FLT LT	Flight Lieutenant
FLT SGT	Flight Sergeant
FOB	Flying Order Book
FTS	Flying Training School
GCA	Ground-Controlled Approach
GH	General Handling
GP CAPT	Group Captain
HQ FTC	Headquarters Flying Training Command

IAT	International Air Tattoo
IF	Instrument Flying
IFIS	Integrated Flight Instrument System
ILS	Instrument Landing System
IMC	Instrument Meteorological Conditions
IRE	Instrument Rating Examiner
JPT	Jet Pipe Temperature
J/T	Junior Technician
KTS	Knots
MB	Martin-Baker
NCO	Non-Commissioned Officer
OR946	Operational Requirement 946
OC	Officer Commanding
OCU	Operational Conversion Unit
OR	Operational Requirement
PAI	Pilot Attack Instructor
P STAFF	Personnel Staff
PFL	Practice Forced Landing
QFI	Qualified Flying Instructor
QRB	Quick Release Box
RAF	Royal Air Force
RN	Royal Navy
RPM	Revs Per Minute
RTB	Return to Base
R/T	Radio Telephony
RUNWAY DUMBBELL	A circular area at the end of a runway that allows aircraft to turn around
SAM	Surface-to-Air Missile
SATCO	Senior Air Traffic Control Officer
SCT	Staff Continuation Training
SGT	Sergeant
SQN LDR	Squadron Leader
STN CDR	Station Commander

STUPRECC	Speed, Trim, Unlock, Power Off, Raise the Guard, Exhaust the Accumulators, Check the Controls, Check Trim
TACAN	Tactical Air Communication and Navigation
TRAPPER	Examiner
USAF	United States Air Force
U/S	Unserviceable
UHF	Ultra-High Frequency
VHF	Very High Frequency
WG CDR	Wing Commander
WINGCO	Wing Commander
WRAF	Woman's Royal Air Force

ACKNOWLEDGEMENTS

We would firstly like to thank all those who submitted contributions for this book, not all of whom had their stories publsihed. To them, we retain your very welcome stories and *Gnat Boys* 2 beckons. The overall response to our trawl for information, and interest shown in *Gnat Boys* has far exceeded our expectations. We extend our thanks to ACM Sir Richard Johns for agreeing to write the foreword.

For photographs, we would like to acknowledge in particular Jonathan Baynton, John MacWilliam and Chris Parker. With special mention to Ray Deacon for being a major resource of both photos and knowledge. All effort has gone to credit correctly all photographs and other material. If anyone has been omitted, we would like to apologise.

We would also like to acknowledge the incredible support, help and advice provided by all at Grub Street, in particular, John Davies, Natalie Parker and Myriam Bell. They have played a very great part in the production of what we consider to be a superb book.

Tom Eeles would like to thank:

- Ben Dunnell, editor of *Aeroplane* magazine, for allowing the use of photographs and text from the 3 September 1954 edition of *Aeroplane* magazine;
- Pen & Sword Books, for their permission to reproduce text from *RAF Little Rissington, the Central Flying School Years 1946 -1976* by Roy Bagshaw, Ray Deacon, Alan Pollock and Malcolm Thomas;
- Air Marshal Subhash Bhojwani of the Indian Air Force, and Captain Mika Rauna, military attaché of the Finnish Embassy, London, for providing details of Gnat contacts in their respective countries;
- Oliver Wheeldon, of the Heritage Aircraft Trust;
- Finally my long-suffering wife Julia, and Buster the golden retriever, for allowing me to spend hours on the computer when, in their opinion, I should have been doing something more exciting with them.

Rick Peacock-Edwards would like to thank:

- Ellen Eccles, widow of Bob Eccles, for providing so much information about her husband with whom I did my own flying training;
- My long-suffering wife of 48 years, Tina, for her patience and understanding.

INDEX

PERSONNEL

PLACES

SQUADRONS AND UNITS

MISCELLANEOUS

RATE OF CLIMB

Thrilling Personal Reminiscences from a Fighter Pilot and Leader

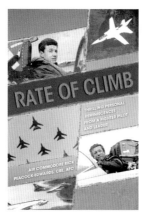

9781911621461 | £20.00

Rate of Climb is an action-packed account of a foremost flyer's life with endless good stories. Rick's compelling recollections reveal a life of considerable achievement, in a very personal book capturing the ties of airmanship that the author has been privileged to share. A must for all lovers of derring-do in the air.

PRAISE FOR *RATE OF CLIMB*

"This exciting hardback is filled with endless great stories and colourful characters to match."

Denise E. Parker, *Air Cadets*

"Clearly an aviator's aviator, the author writes with humour and candour about the thrills and tribulations of his time as a front-line pilot and his important staff posts."

Britain at War (Book of the Month – June 2020)

"'RPE' has produced a typically entertaining read"

Ben Dunnell, *Aeroplane*

"It is a fascinating tale of flying, friendship and fun."

Historic Aircraft Association